T0385618

*Revolutionary Life*

# Revolutionary Life

## The Everyday of the Arab Spring

ASEF BAYAT

HARVARD UNIVERSITY PRESS

*Cambridge, Massachusetts & London, England*

2021

First printing

*Library of Congress Cataloging-in-Publication Data*
Names: Bayat, Asef, author.
Title: Revolutionary life : the everyday of the Arab Spring / Asef Bayat.
Description: Cambridge, Massachusetts : Harvard University Press, 2021. |
    Includes bibliographical references and index.
Identifiers: LCCN 2021016270 | ISBN 9780674987890 (hardcover)
    Subjects: LCSH: Arab Spring, 2010– | Egypt—History—2011– | Egypt—
    History—Protests, 2011–2013. | Tunisia—History—Demonstrations, 2010– |
    Egypt—Social life and customs—20th century. | Egypt—Social life and
    customs—21st century. | Tunisia—Social life and customs—20th century. |
    Tunisia—Social life and customs—21st century.
Classification: LCC JQ1850.A91 B38 2021 | DDC 909 / .097492708312—dc23
LC record available at https://lccn.loc.gov/2021016270

# Contents

*Revolutionary Life*

# Introduction

HOW DO WE TELL THE STORY OF REVOLUTION? The standard narrative focuses on the state, high politics, the palace, and pashas to examine the outcome and gauge "success" or "failure" of revolutionary movements. This perspective is undeniably crucial for any understanding of revolutions, including the ones that rose up from 2010 and have collectively been called the Arab Spring. The remarkable uprisings that spread throughout the Arab world signaled the emergence of a new generation of twenty-first-century revolutions that were rich as *movements* but woefully poor as *change*. No wonder that by the middle of the decade, most observers described these revolutions as outright failures. This appraisal may ring true if we take a macrostructural, political, and state-centric perspective to look at these historical experiences. The picture, however, becomes more complex if we shift the lens to observe and examine what happened in the social realm, in the everyday life, and among the grassroots. This book is an attempt to offer a different way of thinking about revolution by focusing not simply on the elites, the state, and regime change but also on what the revolution meant to the ordinary people, to the poor, the marginalized youth, women, and other subaltern groups in their everyday life. The story of revolution, then, is not just what happened at the top; it is also the tale of what went on at the base—in farms, factories, families, and schools; in social relations governed by old hierarchies; in people's subjectivities; and in the practices of everyday life. At the core of this inquiry is not just what the revolution did to the everyday, but equally what the everyday did to revolution. Never mind that these two domains of human experience are hardly separate even though they are invariably seen as such. This book brings together and bridges the analytical disconnect between *everyday life* as the realm of the ordinary, the mundane, and the routine, and *revolutions* as the domain of the extraordinary, the monumental, and rupture.

The idea of this book came to me just a few weeks after the uprisings in Tunisia and Egypt. This was roughly a year after I had published *Life as Politics: How Ordinary People Change the Middle East*, in which I discussed how unassuming "nonmovements," those collective actions of noncollective people, were important players in pushing for cumulative change in the countries of the Middle East under authoritarian regimes, neoliberal economies, and moral surveillance. Now, in light of the uprisings, I was confronted by a host of questions from journalists, activists, and academics about what role, if any, those "nonmovements" had played in these extraordinary revolutions. At the time, I had no clear idea. But the question was intriguing enough intellectually and politically to push me to explore further the nature and dynamics of these remarkable political uprisings. I have been engaged in this journey since March 2011, when I began my field research in revolutionary Egypt and Tunisia, continuing with a half-dozen fieldtrips during which I attended events, rallies, and street protests; visited popular neighborhoods, street markets, labor unions, research centers, and political parties; and held conversations with activists, academics, officials, as well as ordinary people in cafés, households, organizations, universities, and the streets to secure oral histories of the events. I further collected a substantial amount of archival materials including reports, tracts, surveys, local papers, video clips, and social media posts.

As I began to analyze data and put my findings into writing, I found certain things about these revolutions puzzling, things that I felt differentiated them from their twentieth-century counterparts, such as the Nicaraguan or especially the Iranian revolution of 1979, that I had observed and studied. There were certain novelties in the Arab revolutions that were mostly absent in the previous ones. The revolutions in Tunisia, Egypt, or Yemen, for instance, were organized more horizontally without a clear unified organization, charismatic leaders, any clear ideology, or intellectual articulation. Indeed, these new revolutions were more peaceful and pluralistic in mobilization but far less radical in terms of causing deep change than their earlier counterparts. Consequently, I felt compelled to write a book reflecting on the meaning of the Arab revolutions from a historical and comparative perspective before I completed the book that you have in your hands. That other book, *Revolution without Revolutionaries: Making Sense of the Arab Spring* (2017), adopted a mostly macropolitical, state-centric, and historical approach, which, although indispensable, left aside some fundamental questions. What did the revolutions mean to the average person on the ground in terms of everyday life? How did the revolutions seep into communities, schools, and the private realm? How did they affect popular consciousness, relations of hierarchy, and norms? What happened to the "social question" of poverty and inequality? How do we account theoretically for the place of subaltern groups in the revolutionary events? And, ultimately, how can we establish an analytical link between the everyday life and revolution? The current book, *Revolutionary Life: The Everyday of the Arab Spring*, takes the radically different lens of a microperspective in attempting to address those very questions. It focuses on the everyday of the Arab Spring, highlighting the social side of the revolutions and looking at the subjectivities, practices, and popular politics at the grass-roots level.

This has not been an easy or, for that matter, a quick book to write. It is not just that the study covers a lot of ground, the experience of two revolutions, examining the life and politics of multiple social groups including the urban poor, rural subaltern, marginalized youth, women, and others. The greater challenge lay in how to organize a massive amount of data in accessible and intimate narratives that at the same time yield meaningful analyses and necessary theorizing. I wanted the book to account for structures but also narrate everyday struggles, and to be comparative yet attentive to the integrity of each experience, analytical but also accessible, historical as well as theoretical, concise yet rich with details. Whether I have successfully met these challenges, I leave it to the readers to judge.

This, then, is not a conventional ethnography, which would have yielded deeper insights into the dynamics of a situation, group, or habitat but would have fallen short of covering multiple groups, several sites and situations, and larger processes. The work I set out to do in this book required multiple methods of inquiry and manifold modes of data collection including qualitative, quantitative, observational, archival, and oral history. However, I have to admit that some of the deepest insights for me have come from my experience of living and working for some seventeen years in the region, Egypt in particular, prior to the uprisings. A long experience of living and working in a place can be an asset for any inquisitive observer to acquire critical knowledge about that place, for it is through the actual living, and not just observing, that delicate cultural registers, subtle codes, and intricacies of individual and social life may be detected. This background knowledge about the region has been essential for my understanding of the subsequent events and processes that unfolded during and after the uprisings.

This volume covers the events mostly from the immediate prerevolution years through 2015 and later when Beji Caid Essebsi, a minister from Zein al-Abedine Ben Ali's regime, was elected as president in Tunisia and when General Abdel Fattah al-Sisi already presided over Egypt. The comparative outlook between Tunisia and Egypt is used to explore how and to what extent the "success" (Tunisia) and "failure"

(Egypt) of a revolution may affect the everyday life, in particular the lives of the subaltern subjects. Tunisia and Egypt are often seen in terms of difference and contrast—Tunisia, a country of 10 million people, liberal, secular with progressive women's rights, and ruled by a police state entailed a liberal democracy; whereas Egypt with its 80 million population, conservative sensibilities, religious population, and strong civil society experienced military rule and autocracy. This book will show that despite these differences, Tunisia and Egypt experienced striking similarities when it came to the revolutionary dynamics and the predicament of the subaltern life—the poor, marginalized youth, women, and the provincial population. In both countries, the revolutions were marked by a liberal outlook, nonradical and refolutionary strategy, and a political class invariably detached from the ordinary citizens who were preoccupied primarily with social justice, self-rule, and radical change. The astonishing disenchantment with the revolution and high politics in both countries might be surprising given their different political trajectories—Tunisia toward democracy and Egypt toward autocracy. However, it may be less surprising when one considers the elites' very similar socioeconomic vision and their attitudes toward the subaltern. The key difference lay in the fact that democracy in Tunisia by default allowed popular struggles around social justice and inclusion to continue, whereas autocracy in Egypt stifled any form of collective mobilization. Yet the revolutions in both countries left their undeniable imprints on the social fabric and fostered lasting changes in the personal and social worlds.

In what follows (Chapter 1), I set the stage for an analytical perspective that allows the relationship between the everyday life and revolution to be examined. I will then elaborate on the proposition by narrating histories of subaltern engagement in the Tunisian and Egyptian revolutions of 2011. I begin with an analysis of the struggles of the poor, marginalized youth, women, and social minorities in their everyday lifeworld before the uprisings (Chapter 2) and examine in detail how these social groups became involved in the uprisings (Chapter 3). I then move to illustrate how each subaltern group, notably the poor (Chapter 4), women (Chapter 5), and youth (Chapter 6) figured in the postrevolutionary moments and how their lifeworld became part of the revolutionary landscape. Chapter 7 highlights the revolution of the social, detailing certain novel subjectivities, imageries, practices, and ways of living that challenged old power relations and hierarchies. I conclude (Chapter 8) by discussing some of the enduring gains as well as the structural obstacles against the revolution of the subaltern and the transformation of the social.

Chapter *1*

# Everyday Life and Revolution

On December 16, 2010, Mohammed Bouazizi, a poor street vendor, set himself on fire in the depressed Tunisian town of Sidi-Bouzid after the police abusively confiscated his scale and vegetables because he lacked a permit. The incident set the stage for the spectacular Arab uprisings that were to engulf the Arab region with a ferocity and magnitude unseen before. The monthlong uprising in Tunisia by poor people, youths, provincial population, and middle-class professionals toppled a long-standing dictator, Zein al-Abedine Ben Ali, who had presided over a police state for more than two decades. Egyptians were watching the events in Tunisia with great interest and enthusiasm. Within two weeks, they began their own uprising on January 25, 2011, when tens of thousands of protesters poured into Tahrir Square in Cairo. The crowd, spearheaded by young activists, occupied the central Tahrir Square for the following days and nights, while massive protests spread into other cities and towns. Unable to tackle the crowd, the police retreated from the public scene giving way to the military to deploy its forces onto the streets with signs of neutrality. Within two weeks, another autocrat, President Hosni Mubarak, was forced to step down. Egyptians were still relishing their revolutionary honeymoon when mass revolts overtook Libya, then Yemen, Syria, Bahrain, and other neighboring countries. In total, nineteen Arab states went through popular protests. In the end, four dictators (in Tunisia, Egypt, Libya, and Yemen) were toppled, while the Syrian president Bashar al-Asad was brought to the brink. The affluent monarchies and sheikhdoms in the Persian Gulf such as Saudi Arabia, United Arab Emirates, and Oman felt the shockwaves of the revolutions. Their response included appeasing their citizens through handouts or reforms, while attempting to sabotage the revolutions elsewhere in the region. But the uprisings did not cease. They continued later in the decade, this time in Sudan, Algeria, Lebanon, Iraq, and Iran. This new wave resulted in the ousting of two more autocrats in Sudan and Algeria and the resignation of the prime minister in Lebanon. Sudan undertook a negotiated transition to civilian rule, while the uprisings in Iran and Iraq faced severe crackdowns. The continuing protests in Lebanon, Algeria, and Iraq for meaningful change were halted by the global COVID-19 pandemic in 2020.[1]

The uprisings, and here I focus primarily on Tunisia and Egypt, occurred broadly in the context of structural changes the Arab societies experienced since the 1990s, when the regimes began to liberalize their largely welfare-oriented economies. First, Arab societies became more urban (65 percent in 2010) and globalized. Urban life generated desires, demands, and rights (such as paid jobs, decent shelters, urban services, and respect) that the regimes failed to fulfill for a large portion of the inhabitants. Meanwhile, the creeping urbanity in the countryside (e.g., institutions, communication, consumption, literacy) brought the rural life into orbit of national politics. Second, demographic shift made these societies excessively young (70 percent under 35). Most of the youth faced economic and social constraints but found greater opportunities in schools, streets, or in media to forge collective identities and dissent. Third, these urbanizing and youthful societies had become substantially literate (over 90 percent of those age fourteen to twenty-four). The proliferating universities produced millions of graduates who, unfortunately, found meagre opportunities in the liberalized economies.

By 2010, the region had the highest rate of unemployment in particular among youth (over 25 percent) in the world. An outcome of this uneven development was the growth of the "middle-class poor," a paradoxical class that enjoyed college degrees, knowledge of the world, and middle-class dreams but was pushed by economic deprivation to live the life of the poor in the slums and subsist on precarious jobs. Economic marginalization coupled with political repression underscored widespread dissent which the middle-class poor embodied. With the expanding electronic media from the mid-2000s, an unprecedented opportunity emerged for the opposition to connect, expand, and mobilize toward what came to be known as the Arab Spring.

The downfall of the dictators in the Arab uprisings generated great hope, happiness, and yet much anxiety and uncertainty among activists and the ordinary. Once Ben Ali fled Tunisia, an interim government took power. It included ministers from both the opposition and officials of the old regime. Political prisoners were released, while the political police and Ben Ali's party were abolished. But widespread protests continued to demand meaningful reform and disband the agents of the old regime from the new government. On October 23, 2011, Tunisians elected deputies for a Constituent Assembly to draft a new constitution. The Islamic al-Nahda Party, led by Rachid al-Ghannoushi, captured most of the seats. Meanwhile, a new coalition government composed of al-Nahda and two secular parties assumed power. After months of intense debate, the new constitution was ratified in January 2014, guiding Tunisia's path to a pluralist democracy. But the rise of radical Islamists and the popularity of al-Nahda alarmed the secular constituencies. The killing of two prominent secular activists in 2013 caused a civil strife, leading al-Nahda to hand over power to an interim government in October 2013, following a historic accord brokered by the national labor union UGTT. In the midst of national discord and social unrest, the 2014 elections gave the parliamentary majority to the old establishment parties, and the presidency to Nidaa

Tounes's Beji Caid Essebsi, a prime minister from Ben Ali's regime. This political trajectory sidelined the revolutionaries and caused deep cynicism about electoral politics and disenchantment of youth many of whom opted to emigrate or join ISIS.

In Egypt, the Supreme Council of Armed Forces (SCAF) replaced President Mubarak; it dissolved the parliament and suspended the constitution in a plan to oversee transition to civilian rule within six months. But it would take two turbulent years before a new elected government, led by Muhamed Morsi of the Muslim Brotherhood, took office in June 2012. The SCAF rule faced incessant street protests caused by delays to the transition, repression of dissent, sexual assaults on female protesters, and lack of a serious transitional justice. Even Morsi's presidency, a fairly open political time, failed to bring calm. His Islamist leanings, reflected in the new constitution, alarmed the liberals, leftists, and Coptic Christians who fearfully imagined Egypt adopting an Iranian-style Islamist regime. The "deep state"—the judiciary, intelligence, and the military, among others—remained defiant to Morsi, whose incompetence in governance had already caused much social unrest. The discontent grew in the summer of 2013 into a nationwide movement, or *tamarrod* (rebellion), to demand dismissing the president. The military, led by General Abdel Fattah el-Sisi, rode the wave by inserting itself as the leader of the anti-Morsi "revolution." On July 3, 2013, el-Sisi forcibly ousted Morsi in a military coup. He annulled the constitution and installed an interim civilian government to undertake new elections for new president, parliament, and constitution. In a violent crackdown that left more than 1,000 dead, the generals began to quell the defiant Muslim Brothers, while President Mubarak and his son were set free. When General el-Sisi won the presidential elections in May 2014 and the parliament fell to the pro-Sisi deputies, the counterrevolutionary restoration was complete. It was only a matter of time for the extraordinary repression to hunt not only the Muslim Brothers but also the left, liberal, and revolutionary activists or anyone who defied the new rule.

## A NEW GENERATION OF REVOLUTIONS

I had lived through and witnessed two revolutionary episodes—first, the revolutions of 1979 (in Iran and Nicaragua) when I was a student activist, then the Arab revolutions of 2011, especially in Egypt, where I lived and worked for many years before its revolution. As I eagerly observed the Arab revolutions unfolding, I became increasingly perplexed by how different they were from the ones I had seen and studied before, notably the Iranian Revolution. To begin with, the Arab uprisings were happening in a region that conventional wisdom among Western and local experts alike had deemed stable, as ensured by "authoritarian durability."[2] Second, these revolutions were carried out by the ordinary people, with virtually no charismatic leaders, no unified organizations, no specific ideologies, and no intellectual precursors— no Vladimir Lenin or Ayatollah Khomeini, no Václav Havel or Ali Shariati. Third, all unfolded with spectacular mobilization and mass revolts in the key urban streets and squares, *midans*, in a manner that became the global model for the Occupy movements that spread through some 500 cities around the world in the early 2010s.

And yet, these revolutions caused little break from the old orders. Little changed in the institutions of the old regimes. In Egypt, the intelligence apparatus, powerful business circles, elite cultural organizations, and the military largely retained their old culture and top personnel.[3] So did the economic structure and policy circles. Instead of revolutionaries, the military took over the government to oversee transition to a civilian rule but only overthrew one, led by President Morsi, when it came to power. Even in Tunisia, an electoral democracy seemed to take shape, but it was rendered severely fragile by the fact that so little changed in the social and economic visions, and so little was done to the popular quest for social justice. The revolution did establish free elections, speech, press, and organization. But the prerevolution parties, private media, and "parallel state"—the security sector, business elites, and local mafia that had served as the de facto authority before the revolution—continued to wield power. The post-revolution economic policies mostly reproduced the logic of the pre-revolutionary regimes. Continuity from the old order was felt so deeply that a local observer described the revolution as a "failed coup."[4] At best, according to the author and politician Ayad Ben Ashour, the revolution was continuing.[5] Hannah Arendt once opined that the collapse of authority and power becomes a revolution "only when there are people willing and capable of picking up the power, of moving into and penetrating, so to speak, the power vacuum."[6] In neither Tunisia nor Egypt did a real power vacuum develop because state power did not really collapse and no insurgent group was willing and able to seize power. The revolutionary protagonists, those who initiated and pushed the uprising through, generally remained on the margins of governmental power. In fact, for the most part, they were not planning to ascend to power. Even though some realized later that they should have presided over the government, they lacked the means and the resources: organization, powerful leadership, a strategic vision, and some hard power to wrest power from the old regime.

I have suggested that the Arab Spring represented a new generation of twenty-first-century revolutions that were rich as movements but poor in terms of change. They thus departed significantly from their twentieth-century counterparts, such as those in Cuba, Nicaragua, Iran, or even the "negotiated" anti-communist revolutions of 1989. What transpired in Tunisia, Egypt, Yemen, or similarly Burkina Faso in 2014 and Gambia in 2016 were not revolutions in the sense of the societal *changes* that begin with the rapid and radical transformation of the state pushed by popular movements from below. Rather, they were "refolutions," that is, revolutionary *movements* that emerged to compel the incumbent states to reform themselves. Refolutions in this sense are unlikely to cause fundamental transformation. For the states, when left to themselves, may not undertake meaningful change unless they receive effective political pressure or coercion. In fact, the postuprising

Arab states largely resisted reforming their personnel, culture, and relations and thus broadly kept the status quo.[7] Unlike the radical ideological revolutions, refolutions naturally give rise to nonhegemonic and fairly pluralistic regimes because the persistence of multiple power centers including those from the past regimes as well as a resurgent civil society prevent these regimes from monopolizing power. This might pave the way for the establishment of a pluralist democracy. But precisely such a fluid structure renders regimes vulnerable to counterrevolutionary sabotage and resistant to the pursuit of meaningful change. This understanding of "refolution" is therefore different from that of Timothy Garten Ash, who originally used the term to highlight the peaceful and negotiated character of the otherwise full-fledged 1989 revolutions in Eastern Europe where, unlike the Arab world, the state, ideology, economy, and mode of governance underwent a profound transformation.

Why were the Arab revolutions different? As part of a new generation of revolutions, they occurred at a paradoxical, post–Cold War moment. Neoliberal policies had caused extraordinary dissent and the prevalence of new communication technologies had greatly facilitated political mobilization on massive scales, and yet the very idea of revolution as representing deep change had dissipated. In other words, the possibility of spectacular mobilization and mass uprisings increased, but there was little strategic, let alone "utopic," vision about how to transform the status quo and what new social order to achieve. In fact, all of the key revolutionary traditions of the twentieth century, chiefly anti-colonial nationalism, Marxism-Leninism, and militant Islamism, were by now undercut, while the (neo)liberal ideas expanded globally.[8] Thus, instead of the earlier ideals of equality, welfare state, popular control, and revolution, there developed an explosion in the ideas of the individual, human rights, NGOs, market, and (neo)liberal reform—a paradigm that simultaneously entailed the *dissent* of the marginalized and *deradicalization* of the political class.[9] This global (postcolonial, postsocialist, and post-Islamist) era had, in short, created conditions for the rise of "revolutions without revolutionaries"—a sentiment captured by the veteran Lebanese author Fawwaz Traboulsi in the book *Thawrat Bila Thuwwar.*[10] What transpired were, in the words of the Syrian thinker Yassin al-Hajj Saleh, not the movements of the *thuwwar*, revolutionaries with vision of alternative social order, but of *thaerin*, those who wished to change the status quo without a clear idea of what should come next.[11]

## EVERYDAY LIFE AND REVOLUTION

I have already elaborated on these propositions in my *Revolution without Revolutionaries: Making Sense of the Arab Spring* (2017). That book took a macro, political, and comparative historical outlook to understand the meaning of the Arab Spring revolutions historically. It considered altering the state, ideology, and mode of governance as a fundamental element in the revolutionary outcome. But here in this book, *Revolutionary Life*, I radically shift perspective to suggest that revolutions are more than just the transformation of the state or regime change, however indispensable they may be. Revolutions have also a social side, the level of the grassroots, the everyday. By this I mean transformation in people's subjectivities, expectations, relations of hierarchies, as well as alternative practices in farms, factories, neighborhoods, schools, the streets, and in private realms. Here, I am looking at revolution in terms of an "event" in the sense of Alain Badiou, a condition of rupture in the routine of life that may give rise to open-ended possibilities, a condition in which people may come to imagine a different order of things.[12] Thus, the story of revolution is not just what happens at the top; it is also the chronicle of what transpires in the underside of society—in the everyday, among the grassroots, in ideas and practices, in the meanings and norms that together shape what might be called the everyday lifeworld.[13] This level of analysis is indispensable, for it is here that concerns for the "social question," distribution, property relations, as well as recognition of social difference, gender dynamics, and justice find tangible expressions. It allows us to see what the revolution means to whom, and how the image of revolution among ordinary people—the poor, marginalized youth, women, and others—may differ radically from that of the political class or the "leadership" that often come to "represent" the revolution. In addition, it is this everyday lifeworld that can help complicate the question of revolutionary "failure" and "success" in that a "failed" revolution may not be entirely failed if we consider significant transformations that may transpire at the level of the "social." After all, the very incidence of revolution may condition and compel even the repressive counter-revolutionary regimes to adopt social policies in favor of popular expectations. On the other hand, a "successful" revolution with a new political regime may not be adequately successful if the old habits, subjectivities, relations, and institutions continue. Finally, attention to the subtleties of everyday and popular politics allow us to explore how a surprising revolutionary movement may emerge from the underside of societies that appear safe and secure. The central question to explore, therefore, is how to account for the relationship between ordinary lives and extraordinary revolutions, between the social and the political, between the routine and rupture, between the mundane and the monumental, and between popular politics and unexpected uprisings.

This social side of the revolution—the grassroots, the everyday, and popular struggles—are largely missing from the analytical schema of the prevailing scholarship on revolution. The major scholarly works assembled in the four generations of revolutionary theories are mostly concerned with macrostructural analyses, with little take on the everyday life and popular politics, particularly on how the grassroots get engaged in spectacular revolutions, and in turn how revolutions refigure the everyday lifeworld.[14] Within the Marxist tradition, Barrington Moor placed capitalist modernization at the heart of revolution, suggesting that revolution happens when people suddenly wake up and their anger gets channeled through a revolutionary vanguard organization. Theda Skocpol argued against "voluntarism" stressing the role of structural factors. Even the fourth-generation theorists such as John Foran, Eric Selbin, and Jack Goldstone, who moved beyond the why of the revolutions to highlight their how, continued with mostly macroperspectives. George Lawson's impressive historical and comparative synthesis, *Anatomies of Revolution*, makes only a passing reference to the everyday habits, norms, patriarchy, and hierarchy, primarily to indicate resistance to change.[15]

Scholars of "nonviolent revolutions" such as Maria Stephan, Erica Chenoweth, or Sharon Nepstad, however, do highlight the role of ordinary people in causing revolution.[16] To demonstrate the efficacy of nonviolence, they argue that power rests not in the regimes but in the people, who make regimes powerful by, for instance, working, paying taxes, or obeying laws. When people withdraw their power through such acts as strikes, boycotting, or civil disobedience, regimes fall.[17] These are important insights, but the primary focus in these analyses lies on the consequences of popular resistance on hard power. The question still remains as to how these people get engaged in such acts of resistance in the first place, and how their lives are affected by their own extraordinary rebellion.

In the perspective of revolutionary practitioners such as Karl Marx, Lenin, or Rosa Luxemburg, people's engagement in revolution broadly had to do with the structural contradictions of capitalism, or the conflict between capital and labor, that would condition the proletariat (and not simply the "poor") into gaining class consciousness, thus becoming the agent of radical transformation.[18] While Luxemburg stressed workers' self-organization in socialist movements and the "general strike" as a way toward insurgency, Lenin insisted on a "vanguard party" of mostly intellectuals who were to direct the masses into the revolutionary fold, involving them in insurrection. Lenin shunned everyday struggles as "economism," a reformist deviation from revolution, but

Luxemburg saw in reformist battles a pathway toward radical politics by pitting workers against capital.[19] Marxist revolutionaries such as Alexandra Kollontai and Clara Zetkin attempted to bring the idea of revolution into the private realm, the everyday of gender, family, love, sex, and personal relations—concerns that the Bolshevik paradigm of "class struggle" had serious difficulty embracing.[20] Even though later revolutionaries such as Che Guevara bypassed both class struggle and party politics opting instead for guerrilla warfare, their foco strategy remained acutely voluntarist. Guerrillas were to act as both the "engine" of the revolution driving the masses into armed revolution against the dependent regimes, as well as the "engineers" of a "new man" and culture freed from capitalistic values.[21]

Clearly, then, the macrostructural scope, vanguardism, and heroic voluntarism of these revolutionary strategists left little room for the ordinary actors, everyday politics, and culture to play their parts in revolution. The turn was left to the Italian revolutionary theorist Antonio Gramsci, who in a sharp departure from economic reductionism, vanguardism, and the Russian road, extended the arena of struggle beyond the "point of production" into the "civil society"—the everyday, associational life, ideas, culture, and arts. To transform the state, Gramsci contended, one should not resort to "frontal attack" or "insurrection" as in 1917 Russia but to the "war of position" or transforming civil society because "in actual reality, civil society and state are one and the same."[22] For Gramsci, then, revolution meant waging relentless struggles in civil society to build hegemony in favor of a new social order. Gramsci's idea of revolution was highly original and instructive in incorporating the social sphere wherein cultural norms and values are contested and new ones are cultivated. But it is a mistake to overlook its historical specificity. For as Gramsci himself emphasized, his theory drew on the contingencies of liberal democratic Europe, not despotic 1917 Russia; nor, I might add, contemporary autocratic Middle East where both the "civil society" and struggle for hegemony assume more complex dynamics, and where "insurrection," both as a historical possibility and theoretical question, continues to hold relevance.[23] In Gramsci's schema, the relationship between the "civil society" and "insurrection" remained unresolved.

We can still gain much insights from the scholarly genre that Gramsci's perspective has in part inspired—that is, "everyday resistance." This scholarship has sparked a rich body of work on the intricacies of counterhegemonic struggles by the subalterns in the quotidian and civil sphere.[24] Michel de Certeau's classic *The Practice of Everyday Life* has unveiled the capacity of the ordinary people to subvert and appropriate the elites' "strategies" of domination through what he calls "tactics."[25] For instance, while the Islamic regime in Iran deploys elaborate "strategies" of ideological hegemony through rituals of mourning (to commemorate the death of the Prophet's grandson, Hussein), some young Iranians appropriate these rituals turning them into evenings of fun and sociality, a "tactic" that I have called "subversive accommodation".[26] The more influential contribution in resistance studies, however, came from James C. Scott whose notion of "everyday resistance," built on the study of poor peasants in Malaysia, revealed the discreet ways (e.g., tax dodging, sabotage, spreading rumors, or pilfering) in which the subalterns could deny claims that elites make on them or advance their own claims on the elites.[27] Such a perception of "resistance" went beyond peasant studies penetrating a variety of fields such as labor studies, identity politics, women's studies, education, or digital communication, and inspired the influential "subaltern studies" historiography in South Asia. Altogether, they established a productive venue to understand the subaltern politics broadly. But serious questions lingered. Matthew Gutmann, for instance, questioned the reduction of popular politics in Latin America to simply such acts of "everyday resistance,"[28] in particular when it is not clear where these acts can take the resisters, and how, if at all, they might transform the life of the actors and their societies.[29] Although Scott did point to both "hidden" and "open" resistance, he did not elaborate on their connection beyond a reference to the metaphor of coral reef.[30] If indeed, as Mona Lilja and Stellan Vinthagen suggest, "resistance" is an umbrella concept including different things ranging from riots and revolution to mimicry and slander, the relationship between them are not examined nor, for that matter, the links between "resistance" and sociopolitical change.[31]

It is clear that in general there is an analytical disconnect between works on contentious politics / revolution and those devoted to everyday life and popular politics. Perspectives on revolution have mainly ignored the everyday lifeworld and those of the latter overlooked revolution.[32] This book hopes to bridge the gap by looking at the everyday of the Arab Spring. I wish to propose a new way of thinking about revolution— more precisely, "refolution"—and the everyday, exploring how the ordinary people matter in the extraordinary revolutions, how the routine figures in rupture, and how the revolution remakes the everyday. To this end, I narrate histories of political engagement by the poor, marginalized youth, women, and social minorities in the experiences of 2011 revolutions in Tunisia and Egypt. As I will elaborate below, my Middle Eastern perspective begins with an understanding of the intricacies of local life in the Arab undersocieties, where the subalterns generate their own norms and narratives through intimate collectives, dispersed networks, and elusive nonmovements in the shadow of the authoritarian states, hostile economies, and stern moral authorities. But these very subaltern groups and their dispersed daily struggles come together through their opaque networks to forge, in opportune moments, a collective and contentious force, coalescing with the uprisings that their very participation enhance and empower. The fall of the dictators, the rise of a new consciousness, and a sense of entitlement propel popular energy, initiatives, and imaginations of unparalleled novelty, scale, and intensity. Routine gives way to rupture, hiddenness to openness, passives turn active, and the ordinary becomes extraordinary as subjects begin to imagine and act on different futures. But as these radical acts and ideas come to challenge the new elites and their institutions, the latter push the subalterns to revert gradually back to the undersocieties, the opaque sphere, from which they had augmented their journey toward the unexpected revolutions. Yet, in the process they spearhead significant changes.

Who are the "subalterns" or the "ordinary people," the terms I use here interchangeably? By these terms, I mean groups such as the urban poor, marginalized youth, women, and social minorities who stand at the margins of the socioeconomic, cultural, and patriarchal structures—the power structures that attempt to deny them the voice to speak. The "urban poor" refers to the low-income, low-skill, and low-status working people who usually crowd in the informal lifeworld and working life. Rural poor include small-holders, tenants, and landless tillers. There is a growing category of college graduates with middle-class aspirations who are pushed by unemployment and precarity to live the life of the poor. I have called them the middle-class poor. As such, the "middle-class poor" may not be characterized as "subaltern," strictly speaking, because of the affordances they enjoy (such as access to media and educational institutions, as well as presence in the public sphere) to voice their grievances. Yet, they are deeply embedded in subaltern economic life and serve as key players in linking subaltern life to the wider political landscape.

I realize the complexity of categories such as "women" or "youth" as they are internally differentiated along class, status, or racial lines. However, here I have in mind their broadly shared position of subordination in relation to patriarchy, ageism, and moral authority. Ordinary and elite women may be subject to the same discriminatory treatments in, say, being forced to wear the hijab, to divorce or to surrender custody of children; yet elite women have no doubt wider possibilities to offset such treatments. Even though my central focus in this book is on the lifeworld of the marginalized and the subaltern in the revolutions, I also pay attention to activism and organizations of women, youth, artists, and social minorities more broadly. An adequate understanding of the subaltern lifeworld and popular politics is not possible in isolation and abstraction. We need to highlight their *relations* to more familiar groups, organizations, or forms of politics. Thus, although this book focuses primarily on the lifeworld of the ordinary people, it also discusses the *connections* of these ordinary people to organized activism, civil associations, and social movements. Here, I take "ordinary" to mean not only nonelite subalterns but also "nonactivist" individuals to distinguish them from the "activists," those who spend part of their time engaging in *extraordinary* activities such as organizing or petitioning beyond the daily routine of their lives. All of these subaltern groups and their struggles are in one way or another entangled with the state, its institutions and governmentality. However, in this interrelation, I focus on the subalterns and their lifeworld rather than the logic of the state response.

## UNDERSOCIETIES

In exploring the question of surprise in revolutions, the sociologist Jeff Goodwin asks why no social scientist or think tanks such as the Fund for Peace that monitor conflicts and instabilities around the world could foresee the coming of the Arab uprisings.[33] Indeed, as Timur Kuran had argued earlier, it is simply impossible to predict precisely when and where revolutions may occur.[34] Since people usually hide their private preferences of likes or dislikes in public out of fear or shame, Kuran suggests, the opposition remains hidden from ears and eyes of both adversaries and observers. And when an event triggers action and a small number go into the streets, a "revolutionary bandwagon" may follow, and others including former supporters of the regime may join in the crowd. In a more intriguing way, Charles Kurzman suggests that people may join revolutionary protests if they know that many others will do the same. But they cannot know in advance partly because people's opposition is not known ("preference falsification"), and even if their opposition is evident, it is not certain that they will express it openly.

They usually remain unsure, changing their decisions momentarily by news or rumors, just as the opponents would not know what tactics to use, when to resist, or when to compromise. In short, people's behavior is contingent.[35]

What if people express dissent, but it goes unnoticed or overlooked by elites, authorities, or observers as simply everyday bickering of little political significance? The debate on the "surprise," valuable as it is, focuses primarily on moments of flare-up, not on how monumental uprisings may emerge in societies deemed stable and ensured by "authoritarian durability." It cannot account for the underlying but invisible dissent brewing in societies that otherwise appear sound and secure. To this end, we need to understand the dynamics of life in the underside of the Arab societies, the everyday social fabric, wherein people forge their own public, create their own norms and narratives, and fashion their own reality in negotiation with those of the "normal" society that the elites and officialdom represent. Such effort is necessary because the known perspectives on the Middle Eastern societies— mosaic and culturalist view, labor-capital outlook, or civil society approach—seem ill-equipped to highlight the subtleties of conflicts and solidarity formation among the subaltern subjects.

The primordial and culturalist undertone of the mosaic perspective stressing the fracture of society into communities, sects, religions, or ethnicities misses the subtle workings of material and nonmaterial interests, class, and power in the subaltern lives.[36] For instance, the culturalist outlook of Orientalist writers such as Bernard Lewis cannot see the Muslim subaltern as capable of imagining revolution beyond the "Battle of Karbala" or outside of a religious frame in terms of a struggle for this-worldly justice.[37] On the other hand, the labor-versus-capital lens of reductionist Marxism tends to downplay or otherwise reduce the multilayered sources of subaltern dissent (gender, age, status, or social standing) to simply class belonging and remains oblivious to varied forms of solidarity formation.[38] The "civil society" outlook that flourished after the cold war with the promise of development and democracy failed to capture the reality of the Middle Eastern undersociety. Even though the trend fostered establishing countless civic associations including some with effective critical work, the idea of "civil society" was essentially reduced to NGOs anchored on the broad neoliberal rationale. Even Hisham Sharabi's innovative characterization of Arab society as "neopatriarchy" cannot help due to its focus on traditional hierarchies clothed in a "pseudo-modern" veneer.[39] In neopatriarchy, the father figure maintains the ultimate power, whether in the image of the "modern" state or in the "civic" realm—the family, clan, and religious sect. The key social unit, family, generates obedience, diminishes autonomy, and thus reinforces the system of patronage. Sharabi's overemphasis on the politics of "mass" encompassing family, clan, and sect overrides the silent, subtle but serious workings of class, interests, and dissent in the underside of the Arab social fabric.

I am envisaging a model of society with a double life: one expressed in the official, elite, and open sphere that gives the appearance of normality, stability, and status quo; the other in the subaltern, informal, and opaque sphere, hidden from the average observer or otherwise seen as aloof and abnormal. Here in these undersocieties—under the shadow of the autocratic regimes, hostile economies, and moral control—the subaltern groups build and engage in enduring networks grounded in kinship, friendship, worship, and working life to sustain livelihood, while resorting to the elusive nonmovements to advance claims, cultivate norms, and enhance life chances. The conflicts and collectives emerging out of these settings (over sustenance, norms, rights, recognition, or alternative lifestyle) shape the subaltern engagement in individual or collective, hidden, or open struggle. For most of these people, their neighborhood provides the primary context of action and imagination. Even though many people may work in offices, farms, factories, or college campuses with their associated conflicts and struggles, their neighborhood allows them more intimate and intense interactions and more extended networks of connectivity and support. Kinship ties get reinforced despite, or perhaps because, of the growth of modern individuation and mobility. Kin members or those with shared communal ties increasingly opt for a nuclear family and love marriage but strive to inhabit in proximity, in the same neighborhood or even apartment buildings, to ensure support and share responsibility.[40] Religious times and spaces—mosques, Friday prayers, or semiprivate women's *halaqat*— facilitate assembly, exchange, and identity and serve to mobilize mutual support as well as broader collective actions. Yet these traditional settings also structure the social control of women and young men who often undergo everyday police surveillance.

Thinking with Jacques Derrida on a bygone friendship, a commentator writes how in this age of social media and superficial relations, the "idea of friendship seems almost quaint, and possibly imperiled."[41] Not in the Arab undersocieties. For most young people there, friendship remains the chief entity to build identity, security, survival, as well as contentious politics. Friendship underlies relation of trust, loyalty, and solidarity; it is nourished by affective and reciprocal bonding forged in everyday life and enacted in the homes, schools, cafés, or street corners. Embedded in friendship is a restoration of a sense of childhood even in adults who may behave like carefree and playful children. This make friends similar to siblings albeit without the latter's hierarchy and rivalry. Friendship is different from and goes beyond comradery which underlines the sameness of those who share a political commitment and is marked by equality, discipline, courage, and enthusiasm.[42] Friendship is more affective, intimate, and enduring, bordering on kinship, but it can intersect with comradery. Friends embody company and sociality in normal times and a source of support and survival in times of crisis. But my emphasis here is on the role of friendship in contentious politics. I am not invoking Derrida's notion of friendship as the basis of future democracy.[43] Rather, I am thinking in a more immediate sense that the fundamental elements of trust, solidarity, and loyalty in friendship serve as an invaluable asset to ensure safety and security when confronting the regimes of surveillance and suppression.[44]

Closely associated and often identical with friendship is the *shilla* (clique), close-knit and exclusive small groups of individuals sharing common values within a much larger group, as in a workplace, school, neighborhood, or an army barrack. Here, I do not mean the kind of self-serving "small groups of friends united by bonds of personal, economic, and / or political interests" described by Robert Springborg— those active in business or bureaucracy and who try to enhance their own exclusive interests to the extent of corruption.[45] Nor, for that matter, do I have in mind gangs or the *futuwa*s of the modern Middle East that are well-organized and hierarchal groups typically engaged in criminal and chivalrous acts centered on particular urban territory, most commonly in the urban undersocieties. Rather, I am referring to the mostly altruistic *shilla*s that center on sociality and support from which local leaders may emerge. I am pointing to those innumerable small (ten to fifteen members) and informal private or semipublic cliques and collectives within which ordinary people connect, socialize, deliberate, develop trust, and often generate alternative norms and narratives. An Arab youth survey by the German Friedrich Ebert Foundation found in 2016 that over 60 percent of the Arab youth (between sixteen and thirty) including 63 percent in Egypt and 72 percent in Tunisia belonged to a *shilla*.[46]

The Yemeni khat-chewing assemblies or Kuwaiti *diwan* are adequately known and well studied.[47] So are the Iranian *doureh* (exclusive male private gatherings) or *patouqs*, the place-based circles of intellectuals, friends, or workmates, who may assemble regularly in coffee shops, malls, or restaurants to bond, socialize, or discuss political and literary matters, perhaps something similar to Robert Putnam's bowlers.[48] But in Saudi Arabia, where political control is embedded in an intransigent patriarchy justified on Wahhabi Islamic doctrine, young Muslim women generate their own spaces within the system to challenge sex segregation, while the young devise ways to assert their youthfulness through as-sociations of their *shilla* or in open public spaces. Amelie Le Renard's ethnography gives us a glimpse of how educated Saudi women have been transforming urban societies by creating their own professional, con-sumerist, as well as nonconformist lifeworlds.[49] Groups of women ini-tiated "push normal" to challenge sex segregation in public by, for instance, strolling in male-only spaces, art galleries, and work areas, not to mention their home-based associations. A young male who lived in Riyadh related to me how "we were trying to make our own youthful spaces, *shillas,* in clubs, schools, or friendship gatherings in homes to watch movies, play games, discuss issues, and make friends with girls."[50] Pascale Menoret, reporting from the Saudi Arabia activist world, shows how "groups of ten or twenty friends who share a common goal and meet regularly in a given place, apartment, coffee shop, or private rest house *(istiraha)"* had created their own world under the shadow of the regime's surveillance.[51] During my visit to Riyadh in 2013, I could see how groups of young boys and veiled girls hung out in the malls eyeing each other, sending messages in the forbidding spaces. The boys stated to me that they had formed their own "societies" in the malls, gymna-siums, and private homes where they socialized, watched banned movies, and deliberated social issues.

These cliques and collectives lie somewhere between the Haberma-sian notions of the "private" sphere of family and intimacy and the "public" sphere of civil interaction and rational deliberation. Consider, for instance, how the public acts of organizing and mobilizing for so-cial movements are often initiated by exclusive circles of friends and *shillas.* Yet in terms of worldview, such collectives echo aspects of "coun-terpublics," the parallel discursive arenas where the subaltern groups establish alternative narratives about their identities, interests, and needs, different from those of the elites and officialdom.[52] These hybrid cir-cles may give us a clue as to what goes on between the underside and overside of these societies.

But beyond these *physical* interpersonal cliques, collectives, and networks, a large number of subaltern groups simultaneously get involved in certain inaudible, individualized, and elusive acts of claim making that I have called nonmovements.[53] They are the dispersed but contentious practices of individuals and families in everyday life who struggle to enhance their life chances often in a quiet and discreet fashion. For instance, urban poor families strive to acquire land to put up a shelter, gain access to urban amenities, consolidate their communities, and earn a living in the vast street subsistence economy. These efforts often involve encroaching on the state, property holders, public spaces, and public order and are thus deemed subversive and unlawful. Meanwhile, Muslim women are engaged in daily struggles at home and in educational institutions, workplaces, and court houses to secure justice and equal rights in decision making, personal status, work relations, and presence in public space. Sexual minorities tend to establish discreet relations to build collective identity and practice alternative lifestyles. And youths take every opportunity, at times through the Foucauldian "counterconducts," to reclaim their youthfulness, affirm their autonomy, challenge the social control of elders and moral authority through destabilizing lifestyles and subcultures, such as premarital sex, *urfi* or non-official marriage, living separately from parents, youthful religious rituals, and street corner assemblages.[54] These mundane practices by very large numbers of people entail significant changes in the subaltern lives and their societies, in urban fabric and governance, citizenship rights, resource distribution, in lifestyles, and in norms and rules.

As such, these practices are not meant as deliberate acts of defiance or even as a "clear" or "ambiguous message," as in Scott's resistance.[55] Rather, they aim simply to improve dignified lives and secure fairness. Thus, the power of nonmovements rests not on the unity of actors to put pressure on authorities to concede, as in the conventional social movements. Rather, it rests on the power of big numbers, the consequential effect on norms and rules in society of many people simultaneously doing similar, though contentious, things. Yet the actual process inevitably involves these subalterns encroaching on power and property, challenging patriarchy, breaking laws, and defying norms. The ensuing processes (confrontation, negotiation, ostracism, repression) condition the subaltern actors to reflect on the meaning of their doings and the adversaries' response, to ponder about law and justice. They become "political." They begin to utter the language of rights, speak of "us" and "them," and venture collective resistance, all of which prepare them to potentially engage in broader political movements when they arise. The social, economic, and cultural changes they steer, and the undeniable facts they create on the ground, result in establishing new norms and rules in society. For instance, the poor people building homes or subsistent business illegally and without paying tax, the young people pursuing subversive lifestyles and subcultures, or women becoming public actors and claiming gender justice in education, work, and personal status all become de facto (counter)norms to which the political and moral authority have to respond. These de facto norms may end up being accepted or officially recognized. This practical process of generating norms that may follow legal change reflects what the German constitutional lawyer Walter Jellinek described as "the normative power of the factual," or the ability of certain kinds of facts to create norms. It equally echoes "the factual power of the normative," or the ability of norms to shape facts, as proposed by Hermann Heller.[56] Yet our stories speak more to the factual and normative power of the subaltern acts in everyday life.

The result is change neither in the sense of conscious and coordinated efforts by politicians, planners, and other powers, nor that which is caused by Latourian things, objects, or natural processes. Rather, this is change in a rhizomatic, associative, and performative sense, pushed by millions of ordinary humans in their everyday lives through a vast temporal stretch in which, as the German curator Katrin Klingan puts it, "time means production."[57] Here, change appears as "multiple temporalities folded over one another in our everyday social fabric," a cumulative process that "reclaims time, not as a linear process of producing results, but as a continual, constantly transforming stop-motion of improvisations, variations and alterations." As if an effect of the Anthropocene, "social space becomes akin to the geological record, striated, with the record of nonmovements accumulating horizontally." But as I will show later, such gradual transformation may be disrupted by eruptions and mutations when nonmovements turn into formidable social movements or merge into revolts and revolutions.

How do we characterize these disparate practices, networks, cliques, collectives, and sentiments embedded in the underside of these societies? Are they not the Middle Eastern version of what Havel, drawing on the Soviet bloc, called "hidden sphere"—that is, the private realm of individuals who communicated the "truth" between themselves but separate from and against the Communist state and its omnipresent propaganda machine?[58] Writing on the paradox of the Soviet collapse that came both as a surprise and yet expected, the anthropologist Alexei Yurchak argues that although the Soviet system—its values, institutions, and discourse—appeared to be normalized and stable, it nevertheless offered spaces (such as discourse of equality, justice, community, or selflessness) within which the Soviet citizens functioned, interpreted, altered, and subverted meanings by creating their own reality different from what the authoritative discourse or officialdom had imagined. The system induced not only citizens' attachment but also their alienation; it seemed stable and durable but in fact remained fragmented and fragile.[59] So the Soviet citizens were pretending as if they were agreeing with the officialdom. But in fact and in private, they resented that same officialdom. They were engaged in "performative" acts of voting, marching, singing the anthem, or joining organizations. But they gave different meanings to these authoritative political rituals.

There is much in the notion of "hidden sphere" that resonates with the contemporary Arab or Iranian undersocieties. But the sphere that the Arab or Iranian subalterns have created is not hidden, nor is their dissent silent. First, the regimes in the region, despite being autocratic and repressive, have not been totalitarian as Eastern Europe was. The Arab or Iranian societies have enjoyed myriad socioscapes or ambiguous (spatial, legal, institutional, and discursive) zones that the subaltern use to push for their claims. These include, for instance, exploiting vague laws, unclear public-private distinction, official corruption, or sexual fluidity. Moreover, ordinary people speak out, pester, and complain in public—in taxis, buses, or street corners. In fact, the region has enjoyed a powerful "political street."[60] Subaltern groups may formally show compliance to avoid risks, but they remain deeply cynical privately and critical publicly. They may participate in official events, consume state media, and turn out to vote for the autocratic rulers, but in their subsocieties they quietly create their own reality, crafting alternative meanings, norms, and narratives often in opposition to the authoritative discourse and practice. Whether or not this reflects Gramscian take on the subaltern "contradictory consciousness" is perhaps immaterial—at best it has the appearance of contradiction.[61] What matters, rather, is that when the political breakthrough emerges, these subaltern groups may rise from their undersocieties against the very rulers for whom they cast their votes not long before.[62]

What primarily marks these undersocieties is not hiddenness; it is opacity. They are not invisible but illegible. And this lies at the center of their strength and the political surprise that may transpire. Millions live in the informal communities that rarely use official maps, street names, home numbers, or regular thoroughfares. Their economic life remains a mystery to outsiders and their politics unintelligible. But the whereabouts, relationships, and doings of people of these communities are internally known to one another. People intensely socialize, exchange news, mediate, and interfere; they lend and borrow money, goods, or services. These intertwined lives accumulate an exclusive local knowledge that remains internal, mostly denied for the elites and authorities, who after all tend to have faint presence in these settings, except perhaps for the repressive police. In the early 1990s, the Imbaba neighborhood of 800,000 inhabitants in the heart of Cairo was being run by the Islamists' "government within the government" of which the officials had remained unaware. Only after a foreign journalist broke the news did the government move in to make the area "transparent" by installing street names and home numbers, generating maps and "development projects."[63] Opacity is power; it is the flip side of the panopticon.

Even more than the *physical* space and lifeworld, opacity defines the very texture of the subaltern nonmovements, for no identifiable person or group is responsible for them. There is no leader and organization, no slogans or ideology, no banners and no marches. They come to life when countless dispersed individuals and families, structured in the routine of daily life, take up similar seemingly mundane practices to make their lives better. Aspects of such ambiguity may find echoes in digital activism. For instance, in 2018, the online campaign of boycott "Let It Rot" and "Let It Curdle" against the austerity programs in Morocco managed to slash the sales of fuel, dairy products, fish, and others, but it was not clear who among the two million active promoters initiated or led the campaign when it spread and gained the support of 57 percent of the population.[64] Yet, as the states extend their surveillance over the virtual world, the digital nonmovements become more vulnerable to exposure than those on the ground.

Here in this "opaque sphere," the subalterns move back and forth between the private and public realms, the closed cliques and open institutions, nonmovements and collective resistance, silence and voice, compliance and rebellion. The opacity is not usually a deliberate strategy to confuse; it is part of the subaltern lifeworld that renders their subjectivities unreadable and their behavior unpredictable. This politics of opacity lies at the heart of the subaltern resilience, for it denies the opponents of the strategic knowledge about the subaltern lives. There was a time in the 1960s and 1970s when the political movements deliberately went underground in order to conceal and deny knowledge of their operation to the opponents but were deemed unlawful and subject to crackdown. Police often deployed infiltrators to these organizations to gather intelligence. Today, the overly exposed open movements (with their personnel, programs, ideas, and strategies all out on the internet or social media) may enjoy extraordinary reach and mass support but are vulnerable to political surveillance and strategic frustration.[65] In comparison, subaltern everyday politics has the advantage of appearing illegible and ambiguous without, however, being seen as necessarily political, oppositional, or subversive.

Thus, the dynamics of the everyday lifeworld expressed in the workings of the networks, cliques, collectives, and nonmovements keep the participants engaged and alert while carving off pieces of opportunity in their favor as the repressive regimes would prevent them from forging open and organized mobilization. So while the regimes are able to subdue "collective actors" (political parties or organized and open movements), they are unable to prevent the "collective actions" forged through these diffused socioscapes in which parallel realities—institutions, norms, and narratives—distinct from the official accounts may develop.

## FROM ORDINARY TO EXTRAORDINARY

How does the everyday lifeworld described thus far get entangled in extraordinary uprisings and revolutions? How do its undercurrents, institutions, and actors figure in postrevolution moments? And how, after all, do the ordinary people preoccupied with the routine of daily life turn to do things of extraordinary magnitude? Surely, ordinary people often deploy their past skills and experience of collective protests to engage in new ones, as many observers have noted.[66] This is particularly true of local leaders, labor activists, women, and human rights advocates with the experience of activism, strikes, and street politics. But most participants in revolutions usually hold little experience of open protests, let alone prior ideas about revolution; they typically develop such ideas and experiences in the process of struggle. On the other hand, it is always tempting to think of revolution in terms of Gustav Le Bon's "psychological crowd" to which people are driven by the force of spontaneity, contagion, and subconscious instincts and in which individuals lose their individuality and melt into one unified whole.[67] Beyond the fact that this view overlooks the participants' rational, moral, and affective motivations, it cannot see the more complex processes than pure psychology and animalistic impulses at work.

As Alain Badiou has argued, a revolutionary movement does not spread by contagion or contamination; it does so through "resonance."[68] Something happens there that resonates or means something familiar with people over here and spurs them to act. This may help us understand how a feeling of common destiny and collective imaginary emerges during an uprising. Writing on the Egyptian revolution, Ayman El-Desouki attributes this common feeling, this "connective agency," to Egypt's cultural register of *amara*—"signs and tokens of a shared destiny," or an ethics of solidarity, that is embedded in people's cultural memory.[69] This is an interesting cultural take. But all revolutionary uprisings, not just those influenced by the Egyptian notion of *amara*, espouse such a feeling of shared destiny and connective agency. In fact, it defines the very basis of the "revolution as movement." Beyond affect and cultural traits, it is also crucial to understand the actual mechanisms, social ties, and networks that connect people to one another in normal and exceptional times.

It has now become customary to attribute connectivity in movements to the logic of information technology. Manuel Castells has identified a shift in late-modern societies from interpersonal ties to large-scale fluid social networks.[70] Others view a shift from collective action to "connective action" characterized by, among others, the logic of personalized public engagement.[71] It is undeniable that digital technology has left a profound impact on the workings of the contemporary social movements and revolutions. It has enabled the mobilization of vast constituencies, connecting diverse identity groups and networks, albeit thinly, more widely, and rapidly than ever before.[72] It certainly played an important role in shaping the mobilizational modes of the Arab Spring. But we must not overlook the digital divide that disfavors the poor, provincial, elderly, and illiterate. Even though some 85 percent of population in both Tunisia and Egypt used cell phones in 2010, just 15 percent in Tunisia used Facebook (4 percent in Egypt), and only 500 persons Twitter (40,000 in Egypt).[73] Nor, for that matter, should we underestimate the physical and the collective in favor of the digital and individual. Indeed, physical interactions and collective networks on the ground were instrumental in the Arab revolutions, not only in parallel with but also as part and parcel of the digital realm.[74] The image one gets from this understanding of "connective action" is that the dispersed and atomized individuals are joined together through the technological affordance we call social media mechanism. But in the Middle East and perhaps elsewhere, individuals, if they get connected at all, do not get connected simply as individuals but as members of the already-existing collectives like *shillas*, cliques, friendship circles, kinship networks, and not to mention, the web of social nonmovements. Here, individuals serve as mediums connecting these everyday collectives, physical entities, and activisms to the virtual web of wider publics. I suggest that the flexible dynamics of nonmovements—operating both on the ground and in the digital realm, stretching out, mutating, and shifting back and forth— play a crucial part in mediating the everyday lifeworld and revolutions.

In their basic form, nonmovements are the collective action of non-collective actors who are directly related to one another through tacit communications, or passive networks, which in turn is triggered by recognizing their commonalities in public spaces.

For instance, the hypothetical street vendor Abdallah from Tadamun in Tunis would recognize his shared position with other vendors even though he may not know or talk to them. In the same fashion, the unemployed college graduate, Hmed, who frequents the street cafés of his neighborhood with his friends and *shilla* would identify their common misfortune with others of similar demeanor sitting around in the café

Figure 1.1.   A Nonmovement

without even speaking to them. Or think of Asmar who, in a family court in Tunis trying to seek divorce from her abusive husband, would feel a shared agony with other women in the waiting room by merely noting their anxious expressions. Each of these situations displays moments of developing passive connections and forging collective sentiments among individual actors in local and physical settings.

The information technologies, when deployed, would change these dynamics and open new possibilities. First, they would extend the space of connectivity beyond one's locality to distant geographical spaces. Second, the information technologies would tie the physical to the digital. Finally, they would link the elusive nonmovements to the circles of cyberactivists and organizations. So the unemployed college graduate Hmed can now serve as a medium to connect his jobless *shilla* and his unwired poor family to a wider world of similar people through blogging or membership in a Facebook group. In a similar way, Asmar's sense of common identity and anguish can be extended beyond her intimate friends or the court room with those of other women in similar positions as she hears or reads their stories put out in the media or by activist circles.

What happens in the time of popular uprisings? These subaltern collectives and networks take on new dynamics during the extraordinary political upheavals triggered by incidents like the self-immolation of Mohammed Bouazizi in Tunisia in 2010, the January 25, 2011 protest in Egypt, or the levying of tax on the use of WhatsApp in Lebanon in

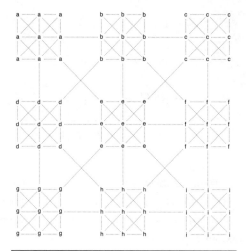

Figure 1.2.   Network of Nonmovements

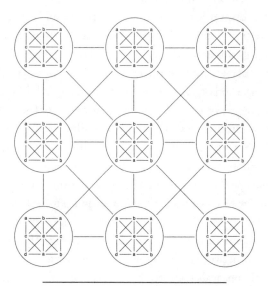

Figure 1.3.   Network of Cliques

2019. On the one hand, local *shillas*, friendship circles, or family units become political actors operating between the on-the-ground and cyber networks.

At the same time, information technologies allow the dispersed non-movements (such as youth, the poor, women, social minorities, and others) to interconnect, forming something like a broad network of networks.

Thus, Hmed, who sits with his fellow clique in the local cafés to organize protests or prepare signs in the neighborhood, may link up through his social networking with Asmar's women's circle, who in turn may learn of Hmed's network and those of others connected to him, including those from Tadamun where the street vendor Abdallah works. All these individuals in these vast networks may eventually join together in the physical streets of the uprising.

This gives us a cue to explore how the subaltern everyday struggles came together in the Arab uprisings to forge a collective and contentious force coalescing with the political mobilizations that had been initiated largely by young activists.

Why should individuals like Hmed, Asmar, and Abdallah with different concerns and in different nonmovements come to feel and act in unison? What would they share at such moments of political upheaval? It may have to do with their overlapping interests and positionalities, or interpositionality. For instance, our Abdallah who is a street vendor may also be the father of a college graduate like Hmed, who is both young and unemployed. And all of them are subjects of police violence. Interpositionality is certainly important, but it cannot on its own follow collective action. It needs to be activated, to be felt and internalized, in order to find meaning. The key to the birth of the collective agency is the spirit of the moment, a sudden extraordinary constellation of voices, networks, and energies that activates overlapping interests and positionalities and renders disparate subaltern groups to share a feeling of collective pain and prospect. Something happens somewhere to some

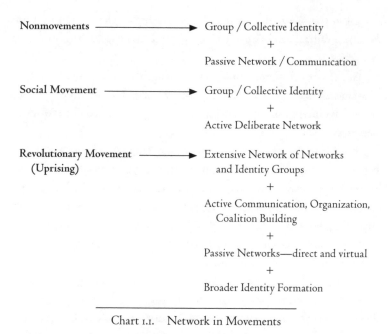

Chart 1.1.   Network in Movements

individuals or groups that resonate with others elsewhere and they take on its meaning. Asmar, Abdallah, and Hmed may read about, hear about, or see the predicaments of fellow subalterns, which may come to resonate with their own experience of subalternity as subordinate women, vulnerable street vendors, and unemployed youth. The visual dimension of relating to distant others has become critical. The "new visibility," the ability of individuals to witness happenings through countless images and video clips, adds a new layer to this shared feeling.[75] From such a complex process may emerge the collective agents poised to engage in collective action and possibly even revolution.

Most revolutions "begin" with narrow protests, such as housewives demanding bread, intellectuals asking for freedom of expression, or young people raging against police killing of a colleague. But only few protests, however widespread, may develop into a revolutionary uprising. In 2017–2018, tens of thousands of Iranian workers, students, farmers, middle-class poor, creditors, women, and others concerned with the environment took to the streets in more than eighty-five cities for ten days before the government's crackdown halted the rebellion.[76] Some observers considered the events as a prelude to revolution. It was not. For even though connected and concurrent, the protestors mostly focused on their own particular claims—workers for delayed wages, farmers for drought, creditors for lost savings, and the young for jobs. As such, theirs was not a *collective* action of a united people but *connective* actions of parallel concerns—a simultaneity of noncollective actions that only the new information technologies could generate.

Popular protests become a revolutionary uprising ("revolution as movement") when the diverse constituencies—workers, women, youth, ethnic, religious, or social minorities—come to eclipse their particularistic claims in favor of broader calls for greater good for all— dignity, democracy, or justice. A revolutionary spirit arises when these social groups temporarily cease to be workers, women, youth, or ethnic minorities and become equal parts of a singular entity they call the people. Identities fade in favor of an affective and strategic urge for unity and collective equality. Women relinquish claims for gender rights, youth for youthfulness, workers for fair distribution and self-realization, or social minorities for recognition, only to resurrect them in earnest once the dictators are gone and the urge for unity is dissipated. But segments of the poor may begin an early practice of "their revolution" in villages or urban backstreets by seizing land, property, and opportunity or forming cooperatives. This "opportunism" of the poor may evoke Arendt's misgivings about the claims of the poor for distribution and leveling (the "social question"), which she thought would spoil the revolutions leading to tyranny.[77] But one might perceive it differently in terms of the popular desire to realize "future in the present." The more salient expressions of this "future in the present" include the "liberated zones" of the revolutionary wars—for example, in Mexico's Chiapas or the "liberated squares" in urban uprisings, as seen by some in the Occupy movements of the early 2010s. These display the kind of social order that the rebels appear to desire: popular control, democratic self-governance, horizontal decision making, self-help, and altruism.

Clearly, then, revolution is not limited to the strategic matter of how movements evolve and networks interconnect. It is also an affective and cognitive process involving a sudden shift in the structure of feelings and thinking, expressed most vividly in popular politics in the post-revolution moments. The very experience of the uprisings—moments of solidarity, sacrifice, unity, and equality—generate in the ordinary people a new consciousness, a novel perception of the social world, which enables them to imagine, expect, and do things that they had never done before. This informs and implies the "event" of the revolution, a condition that gives rise to an "experience of enlightenment," an uncommon novel awareness, a kind of gnosis.[78] With the fall of dictators and the collapse of police control, ordinary people experience a liberating loss of fear and a powerful sense of entitlement. These in turn propel popular militancy of unparalleled scale and intensity, which comes into conflict paradoxically with the powerful desire for stability and normalcy at a time when people face disrupted economies, disturbed state administration, and elite backlash. Subaltern groups now strive to intensify their everyday claims, moving further to challenge many established hierarchies in a manner that is no longer dispersed and discreet as before. The elusive nonmovements turn into more organized social movements: open, audible, and collective campaigns.

Thus, women set out to subvert some of the enduring gender norms both in discourse and in practice. They work in or establish associations, build coalitions, lobby, and organize street protests. Students rise up against the austere education order and hierarchy by calling for change in schools and college campuses. Ethnic, religious, and sexual minorities activate their networks, come together, and claim recognition. In the meantime, subaltern youth exhibit an extraordinary urge to "do something" for their reborn nation. Their collective efforts find expressions in local self-rule and development initiatives in urban neighborhoods, organizing grassroots democracy in villages, and pressing for change through street protests. For the poor, now empowered and entitled, respect and redistribution become key claims which they pursue in earnest. Informal communities witness an upsurge in neighborhood committees to organize local life and social development. In the meantime, the urban poor embark on aggressive and extensive encroachment, extralegal constructions, occupying state housing, tapping on urban amenities, while organizing to defend collective gains. Street vendors proliferate as they freely encroach on the strategic urban streets to make a living or further their lot. Critical outlooks get displayed in the explosion of revolutionary aesthetic, arts, graffiti, and music. While workers purge oppressive managers and take control of plants to run through work councils, small farmers expropriate farmlands or build cooperatives to farm, manage, and take the revenue. Efforts to create new syndicates and unions among small farmers, street vendors, and wage earners find extraordinary currency. Indeed, the radical claims of the poor place the "social question"—property rights, redistribution, and self-rule—on the revolutionary agenda. These radical moves sooner or later provoke the fury of the new elites, deepening the political strife between ordinary people and the authorities who preach stability and normal life. In these turbulent postrevolution times, elites, opportunists, and agents—domestic or foreign—strive to take advantage of the moment as much as the subaltern subjects do.

Yet this episode of intense and open mobilization is likely to subside in favor of a return to the opaque undersociety, a strategy that is perceived to better serve the grassroots needs. For when the old power structure, a feature of the refolutions, remains unaltered, the politics-as-usual adopted by the new regimes is likely to offset the subaltern gains and frustrate their organized efforts. It would push the subaltern groups to seek merit in the more discreet nonmovements and local trust than open and audible mobilization or trust in the state's protection. Even though the structural capacity of each subaltern group to face its adversaries and cope with revolutionary dynamics differs—I have examined these dynamics in detail for the poor, women / gender, and youth separately in this book—they would mostly resort to direct actions, local self-rule, and reciprocity, while negotiating with the structures of power to enhance their life chances. Such a repertoire may continue until a new political opportunity arises in which these subaltern groups begin a new cycle of collective rebellion.

Is this a retreat to the old ways? Maybe. But these are old ways at a time when the old order, however entrenched, faces new political subjects and novel subjectivities, when the incidence of revolution has caused extraordinary disruptions, empowered the subalterns, and rendered the new rulers more security conscious. The subalterns find themselves in a somewhat new battlefield with shifted players, altered rules of the game, and conflicting desires for both struggle and stability. As grassroots activists become more aware, skilled, and entitled, the ruling elites deploy more vigilance and vengeance. Wounded by the revolutionary assault, dominant groups strive to fight back, consolidate power, impose surveillance, and even restore the old order. This outcome would remind the rebels, in retrospect, how critical it is for the revolution to radically transform the ancien régime and its power blocs in favor of one that embraces an egalitarian and democratic order.

But a prevalent view suggests that no matter how much revolutions alter the incumbent states, in the end they tend to reestablish authoritarian, if not totalitarian, order of a different sort. Thus, in a recent book, George Lawson concludes that despite radical changes that revolutions typically cause, "they are usually major disappointments, often ending in defeat, re-subjugating those who brought them about, and leading to the establishment of domestic tyranny."[79] It is undeniable that many revolutions have indeed resulted in authoritarianism of various kinds, as in Russia, China, Cuba, Algeria, Iran, or Egypt of the 1950s and 2010s. If we take the macrostructural and state-centric outlook, revolutions are most likely to disappoint, fail, even betray dreams. But it may be different if we take, as we do in this book, the social lens, looking at what happens at the grassroots level, in the everyday, at the underside. For no matter what transpires at the top, revolution unleashes dramatic convulsions in society—often giving rise to new thinking, inspirations, and ways of life, new relations of power and property, and new claims for redistribution and self-governance. The recurring proclamations by Arab activists today, even at the height of despair, that "things will never go back to the past," point to certain irreversible if illegible outcomes, certain internalized revolutionary ways of feeling, being, and doing things, which, put together, differentiate these societies from their prerevolutionary past and, at the same time, set the foundation for thinking of different futures when new political openings arise.

*Chapter 2*

# The Subaltern under Autocracies

THE STATUS OF THE ARAB COUNTRIES in the decade prior to the 2011 uprisings was so unsettling that in retrospect the revolutions appear inevitable. Rarely had the region seen in its recent history such a cry for change as it did in that momentous decade. "Everywhere has changed except the Middle East," echoed the sentiment of the time. Arab autocracies from Egypt, Tunisia, Yemen, and Syria to the monarchies of Jordan, Morocco, and the Persian Gulf all appeared deeply entrenched and stable, building alliances with the military, intelligent services, and globalized business elites, while showing little regard for citizens' desire to meaningfully participate in politics. According to the Freedom House, the preuprising Middle East and North Africa region was the "least free in the world," marked by "severe abuses of almost all fundamental political rights and civil liberties."[1]

These autocratic regimes, meanwhile, had begun since the 1990s to transform their welfare-oriented economies into a more neoliberal breed in which some segments prospered extraordinarily, while the fate of others was left to the mercy of the market. In the mid-2000s, the *Arab Human Development Report* deemed the Arab countries to be "richer than developed," suffering from a growing inequality and deep deficits in democracy, development, and gender empowerment.[2] By 2008, food prices had risen, inflation more than doubled the global rate, and unemployment (25 percent) especially among youth had become the highest in the world.[3] Even though the fear of mass revolt pushed the governments in Egypt, Tunisia, and Jordan to provide some safety nets in the form of social funds, nongovernmental organizations (NGOs), and religious charities, such measures appeared too feeble to meet the rising expectations of the increasingly urbanized, literate, and young population.[4]

In Tunisia, President Zein al-Abedine Ben Ali had since 1987 presided over a police state that had closed the major venues of open debate and the free press, in addition to political rights and civil society associations. His autocracy combined secularism with a modernist veneer, liberal social mores, and women's legal rights, and ruling through fear and repression. The regime "allowed an elitist legal opposition, only to show that you could not do much," according to the Tunisian political scientist Hamza Meddeb.[5] But at the same time, it had put in place an economy of consumption which provided loans, cheap cars, popular computers, and other consumer goods for the middle class to enjoy life so long as they remained politically mute. In the meantime, its corporatist policy courted the historically powerful labor organization, UGTT, that organized mostly well-to-do workers, notably the state employees. The idea of "consume and shut up!" had found a discreet charm in this country of 10 million people at the time when neighboring Algeria was burning in a civil war.[6] In this context, the key opposition, the Islamic al-Nahda led by Rachid al-Ghannoushi, received draconian treatment. Repression targeted not just the dissenters but also their families, their jobs, their chance of using institutions, or even of getting married. It instituted a "social death." This system of strict surveillance mixed with welfare structured citizens' obedience, according to an observer.[7]

Egypt, with a population of 82 million in 2010, had been ruled by the National Democratic Party (NDP), since 1980 led by President

Hosni Mubarak under the heavy influence of the military. With the liberalization of the economy since 1990s, Mubarak allied himself increasingly with the new business class and the intelligence apparatus at the cost of demoting the military.[8] His economic liberalization departed greatly from the earlier distributionist policies, increasing inequality and marginalization. By 2010, some 490 Egyptians controlled 25 percent of national wealth.[9] Yet Egypt's autocracy, compared to Tunisia, allowed more space for oppositional parties, press, civil society associations, and somewhat independent judiciary. The militant Islamist opposition, such as Jihad and al-Gama'a al-Islamiyya, was harshly suppressed, but the powerful and highly organized Muslim Brothers, even though illegal, were largely tolerated. Political surveillance, police brutality, and moral-religious repression remained an integral element in the regime's governance.[10] Indeed, since the 1990s, Islamization from below had pushed such secular regimes to court religious conservatism in order to gain moral legitimacy, serving as a pretext to impose social control against dissenting women, youth, leftists, as well as religious and sexual minorities.

Thus, in the 2000s, the subaltern groups—the poor, marginalized youth, women, and social minorities—faced three major challenges—political repression, economic marginalization, and religious-moral surveillance—even though the extent of these challenges in Tunisia and Egypt and the degree of subalternity for each group differed. How did the subaltern groups manage to operate under these conditions? How did they survive, subsist, and subvert? And in what ways did they live their lives while struggling to enhance their life chances? Crowded in the informal, discreet, and opaque undersocieties, the subaltern groups built on the networks of family, kinship, and local collectives to ensure support and survival, while resorting to nonmovements to extend their claims. In this manner, they established communities of life and labor wherein they carved off opportunities to better their lives, resist exclusion, and craft their own reality. However, the dynamics of the subaltern struggles would change from the mid-2000s. A shift in the regional politics following the 9/11 terrorist attacks, the advent of new information technologies, and the rise of "new politics" set the stage for the subaltern groups to extend their networks and adopt more collective, open, and audible protests that ultimately merged into the streams of the uprisings.

## THE POOR

Since the 1990s, the Egyptian political opposition was dominated by the Jihadis, the Muslim Brothers, and a number of secular parties. Mostly aloof from such opposition, the urban poor carried on with their quiet encroachment, surreptitiously and often unlawfully acquiring land to build homes, obtaining electricity and piped water, constructing roads, and organizing garbage collection. They strived to secure work mostly in the vast informal economy, while investing heavily in their children to give them a life better than their own. Between 1998 and 2006, most of the 4.5 million new households, mostly newly married couples, moved into the _ashwaiyyat_ or informal communities, despite the existence of over 10.5 million vacant housing units, whose high prices these people could not afford.[11] By 2006, some 60–65 percent of Cairenes had built life in the _ashwaiyyat_, but problems such as frequent power cuts and water shortage marked their everyday life. Whereas the rich communities in Cairo and elsewhere with vast green lawns and swimming pools expected an uninterrupted flow of water in a country that fell far below "water poverty," some 40 percent of Cairo's population, usually poor, only had access to drinking water for no more than three hours per day; at least four districts received no water at all.[12] Millions depended on public wells for drinking or washing.[13] For those who did have access, the International Monetary Fund–initiated transfer in 2004 of water utilities to private corporations led to the rise, in some areas doubling, in the cost of water, leaving scores of families to depend on the Nile River.[14] More importantly, there was always the lingering threat of demolition and dispossession. Yet residents found ways to get around inadequacies and often resist when the threat came. Frustrated, the parliament expressed helplessness. "We are facing a dangerous cultural legacy from the *ashwaiyyat* which is expressed in 'Go illegal and God will help later,'" deputies lamented. "The encroachment will continue and the government will not be able to confront them legally, while the transgressors will expect that the law will eventually have to adapt itself [to the fait accompli]."[15]

Unlike Egypt's prerevolution 80 million population which had crammed in just 5 percent of the land (Nile valley and delta), Tunisia's 10 million had spread throughout the country in towns and villages that had few informal settlements, such as Tadamon and Sayyeda Menoubiyya in the capital Tunis, which appeared in better condition than those in Cairo. Tunisia had "essentially eliminated all its slums" through a program initiated by the Ministry of Infrastructure.[16] Rather, it was the regional disparity in access to opportunities—between the marginalized interior (*dakhel*) and the better-off coastal towns (*sahel*)—that stood at the heart of the popular dissent. Key resources such as water, mining, oil, and gas were located in the *dakhel*, but products and profit were channeled into the coastal regions for processing, manufacturing, and marketing. Sidi Bouzid, the birthplace of the revolution, was once prosperous, a top producer of vegetables and dairy products, according the geographer Habib Ayeb. But by 2011, it became one of the poorest regions, with a poverty rate of 42.3 percent compared to 24 percent national average, where the large agribusinesses deprived small farmers from the irrigation system.[17] The interior areas such as Ain Drahem in the south and Sidi Makhlouf in the north were believed to be deliberately marginalized for ethnic and tribal reasons. But in general, government policies benefited certain regions and disadvantaged others to the extent that their inhabitants described themselves as "outcasts," not a part of Tunisia.[18] For the provincial poor, the key concerns were not housing, education, or health but jobs, precarity, discrimination, and police brutality in urban areas and access to land, credit, and farming resources in the rural settings.[19] Unemployment and precarity, however, remained the prime concerns. The young people, 30 percent jobless, hanging out in cafés or surfing the internet had become the marker of Tunisia's developmental deficit. One out of three young resorted to informal work on the black market. They earned good income but had to endure the risks of unlawful trade or jobs that were far below their qualifications.[20]

Indeed, most Tunisians subsisted in the informal economy, which produced 38.4 percent of the gross national income. Yet the street traders, 40 percent of the informal workforce, remained strictly outlawed. No permits were issued for street vendors, deemed a hindrance to traffic flows.[21] The French term *vendeurs à la sauvette* or "vendors on the run" reflected the extent of insecurity that gripped the poor traders, who faced constant harassment, fine, beating, or confiscation of their properties.[22] And there was little help from the national labor union, UGTT, which organized mostly the well-to-do public sector workforce, notably the state employees. In Egypt, too, public sector workers were traditionally the most organized; however, with the privatization policies, job seekers were pushed into the informal sector. Over 75 percent of the new job seekers between 2000 and 2005 were engaged in informal and extralegal work, which by 2006 constituted 61 percent of total employment in Egypt (up from 57 percent in 1998).[23] Of this, a vast segment worked as street vendors, spreading often illegally in strategic public places, market areas, central districts, train stations, as well as the backstreets.[24]

In such extralegal fashion, the poor created vast communities of life and labor wherein the ethics of self-regulation, mutual help, trust, reciprocity, negotiation, and kinship ties served their precarious lives better than formal rules, rigid contract, or the discipline of time and space. Even though scarce resources induced competition, envy, and discord, those very "traditional" ethics ensured their survival and operation within their country's modernity. Beyond the local collectives and networks, much of their claim-making efforts remained quiet and individual with some occasions of collective protests, which would invariably invite police repression. Mohammed Bouazizi, the street trader of Sidi Bouzid whose fatal encounter with the police would alter the history of his country, came from such a community.

Indeed, everyday encounters with the police were an integral part of the poor people's life. In Tunisia and Egypt, the police had extensive functions to control outdoor markets, roads, highways, public transport, and back alley neighborhoods. While Egypt's "emergency law" criminalized assembly of more than three people in public, in Tunisia any gathering, including wedding parties, required an official permit. Unauthorized political or civil organization risked severe police punishment. Surveillance pushed the subaltern citizens further into their closed cliques and collectives in the underside of these societies. Yet the specter of the police haunted their lives on a daily basis. In Cairo's community of Imbaba just before the uprising, the police treated the locals like "dirt," extorting, humiliating, and even torturing family members if found guilty.[25] "Suspected" individuals—squatters, street vendors, street children, taxi drivers, strolling youths, bearded Islamists, liberal women, and gays—always felt vulnerable in public for their heterodox habitus or underdog status. They risked paying bribes, abuse, humiliation, and even framing. Young men with shabby clothing and suspicious looks were routinely stopped or taken to police stations for questioning. If they stood up to the police, they were likely beaten up or charged with "drug possession." Reportedly, the authorities fabricated 57,000 cases of drug possession each year in the 1990s.[26] The fictional character *baltagi* (thug), deployed widely in the official and elite circles, summed up the criminal imagery of Egypt's impoverished youth. He was poor, young, workless, and "noncultured" usually from the *ash-*

*waiyyat,* who could be singled out by his mode of clothing, walking, or staring. Officials spoke of 5,000 to 130,000 *baltagis* in the late 1990s.[27] The *baltagi* was also used to describe the lower-class but highly organized and combative soccer fans (Ultras), who later during the 2011 uprising fought fiercely against the security forces and the thugs of the ruling NDP.

Certainly, the poor endured fear, adopted caution, and even appeared submissive, with some like Ahmed Abdou Qutb setting themselves on fire because of overbearing poverty and debt.[28] But they also spoke out and took revenge. If the elites called the underdog male youths *baltagi,* the poor of the *ashwaiyyat* described the police informers as thugs. Speaking out and venting in public was not uncommon. Elderly and subaltern women, in particular, deployed their maternal impunity and "apolitical innocence" to get away with what they uttered. They complained about high prices and power cuts, police brutality and traffic jams. And they mostly blamed the government for these misfortunes. In the prerevolution Tunisia, working-class women like Yusra from Monastir would "angrily recount the unsavoury behaviour of the local despots to her fellow passengers" during her commute to and from the capital.[29] Indeed, the practice of public nagging or venting and voicing grievances in public places was a salient feature of public culture in the preuprising Arab societies, serving as a central element in the making of public opinion. It was a constituent of Arab *political street*—the collective sentiments, shared feelings, and public opinions of ordinary people in their day-to-day speech, irony, and disdain that were expressed casually in taxis, buses, shops, backstreets, or deliberately in public gatherings.[30] Whether the autocratic regimes and political elites were able or willing to hear these dissenting voices may be open to question. But given the regimes' intelligence operations, it was likely that the elites and authorities could hear them but dismissed them as the commoners' everyday "bickering" or a cultural trait of the "pitiable" but "cunning poor" that had little to do with politics. In fact, politics was a trade not just of the urban inhabitants but also of the rural and provincial subaltern.

*Rural Poor*

Rural discontent, particularly in Tunisia, seemed so widespread that some observers deemed the January 14th Revolution to have rural origin, beginning in the mining region of Gafsa. On January 5, 2008, according to geographer Habib Ayeb, young people and their families occupied the office of UGTT in Gafsa to protest the corruption involved in giving jobs in the Phosphate Company to people outside the region. The protest then spread to Erredeief, Umm Larayes, Metlaoui, and other localities. In the ensuing clashes, three people died, hundreds were arrested, and thirty-eight trade unionists were put behind bars. Of course, Gafsa was a mining and not a farming town, but it was farmers who staged a sit-in in Sidi Bouzid to protest the credit policy of the National Bank of Agriculture in July 2010. This followed a month later by the riot of informal traders against the closure of the Tunisia-Libya border that curtailed cross-border informal trades on which thousands of families depended.[31]

Significant social change had rendered the rural subalterns the subject of contentious politics. Life in such villages and rural towns as Mohammed Bouazizi's Sidi Bouzid in Tunisia was not exclusively agricultural. Nor were the inhabitants exclusively farmers residing in desolate traditional rural communities—in Egypt some 80 percent of small farmers (those who owned or rented less than five feddans and relied on family labor) worked outside agriculture to survive. Rather, the villagers inhabited urbanizing rural settings that often enjoyed running water, electricity, phone lines, TV, and shops, not to mention schools, banks, or uniformed police.[32] Visibly stratified, village life had developed both poor wage workers and well-to-do middle classes. Above all, villagers were overwhelmed by the desire and demands of urban consumption patterns. In truth, these communities represent a novel formation of hybrid political economies. For the most part, these rural and agricultural communities were subjected to intense processes of marketization, commodification, and mechanization of large-scale farming colonies. Villagers may hold plots of lands to grow vegetables or raise chickens and goats, but their surpluses are subject to market, and their life dependent on cash, wage work, bank loans, and timely payment of electricity, water, and phone bills. They may be rural, but their children are likely to go to college, be well versed in new media, experience regular travel to large cities, and be in tune with the global consumer culture. In the Tunisian Sidi Bouzid, for instance, mechanization of large-scale capitalist farms was at the cost of the small holders' debt, dispossession, and proletarianization. In fact, farm workers like Mohammed Bouazizi's father, according to Habib Ayeb, struggled on a small plot for "food security." The father's death left a three-hectare plot depending on rainwater and was barely sufficient to feed the family. His uncle, subsequently married to his mother, tried to build a new farm project to enjoy irrigation water. To finance the project, the family took out a loan by mortgaging the land to the bank. But unable to pay the debt, the bank seized their land, leaving them dispossessed. The young Mohammed then moved to work on his uncle's farmland but experienced the very same prevalent course of dispossession. Only then did Mohammed turn into becoming a vendor selling fruits in the streets. His possessions were taken away once again, this time by the police for lacking a permit.[33]

These emerging social formations are bound to leave their imprints on the forms of dissent and political practice. The inhabitants do wish to have access to land and agricultural resources, but they also carry out wage work and operate in the *urbanizing* rural communities that produce dissent rooted in both "rural" *and* "urban" claims. In the Tunisian Sidi Bouzid, for instance, for many years prior to the revolution, the farmers refused to pay for or subverted regular payment of electricity and water bills which, according to Habib Ayeb, caused a sizable decline in the state's utilities revenue. In a sense, farmers were involved in some kind of nonmovement—with thousands of them refusing to pay but doing so individually while being aware of each other's doings. In the meantime, some 150 families waged land squatting, occupying some 400 hectares of the state land near the chemical complex of Gabes.[34] Once they established their occupancy, the intransigent regime repression could do little to deter them from holding on to their new possessions. In sum, social changes of such kinds brought the provincial and the rural into the circuit of the national society and politics, turning them into geographies of wider political dissent.[35] In this process, they began to produce schooling, youth, and youthfulness somehow similar to those of the urban landscapes.

*Middle-Class Poor*

An intriguing feature of the traditional poor families—whether urban or rural, slum dwellers or inhabitants of mud bricks—was that they raised children who attended college and gained middle-class aspirations. In Egypt, 30 percent of youth with college degrees lived in rural areas, in Tunisia, 40 percent.[36] At the same time, middle-class youth with educational capital felt poverty because of prolonged unemployment and precarity. Gone were the days, as in the 1970s, when once graduated, "I got a job in less than thirty minutes at a high school I had requested," as a retired teacher recalled.[37] In Egypt of the late 2000s, college graduates were ten times more likely to remain without jobs than those with primary education. The rate was higher in Tunisia, something similar to Iran of 2016 with 35 percent.[38] The pattern was unmistakably regional, where youth unemployment, most severely among the highly educated, reached roughly twice the world average. Thus, by the time the revolutions arrived, a distinct paradoxical class, what I call middle-class poor, had emerged in the entire region. Not only did this class complicate the status of the "poor" and "middle classes," but it also brought the village and slum lives in contact with college, consumer ethos, and urban culture. With a disposition distinct from both the middle class and the poor, feeling disenchanted and restless, this angry class of our neoliberal times showed the greatest potential for mobilization.

A product of large youth cohort, educational expansion, urbanization, and aggressive economic liberalization, this paradoxical "middle-class poor" holds college degrees, experience of social media, knowledge of the world, and middle-class dreams. But it is pushed by economic deprivation to live the life of the traditional poor in slums and squatter settlements and subsist on family support or on largely precarious and low-status jobs—as cab drivers, fruit sellers, street vendors, or salespersons. A middle-class poor knows and frequents the city centers but lives on the periphery. He desires to wear Nike shoes but has to settle for fake brands. He dreams of work or vacation abroad but feels trapped by the dearth of money and border controls. This is a class that links the world of poverty and deprivation, of shantytowns and casual work, of debt and precarity to the wider world of the college, consumption, and the internet. Its members are acutely aware of what is available in the world and what they painfully lack. Their precarity and limbo is supposed to be temporary, but it ends up being timeless. Neither feeling fully young nor adult, and filled with a profound moral outrage, this class became a critical player in the Arab uprisings.

Before the uprising, Tunisia and Egypt had fairly similar young populations, 40 percent and 37.8 percent, respectively, between fifteen and thirty-five years of age. But with 6 percent of annual gross domestic product allocated to education, Tunisia had a vast literate population: 97 percent of youth between fifteen and thirty. Yet one-third of this educated youth were out of suitable work. According to a sample, some 85 percent of jobs (which were mostly in the informal sector) did not need qualifications, yet were mostly held by people with university degrees. In January 2015, the Tunisian geographer Habib Ayeb advertised to hire two "trainees" for meager "pocket money" in his association OSAE. Within twelve days, thirty-three people applied. Of these, thirty held master's degrees, and three had doctoral degrees. Of the total, twenty-five had several months of professional experience, ten of them associative experience, and most of them spoke at least three languages: Arabic, French, and English. In Ayeb's words, "When three PhD holders apply to a trainee position in a small association without resources, it is a sign of total despair."[39] In Egypt, the subaltern lawyers, those raised and resided in the poor urban or rural communities, personified best the paradoxical status of the middle-class poor. They often failed to find proper legal jobs, resorting instead to teaching, driving, or assisting with everyday legal issues such as rentals, divorces, or contracts. As part of the large pool of the precarious surplus law graduates, they espoused oppositional politics and took the plight of their communities to the courthouses.[40]

The "middle-class poor" was not a new formation. It had roots in the 1980s but expanded since the 1990s when the Middle Eastern economies liberalized extensively. In Egypt of the 1980s and 1990s, segments of this stratum merged into a political class adhering to the nationalist and Islamist sentiments. In Tunisia, some youths in the provinces and the poor communities like Tadamon in Tunis identified with the politics of underground Islamic movement, al-Nahda. Others put their hope in the UGTT or remained indignant until they found an opportunity to explode as they did in the uprising. However, in their quotidian existence, many members of this class, just like the other discontented clusters, were involved in everyday struggles to advance their claims, while creating alternative life norms in their dispersed cliques and collectives.

## YOUTHFUL POLITICS

Of course, a significant segment of the young was part of the middle-class poor. But "youth" as such held broader (gender, class, rural, urban) affiliations, diverse concerns, and varied social imageries. Nevertheless, they all seemed to share certain similar anxieties and claims that had to do with the sociological fact of being "young." They were concerned with claiming youthfulness.[41] Of course, as "citizens" the young like others expressed outrage about the general state of their country, but as "youth" they sensed an additional violation. Although the socially liberal Tunisia allowed the young, albeit mostly male, to experience less moral / religious surveillance, they still shared economic constraints with the Egyptian counterpart on fulfilling their youthful needs. Simply to be autonomous, live on one's own, or fulfill youthful dreams required money and jobs which many (one-third in Tunisia and 40 percent in Egypt) lacked. Thus, political dictatorship rendered them unsafe, economic hardship worried them about their present and future, and moral surveillance put a damp on their individuality and youthful desires.

In 2003, I asked twenty male and female college students from fairly comfortable families to describe their anxieties as young persons. They overwhelmingly feared the prospect of their adult life. Maryam, twenty-one, was "extremely worried about my future career. . . . I am afraid of being without a man."[42] Osama expressed anxieties about not finding a job, wondering how he would meet the social expectations of his parents. Others worried about marriage, family, and their fiancé who "has not worked and still has a long road ahead"; how could they "afford dowry, furniture, reasonable income?" Young men in particular sensed apprehension in their role as providers for the family.

The young—male, female, religious or nonreligious—were also indignant about the suppression of individuality. In a conversation with female students of Cairo University, who prayed, fasted, never tasted liquor, and had no boyfriends "because we are from Upper Egypt," they said their freedoms were restricted especially by parents. "There are lots of things we want to do . . . wear new style pants, makeup, but we can't." "I want to work and have an independent identity," one of them said. "But unemployment does not allow."[43] Maryam wanted to "be freed from the societal chains that make me unable to be independent; to experience enough to face challenges of life and to live my life the way I want to."[44] One young veiled female wanted to "get away from my parents and live a life of my own rules.... They even plan for me to live in their neighborhood after marriage.... I can't tell them to their face, 'Honestly, I want to get away from you.'" This strong desire for autonomy and selfhood that marked even "conservative" youth may explain why just after the revolution scores of women took off veils and left home to live on their own (see Chapters 5 and 7).

Suppression of youthfulness in Egypt did not come simply from parents, religious authority, or dominant culture. It had a lot to do with what Dina called the "oppressive political authority," for the expression of youthfulness was intimately linked to civil rights and its violation agitated many young people, making them conscious of their violated youthhood and the tyranny of the state. Just to illustrate, Baher and her girlfriend met to be together in Alexandria's Montazah Park in 2009, but their moves were watched by the intruding passersby. "We are nineteen. How old do we have to be to take control of our own feelings?" he complained.[45] They managed to find a quieter and darker spot where other couples were sitting, holding hands and whispering. "They were all like us: unmarried, rejected by society, and in financial strains." Not long after, they sat down to imagine their future—wondering "how could we get married without the money to pay for an Egyptian wedding; why was everyone judging us as if we were immoral criminals; what were we doing wrong?"—when the morality police descended upon them, proclaiming that they had committed public indecency. The police took their IDs and wanted to take them to the police station. "If we were arrested, it would be the end of everything: our relationship, our reputations, our parents' trust in us. We would have a criminal record that would haunt us all our lives."[46] Apprehended and terrified, they were set free only after paying a hefty bribe. "That was the first bribe I had ever paid in my life but not the last." It was a price paid by vulnerable youth "denied of the most basic right: the right to express our feelings, the right to be sincere." "Two people with no hope in sight are forbidden by a tyrannical government from loving each other." The story of Baher summed up the status of most young Egyptians caught up between youthful desires, poverty, social control, and political tyranny.

The state viewed youth mainly as a "problem"—potential source of social ills and political danger, of soldiering radical Islam.[47] Officially, the state was to provide the young with "scientific advancement" or technical education to catch up and compete in the world, and at the same time guide them into moderate religion in order to withstand both radical Islam as well as foreign cultural influences.[48] The 1999 presidential decree in Egypt to elevate the Supreme Council of Youths (established in 1965) to the Ministry of Youths and Sports (something Tunisia already had) displayed official anxiety over the "youth problem."[49] The Ministry of Youth with its control of 4,000 youth centers (Tunisia had 380) was to help appease and integrate the young through government loans to enable them to marry and settle down, access to information and communications technology, and technical training.[50] But if the televised annual "dialogue" of the presidents in both countries with their youths was any indication, a deep mistrust separated youths from the states.[51]

The young simply did not trust formal politics and institutions. In Tunisia, only about 4 percent of young people (between sixteen and thirty) were active in formal associations of any sort.[52] "People were so fed up with politics that the idea of being organized was somehow rejected," remembered a cyberactivist.[53] In Egypt, a survey of Ain al-Shams University in 2002 showed that 80 percent of students ignored parliamentary elections, and 90 percent refrained from party politics.[54] Only 10 percent of students were active in the students union, and 66 percent did not even participate in its elections.[55] As one student said, "I would be interested in politics if my voice is heard. . . . [Otherwise] politics would send you to jail."[56] Indeed, scores of political youths were already in the Egyptian prisons; and some 4,000 youths were put to trial in Tunisia, a country of 10 million, between 2004 and 2010.[57] Some Egyptian youths, inspired by the Palestinian second intifada and the outrage over the US invasion of Afghanistan and Iraq in 2001 and 2003, got involved in the less dangerous civic activism. They led organizations such as al-Andalus Institute for Tolerance, Nahdet al-Mahrousa, and al-Ashanak ya Baladi that spearheaded impressive volunteer work.[58] Others joined later in the Life Makers (Sana al-Hayat) led by the lay popular preacher Amr Khaled. The initiative intended to encourage youth to help themselves through entrepreneurial spirit, civic engagement, income generation, and employment.[59]

But the main form of youth activism in both countries lay in their everyday lifeworld. Through local cliques, networks, and nonmovements, the young strived to reclaim their youthfulness and assert their citizenship. Neighborhoods had long been spaces where the lower-class youth formed *shillas* in which they connected, discussed, and socialized. Even those who described themselves as *al-qaidin*, the "sitters" (sitting around in cafés and waiting for things to turn up) would build strong ties within their cliques and local networks. Bonds of friendship and loyalty offered everyday support, forged collective imagination, and ensured safety and security in the risky business of contentious politics. Neighborhood mosques and churches were crucial, especially on Friday prayer times, for the locals to assemble, deliberate, or plan for action.[60]

So a person like Abdelrahman and his friends in Cairo would try to make their own youthful spaces in clubs or friends' homes where they watched movies, played games, made romantic friends, or read and discussed social matters. Female youth in particular spent most of their free time at home hanging out, chatting, or listening to music, thus reinforcing bonds of friendship and common purpose.[61] In Cairo, in 2010, some young groups made initiatives like Lamma or "Gathering," where they assembled in public places such as parks to chat, discuss politics, and read books on specific topics.[62] The young Ala Abdel-

Fattah, who would become a leader of the Egyptian revolution, volunteered with friends to work with the children of the poor Zilzal area of Moqattam or work in al-Nusur al-Saghira summer camps to help enhance deprived children's creativity, awareness of their communities, and their values as individuals. Later in the mid-2000s, the group began discussion sessions and reading circles.[63] Others formed informal cliques in high schools, colleges, student unions, and clubs. Even though watched by the secret police, these activities "gave me a lot of experience and a lot of connections," an activist recalled.[64] Lower-class youngsters used youth clubs (Nadi al-Shabab) to assemble, play, watch films, and discuss.[65] Imbaba's Ultras or soccer fans, in particular, enjoyed strong internal ties, knowing one another and often hanging out together. So when the uprising broke out in 2011, they informed one another to join Tahrir on January 28 to fight the police they detested deeply. Likewise, the state surveillance in Tunisia had pushed the young to go underground, to form communities of cultural activities, music, art, tattoos, or LGBT associations, which all espoused a fundamentally oppositional spirit.[66] Amin Allal reports of the unemployed youths who formed their *shillas* in affordable cafés in the working-class suburb of Tunis where they met, socialized, discussed, and led subversive actions against the police and local authorities.[67] Others received nourishment from discussion groups in bars, cultural cafés, art centers, bookstores, or professional syndicates mostly located on Bourguiba Avenue in Tunis.[68] "People would drink and talk about politics; there was a political life before the revolution," the young Elyssa stated.[69]

Many youth conducts were not meant to be political. Rather, they meant to fulfill certain youthful desires, which nevertheless questioned certain dominant norms. In what looks like the Foucauldian "counter-conduct," young boys and girls, well-off and subaltern alike, drank alcohol, smoked hashish, took on intimate friends, and practiced premarital sex.[70] In a conversation with a group of male youth in Cairo in 2002—who prayed, fasted, believed in sharia as a "medicine to recover humans"—most said they had girlfriends, smoked weed, drank beer, and favored *urfi* or "informal marriage" for sex. But all expressed remorse and repentance. "I pray and fast but do whatever I want to." Most had girlfriends, "but this is a temporary relationship. . . . No one marries his girlfriend," an attitude that infuriated young women. Pious girls took boyfriends, went out in secret, engaged in romance, but did not find these against their faith because they were planning to marry their partners. In the 2000s, the practice of informal or *urfi* marriage—to legitimize sex and get around wedding costs—alarmed parents and politicians. Some estimated that 17 percent of university students practiced *urfi* marriage, deemed as the source of 14,000 fatherless children.[71] The young enjoyed dancing, having illicit relationships and fun but found solace in their faith and prayers. "I do both good and bad things, not just bad things" hoping that the "good things erase the bad things."[72] Some expressed "youthful selfhood" not in counternormal acts of drinking or illicit sex but in a "conservative" mission of taking on the veil against their parents' wishes. "When I decided to wear the veil," said the young Mai, "my mother cried and shouted, 'No way, don't dare.'"[73] Even though they dreamed of husband and family, the girls willfully delayed marriage to prolong youthful time. "I know my responsibilities and limits," confirmed veiled Rania, "so I don't want anyone to guide me or tell me this is right and that's wrong." Through such strategy of subversive accommodation, the young—liberal or conservative—worked within but tried to redefine and reinvent the prevailing norms and traditional means to accommodate their youthful claims.[74]

With the spread of social media, the space and speed of youth connective networks and the scope of their claims took a new turn. Individual blogs (increased from 50 in 2004 to 6,000 in 2006) allowed the young, notably females, to call into question oppressive norms, debate the authoritarian mentality, and express individuality in a somewhat public manner. In doing so, the bloggers connected, debated, and formed larger communities, virtual nonmovements, that linked physical circles to digital activism. Facebook and Twitter broadened these communities of dispersed individuals who were making many similar claims. Even the youngsters of the poor communities quickly frequented the multiplying internet cafés. Muslim Brothers youth ignored their leaders and sheikhs who issued fatwas against blogging. Like Egypt, Tunisia saw a rapid rise of blogs and Facebook use by the young since 2007. When the blogger Fatma Elgierehy was arrested in 2009, a cybercampaign emerged securing her release. "That was an example that you could do something on the internet, a real thing," affirmed an activist.[75] By the close of the 2000s, youth in Egypt and Tunisia shared ideas in the countless individual but interconnected networks that linked cyberactivism to what went on in neighborhoods, colleges, workplaces, and the streets.[76]

## WOMEN AND GENDER STRUGGLES

Of these youths, about one-half were of course young women. But as women, they faced additional challenges rooted in patriarchal attitudes and institutions that targeted the female citizens in general. Conservative social mores, men, and secular states often invoked religion and "moral values" to retain gender inequality that marked many domains of public and private life, including social labor, family, sexuality, and laws. Lower-class women in particular remained more exposed to gender discrimination.

The postcolonial states in both Egypt and Tunisia viewed publicly active women as part of their modernist project, as an element in the building of modern nation. In Tunisia, women were granted in 1957 the right to vote and run for office. Abortion was legalized in 1965 and polygamy abolished; women were allowed to file for divorce and enjoyed access to birth control from 1962. Even though women in Egypt had the right to vote and run for public office, legal discrimination in matters such as the right to initiate divorce, child custody, and inheritance remained. Reforms such as the right to pass nationality to children were adopted only in the 2000s. Even though a signatory, the Egyptian government rejected many articles of the United Nations Convention on the Elimination of All Forms of Discrimination against Women (CEDAW). Thus, Egypt's penal code would still stipulate that a man was guilty of adultery only if he committed the act at his marital home, whereas a woman was guilty regardless of where the act took place. Many women remained the easy victims of honor crimes for which sentences were the most lenient in the legal books. In both Tunisia and Egypt, a large gap persisted between the text of legislations and their actual implementation. On the one hand, the "state was party to most relevant universal declarations and conventions on gender rights and equality," as the anthropologist Hania Sholkamy succinctly argued. "On the other hand, the space to claim these rights was constricted by a state-led hegemony over civilian and public spaces."[77] Women of poor classes in particular remained more vulnerable.

The regimes spoke of the role of women in national development, sponsored national councils or ministries of women affairs, and celebrated Women's Days. But they resorted to repression when they encountered women's critical and independent voices. The Egyptian government sponsored the National Council for Women, headed by the first lady Suzanne Mubarak, in 2000 to work for "women's advancement," but it shut down the Egyptian Women's Union led by the critical feminist Nawal al-Sadawi. When female activists were sexually harassed by the police in 2006 or 2008, Suzanne Mubarak ignored the matter, the Interior Ministry denied it, and the police blamed belly dancer Dina for "provocation."[78] Police detained activists like Omnia Taha and Sara Rizk for calling on citizens to protest government corruption by staying home. Tunisia had a Ministry of Women's Affairs, which most women resented, for it projected the image of modern women in the persona of Ben Ali's corrupt wife, Leila Trabelsi. Even though Ben Ali's constitutional coup in 1987 kept the pro-women laws, his police state used sexual violence to silence dissent. Ben Ali presented himself as "he's the one who liberates women," according to the feminist Ben Slama. "Whereas we know that he mistreated Islamist women and women of the left."[79] Ben Ali's regime blacklisted the female judge Kalthoum Kannou (who would become a presidential candidate after the revolution of 2011) because she spoke out against corruption and authoritarian rule and called for an independent judiciary. The government prevented her from traveling, denied promotions, and transferred her from Tunis to the remote provinces.[80] The regime often used "women's rights" discourse to rally women against Islamist opposition al-Nahda and largely ignored the plight of the poor provincial women. How did women in the prerevolution Egypt and Tunisia manage their unequal position? How did they tackle gender discrimination and enhance their status?

*State Feminism*
Among women activists, the strand with the loudest public voice—that is, "women empowerment"—came from the "gender and development" frame that was intimately linked to development aid, international NGOs, and the United States Agency for International Development (USAID) whose discourse was fundamentally "developmentalist" and often "anti-politics."[81] In many ways, the "NGO-ization" of the women's movement signaled and materialized the decoupling of "gender issues" and popular struggles.[82] In both Egypt and Tunisia, this strand had partially merged with what the scholar Mervat Hatem called state feminism. At best, state feminism focused on women quotas in Parliament, personal status, and similar liberal concerns;[83] at worst, it served as a "liberal progressive" veneer to conceal the illiberal and authoritarian character of the autocratic regimes. Such elitist state feminism did help with some legal changes in favor of women in prerevolution Egypt, Tunisia, Yemen, and Morocco. In Egypt, it included criminalizing female

genital mutilation (FGM) in 2008, parliamentary quota for women, *khul'* (right to initiate divorce), and passing nationality to children. But it mostly remained oblivious to the plight of the lower-class women and their manifold marginal positions such as 18 percent of Egyptian households that were headed by women, or the millions who lacked even national IDs.[84] Many poor women remained unaware of their rights and there was a large gap between feminist discourse and the reality of many women on the ground. "Coping with life's daily burdens is a struggle for the vast majority of Tunisian women who," according to the journalist Mariyam Ben Ghazi, "remain unaware of such privileges and incapable of claiming their rights." She was referring to "an 85-year-old woman who works from dawn to dusk to feed a family of five for less than $3 per day." In Tunisia, inheritance law continued to disfavor women who were entitled only to half of men's share—a practice particularly inimical to poor and head-of-household women. And then there was the sexual harassment that in Tunisia "starts from around the corner from your house,"[85] and in Egypt spread like a social disease infecting the public squares. Certainly, state feminism did open a space for women activists to raise concerns and campaign for gender rights, but when it came to campaign against the repressive secular regimes, the state feminism mostly sided with the status quo.

*Women Activism*
So the task of organizing to improve women's status fell on what Nadje al-Ali described as "the women's movement," which in Egypt meant a blend of formal organizations (such as the New Woman Research Centre, Alliance of Arab Women, Women's Study Centre: Together, and the Daughter of the Land Group) as well as informal groups, networks, and personalities that campaigned for political participation, education, reproductive rights, and against sexual violence, FGM, and Islamist push for more conservative agendas.[86] It embarked on programs

to enhance income generation, bring about legislative change, put an end to FGM, establish shelters for abused women, and raise awareness through workshops, seminars, and publications. Thus, the Egyptian Center for Women's Rights, established in 1996 to provide information and legal aid to poor women, took on the fight in 2005 against sexual harassment which had proliferated in the country.[87] In Tunisia and even more in Egypt, these independent groups were in a sense negotiating with patriarchy, attempting to gain as much as they could under the authoritarian polity and patriarchal sensibilities.

There were, however, serious shortcomings. Groups were scattered and constrained by a dearth of funding, sometimes competing with one another to attract donors. A few were close to the state working under its laws, while others remained critical and combative, at times bogged down in party politics ignoring what it meant for women's lives on the ground.[88] In the 1990s, a key battle for Egypt's women activists revolved around the Personal Status. While feminists like Nawal el-Sadawi supported the law because they saw it benefiting women, the leftist groups close to the Tajammu Party opposed it because they resented President Anwar Sadat and whatever he stood for. In addition, as secular activists, these groups mostly stood apart from the Islamic women's organizations—those revolving around personas like Zeinb al-Ghazali or Safinaz Kazem, who deemed sharia as a path for women's liberation, or the younger activists such as Heba Rauf Ezzat, who espoused a more post-Islamist orientation and pursued their own "Islamic feminist" agenda. Women of Muslim Brothers were concerned less with gender issues and more with broader political, religious, and regional matters. They had formed a distinct lifeworld of their own with their mosques, schools, entertainments, charity organizations, and their underground gatherings.[89]

Tunisian state feminism had already addressed many of the concerns that the Egyptian women activists held, including polygamy and personal status. Tunisian women occupied some 20 percent of the parliamentary seats before the revolution. There were women like Maya al-Jribi who, coming from the student activism of the 1970s, became a major opposition figure rising to the leadership of the leftist Progressive Democratic Party (Hizb al-Demuqrati al Taqaddumi). In her confrontation with Ben Ali's regime, she went on a hunger strike for thirty-three days until achieving her demands. Al-Jribi defended the provincial people in their struggles for justice and democracy for which she was terrorized by the regime's agents. While progressive laws in Tunisia facilitated women's public presence and equal rights, it was a different matter in the private and informal domains—in particular for marginalized women. For instance, in the provincial towns of Sidi Makhlouf in Medenine and Ain Drahem in Jendouba, according to a report, women experienced high unemployment of their men or themselves. But those in Sidi Makhlouf who did work, they began their day at 5:00 a.m. working until 5:00 p.m. to sell cheaper oysters, while others left home at 4:00 a.m. in covered trucks to fish oysters for a meagre daily wage of two dinars ($0.75) in an industry that produced 78 percent of the state income from the fishery sector.[90] Many women were even prevented by their families from working outside the home or taking part in the cultural and recreational activities in public. This was particularly true of many girls who could not attend youth centers or local festivals which had been dominated by men. Health centers refused to provide midwives whom women wished to have for childbirth. When worked as housemaids, women often experienced abuse. Human Rights Watch reported that 47 percent of Tunisian women were the subject of domestic violence.[91] Samar al-Mazghani expressed vividly such everyday discrimination when she wanted to cross the border to Libya with her mother. She was "humiliated" by the custom's officer who required them to have a male companion. "In the Arab world I cannot travel alone," she fumed in outrage, "not because I am illiterate, ill, a criminal or a terrorist, but because I was born a woman."[92]

*Feminism of Everyday Life*

Organized activism notwithstanding, it was mostly left to women in everyday life to defy discrimination, resist abuse, and assert presence in public life often in individual and discreet fashion. Young women like the veiled Egyptian Dalia whose passion for traveling, writing, film-making was suppressed for years by "my mother who is suppressed by Mr. Society" but rebelled in the "manner of Martin Luther King" whom she read. Dalia learned to say no firmly, discussed fiercely, and convinced her elders to allow her to travel, write, and attend classes so that she eventually succeeded to lead a human rights organization in Cairo just before the 2011 revolution.[93]

Indeed, for decades women had pushed their ways to be active members in public life—in worksites, political parties, trade unions, NGOs, and later in the blogs and virtual sphere.[94] In the few years prior to the uprising, scores of younger women in Egypt volunteered in charity organizations, where they expressed their individuality and publicness. Many worked in such organizations as Resala with 25 national branches and 50,000 young volunteers. Over 65 percent of the volunteers were female between twenty and thirty years of age, like Ghosoun or Mona who participated in charity, helped in El-Gamai'yya El-Shar'iyya, trained young children in remedial classes, and later followed the web page group We Are All Kahed Said.[95] Inspired by preachers like Amr Khaled, their activism enhanced their moral / religious selves, asserted their presence in public life, and helped the needy.[96] Older women of active piety, mostly from middle and well-to-do classes, formed their own small-scale *halaqat* where they gathered every week in private homes, chatted, socialized, and listened to female preachers, sheikhas, on religion and ethics of self-enhancement.[97] Even though the ethics espoused by the preachers converged with the conservative tenets of patriarchy, these women forged their own norms of propriety, built their own narratives about society and politics, and crafted their own realities.

In everyday households, married women attempted to extend the domains of decision making wherever they could. A survey of 16,527 married women by the Egypt Demographic and Health Survey in 2008 showed that one-third of the women decided on the daily household purchases alone and an equal number did so together with husbands. On the large purchases, half of them shared the decisions with husbands; and a quarter determined their own health issues and one-half together with husbands.[98] Anthropologist Homa Hoodfar's study showed how Egyptian lower-class women maintained high control over the management of the household. They viewed it as a domain where they could exert exclusive power.[99] Decisions about the important areas of reproduction and working outside the home remained fuzzy, but some indications pointed to women's inroads in these areas depending on education and class.[100] Marriage contracts offered some leeway for women to place their demands, such as working outside the home, before wedlock. Many women resisted spousal abuse through sex and silence—that is, denying claim for intimacy (sex strike) and avoiding verbal contact (talk strike), even though these women usually continued with housework and attending their children.[101] Silence in this context did not mean "exit." Rather, it could serve as a powerful weapon in a way the protagonist of Isabel Allende's *House of the Spirits* deployed after being slapped in the face by her husband, saying, "I will never speak to you again." Widowed women in Egypt resorted to informal *urfi* marriage in order to keep the custody of their children as well as the pension of their former husbands, which a legally registered new marriage would deny them. Women's resistance in courts on divorce and child custody remained widespread.[102]

This is not meant to overread women's resistance. Indeed, patriarchal acts and attitudes kept their grip on much of the lives of women, who were seen as bearers of cultural values and social mores. Many women had serious difficulties in attending street rallies or protests simply because their male guardians would disallow them largely for fear of physical and sexual abuse. Thus, when Asmaa, in her twenties, asked her father to go to demonstrations with him, "No way, you stay here at home. You could be arrested, detained, and . . . ," her father responded.[103] Nor could one deny that ordinary women suffered more institutional discrimination than their male counterparts. Yet, women's discreet and dispersed acts of defiance would subvert or mitigate the practices of prejudice which often perceived and presented so "natural." Theirs, then, were ventures in the art of presence, the courage and creativity to assert one's will against all odds to make oneself heard, seen, and realized. Indeed, in the view of Lebanese essayist Amal Gandour, this is the story of Arab women's struggles. "Regardless of how many stages the experts delineate for us through a history battered by colonialism and harangued by our own aggrieved search for cultural authenticity," she writes, "my sense is that our activism has always been about that art of presence." Of course, Gandour does not overlook women's concerted public advocacy for gender rights. "But that too, inevitably, has had to be a rather genteel prodding of the state, carefully balancing its very masculine sensibilities with emphatic demands for better legal protections."[104]

## SOCIAL MINORITIES

More than any other subaltern groups, social minorities like the queer community had to grapple with legal and social discrimination as they strove to pursue their lifestyle. In both Tunisia and Egypt, same-sex relations were deemed legally wrong and socially reprehensible. The regime in Tunisia treated homosexuality unlawful, curbed activists, and harassed those who sought visibility. Even though no legislation pertained to same-sex relations in Egypt, the police deployed antiprostitution and "debauchery" laws to criminalize the gay and bisexual men. As some queer groups ventured to socialize in the open since the late 1990s, many clubs, bars, and private parties associated with gay life became the target of police raids. Homosexual men were subject to shame, police assault, and prosecution. Legal authorities often invoked religion, public morality, and social norms to indict their defendants. In a high-profile crackdown in 2001, the police stormed a gay-friendly club on the *Nile Queen* boat and arrested fifty-two attendees.[105] The crackdown continued throughout the 2000s. On one occasion in 2004, a seventeen-year-old student received seventeen years in prison for posting his profile on a gay dating website. Unlike Lebanon where a handful of advocacy NGOs took advantage of the ambiguities in law to publicly defend LGBT rights,[106] Egypt did not allow any support group, and in Tunisia not until 2015 did a formal NGO emerge to campaign for queer rights. It was largely with the prevalence of the new social media that a number of websites openly but cautiously spoke of alternative sexual orientations.[107]

But in practice, same-sex lifestyle went on discreetly in the opaque spaces of their subsociety under the shadow of police surveillance. "Before the revolution, I was always worried about the police who might ask for my ID card, asking me what I was doing, where I was going, and so on," described a gay man. "If you wanted to meet up, you had to think six hundred times before doing it; it was very risky."[108] Gay men would recognize one another and communicate through passive networks—gestures, dress code, ways of walking, and eye contact. In public, they knew their particular spots, the "cruising points," particular streets or thoroughfares where they would loiter, meet, or hang out. In the dangerous times of police check or *baltagiyya* assault, the men who may have never met before would alert one another through particular signals suggesting "watch out, there are police or gangs up there." The frequency of contacts made individuals known to one another and so offered a degree of security.[109] Otherwise, there were those who pretended to be gay but "in fact were gang members or even policemen who would take you and rub you." Some parked their cars in dark places to pursue sexual contact.

Socially, the men operated in certain familiar "societies," including rich and poor societies, according to a gay man. Each "society" was composed of loose-knit groups of seven or eight people who pursued a particular fetish—for instance, lower-class men, mechanics, or soldiers. Some were "mannish" and others "girlish." They gathered mostly in private homes, sometimes in *baladi* neighborhoods, or in known spots.[110] In the culture of Egypt or Tunisia, the prevalence of male bonds and friendship allowed such queer groups, including married and bisexual, to develop relationships and join groups without raising suspicion. Indeed, it was this fluidity and opacity of male bonds and homoerotic relations that marked and maintained the traditional queer life. But the modern urge to build an identity, open lifestyle, and voice rendered queer individuals more susceptible. These new types of queer groups differed from the traditional *shillas* per se. Unlike *shillas*, the queer members were not necessarily close friends with deep loyalty, bonds, and continuous relationships. Rather, they were ad hoc groups including both regulars and those coming and going out of the group. Overall, this was a highly dangerous lifeworld, "always risky, and you always walk with your eyes at the back," according to a gay man. Police may encounter them and demand bribe, money, or even sex in exchange for not reporting.[111]

Queer women too had underground lives of their own, but they appeared less conspicuous and more flexible, chiefly because the notion of *shaz*, homosexuality, in the public imagination and official circles referred fundamentally to male homosexuals, not female. This allowed queer women to develop same-sex relationships in an everyday lifeworld that was separated little from conventional life. Individual females found their partners, established relationships, formed cliques of similar people, and navigated easily between their queer existence and the conventional norms. Some remained unmarried against social expectations, others married, and still others took husbands to appear conventional while in fact continuing with same-sex intimacies.[112]

In the narrative of the subaltern life in general, opacity and ambiguity allowed the groups to live their extralegal life and pursue and extend their life chances. It is a source of their empowerment. Yet segments from the queer communities attempted to "come out," be visible, and express collective identity. Surely, visibility was intended to ensure recognition, normality, and security but could in fact make the subjects exposed and vulnerable. Yet the very practice of alternative lifestyle even in the hidden sphere tended to generate a connected, albeit loose, entity, which would coalesce as a self-conscious community to push for its claims when cracks appeared in the body politics of these nations. For this to transpire, queer subjects had to wait for an uprising, a transformation that was preceded by the rise of a new politics.

## TOWARD NEW POLITICS

The mid-2000s saw a shift in popular politics. The changing regional dynamics following the 9 / 11 terrorist attacks, the spread of new information technologies, and the adverse effects of neoliberal policies generated a *new politics* in which the subaltern groups moved to extend their networks of *shillas* and nonmovements and turn their discreet struggles into more open, audible, and collective campaigns. In Tunisia, the regime's neoliberal policies undermined the welfarism that, according to Beatrice Hibou, had conditioned citizens' obedience. The pool of unemployed college graduates, the "middle-class poor," was swelling by annual addition of some 80,000, while few trusted Ben Ali's promise in 2009 of providing 415,000 new jobs by 2014.[113] Meanwhile, the second Palestinian intifada politicized many Tunisians; the UGTT rank and file organized solidarity rallies attracting many students and young people. In 2005, the unemployed formed their own movement and began to agitate in public. The remarkable eight-month strike of the Gafsa miners in 2008 exploded the myth of Ben Ali's "economic miracle," instigating simmering dissent from within the undersociety.[114] Tunisians then came to hear the news of sporadic labor unrests and people setting themselves on fire in the central provinces of Qabes, Qasarain, and Sidi Bouzid.

In this new political climate, youth *shillas* began to come out of the underside to engage in open activism and political mobilization. "We had long been working against censorship and the obstruction of free speech," according to an activist. "We tried to talk about opinion prisoners, torture, and dictatorship."[115] Some gathered on the Facebook page New Generation Movement (Haraka Gil Gadid) in 2009. The youth group Takriz (slang meaning "busting my balls" or fed up and disgusted), rooted in Ultras soccer scenes, created a Facebook group to voice opposition to Ben Ali's regime.[116] The regime failed to prevent the cybermovement Saib Saleh or "Enough!" to mobilize thousands against censorship. They organized a silent assembly on Bourguiba Avenue in Tunis all wearing white T-shirts. Later, in August 2010, they prepared a flash mob in Sidi Bouzid. The youth website Nawat helped create the Tunisleaks, the Tunisian Wikileaks, to override the regime's information blackout. Tunisians in the diaspora linked up and established the Tunisie to circulate news and commentary to which some 600,000 visited. Through social media, such youth activities connected to small farmers who were voicing their public indignation against the lending banks and the government over credit, land, water, and subsidies.[117] They also linked up to workers who were now protesting in greater numbers, including some 1,700 labor protests in 2010 alone.[118] For instance, days before the uprising, workers in the LaiCo company in Tunis protested for pay and pension. SNCFT railway workers brought traffic to a standstill over the attack and arrest by the police of a coworker. Backed by the UGTT, the strike spread to all operations, causing massive disorder in transportation.[119]

In Egypt, the "new politics" was rooted in the Popular Committee for Solidarity with the Palestinian and Iraqi People, and especially the Kifaya democracy movement in 2004 calling for competitive elections.

Activists now focused more on popular mobilization than party politics. They brought campaign onto streets rather than voicing it in institutions, concentrated on domestic political issues rather than international (anti-imperialist) ones, and favored nonideological alliances over party or ideological divides. Professionals, lawyers, judges, students, journalists, college professors, women, and workers waged new campaigns and used to their advantage the language of "democracy" that the George W. Bush administration advocated for the region, following the US invasion of Iraq. Women public protestation in particular frustrated the security forces which, in May 2005, deployed thugs to assault the protesting women in front of the Journalists' Syndicate and Judges Club in Cairo. Dozens of women were subject to sexual attacks, including lawyers, women activists, academics, and journalists like Abeer Elaskary who was kidnapped on her way to cover a meeting of the judges at their club in Cairo.[120] In this new political space, some journalists broke the taboo of publicly criticizing the Mubarak family and his ruling party. Secular and religious women formed new collectives. Youth became involved in civic activism, and labor unrest surged.[121] Youth who established the April 6th Movement to support the striking workers of the Mahalla textile plant in 2008 moved to advocate for democracy through civil resistance. This new political environment served as an opportunity for the poor to undertake collective action.

In 2009, some 150,000 Zabaleen, self-employed garbage collectors in Cairo, refused to collect 8,000 tons of daily garbage (60 percent of the total daily waste) because the government slaughter of 300,000 swine (allegedly for health reasons) had made recycling the waste upon which the Zabaleen depended formidable.[122] The Zabaleen attacked with rocks and bottles those slaughtering these animals, which they personally raised to consume the organic waste they collected. In the meantime, tons of garbage piled up on the streets, revealing the failure of the government to ensure a modicum of urban sanitation. In the same year, when heavy rocks from Cairo's Moqattam hills rolled down to demolish a dozen makeshift shelters in the squatter neighborhood of Duweiqa, the precarious condition of the *ashwaiyyat* came to public attention once again. The government's decision to relocate the residents to a desolate desert township caused profound outrage. Staging numerous collective protests, the residents refused to relocate, instead demanding homes in the nearby locations.[123] Their struggles were to continue well through the uprising. In a different incident, when in December 2009 security forces descended on Cairo's Ezbat Hajjana to demolish some thirty illegal buildings with extra floors, tens of families responded by throwing rocks and rubble from their windows and balconies, forcing the parliament to cease demolition. But the government had targeted 27,000 cases of similar encroachments.[124] The poor residents of Maspero and the Nile islands of El-Dahab and El-Qursaya in Cairo rose against the threat of eviction by the investors close to Mubarak. Meanwhile, mass commotion erupted against plans of slum demolition in Manshiat Naser, Darb al-Ahmar, and Zeinhoum in Cairo as well as other cities.[125]

The more widespread social protests, the "revolution of the thirsty," were yet to come. Through the years, many poor families, through their nonmovements, had encroached on urban services illegally. The heavy cost of unpaid water and electricity had often forced the authorities to formally extend subscriptions to some of these informal neighborhoods, while others continued to use illegally or resort to alternative sources like digging deep wells. Yet once connected, any interruption in what became "urban right" would cause collective outrage. Thus, throughout 2007 and 2008, protestors in towns and villages across the Nile delta poured into the streets to rally over cuts in water flow. Dispatches of massive riot police to quell the protests did not stop blocking highways or cutting railways. Activists from the Kifaya democracy movement and other groups went to poor neighborhoods such as Matarya to help mobilize protests over power cuts, water shortage, and spikes in food prices that had produced deep resentment.[126]

Water was even more vital for the poor farmers, as essential as land, credit, electrical power, or simply security. Cutbacks in any of these everyday necessities brought the rural poor face-to-face with the authorities. In January 2010, some 100 small farmers from Sini carried banners and billboards to Cairo to protest in front of the parliament because the government had blocked water from the Ter'a al-Salam reaching their lands around al-Arish, on the grounds that these were not legitimately their lands.[127] A few month later, villagers of Kafr el-Sheikh blocked Belqas-Hammoud Road, burning tires to cause disruption and bring attention to the shortage of water for crop and consumption.[128] In January 2010, some 8,000 people of al-Arish in Sini took to the streets to protest the killing of a neighbor by armed robbers. The crowd blamed the government for lack of security; they attacked the City Council building, set fire on car tires, and caused massive destruction. Twenty-five protesters were arrested.[129] In a separate incident, a group of villagers in Bani Swaif attacked the governor with rocks and rubble because his office had tried to stop villagers digging the ground to connect electricity cables from the nearby town.[130] In the course of 2009 and 2010, rural Egyptians led 180 sit-ins, 132 demonstrations, and 6 strikes; the confrontations entailed 400 deaths, 2,500 injuries, and 3,000 arrests, according to the Cairo-based Land Center.[131]

The new episode politicized youth more than others, prompting the Youth for Change and then multiple online and offline action groups.[132] Over the years, the young essayist Mariam Bazeed was afraid to use her real name in her writings. "I was afraid of everything. . . . We have imprisoned citizens for the most minor of perceived insults to the system." But she and many others began to feel more daring in the late 2000s. "I now write as myself," she stated.[133] Young activists like Abdelrahman thought that "we can do things big now," a sentiment that found echoes in numerous blogs and Facebook pages.[134] But the actual turning point came with the torture and murder of the young Khaled Said by the police. "It became a matter of safety in the streets," Abdelrahman felt, "as if you could die at any time anywhere."[135] It prompted Abdelrahman and his friends to establish the online network We Are All Khaled Said, which rapidly gathered over 1 million followers. Within such altered political space, the cliques, collectives, networks, and non-movements of the opaque sphere came to the surface, connected through social media and more on the ground in the neighborhoods, and merged into broader political movements.[136]

IN THE PREUPRISING Tunisia and Egypt, the subaltern groups—the poor, marginalized youth, women, and social minorities—had to grapple with repressive governments, hostile economies, and moral-religious surveillance. They endured much hardship in pursuing the life they wished to live. But they did not succumb. Some segments intermittently resorted to social advocacy, civil society activism, and open protests to push for their claims. But most led a life in the social underside that integrally featured close-knit collectives, local networks, and elusive nonmovements. Here in these undersocieties, members built vital networks of support and solidarity that helped them to endure harsh life, make claims, and build necessary trust to venture into the dangerous terrain of fighting the police states. While in public they intermittently showed compliance, vented, and expressed outrage, in the underside they strived to live their lives, resist, make meanings, and build alternative norms and narratives. Thus, although the autocratic regimes were able to suppress the dissenting parties or organized movements, they were unable to prevent the connective actions forged through these diffused socioscapes, everyday lifeworld, wherein the ordinary citizens created their own reality often in opposition to the authoritative discourses. Their voices and deeds coalesced by the end of the 2000s to form the backbone of what came to be the Arab uprisings.

*Chapter 3*

# The Subaltern in the Uprisings

JUST AS HE DID ALMOST EVERY MORNING, the young Mo-hammed pushed his screeching wooden cart all the way to the central market in the depressed Tunisian town of Sidi Bouzid to load it with fruits and vegetables to trade in his local souk. This was how he earned a living since an early age to provide for his five siblings after the death of his father. And the police repeatedly bullied him for being a poor street vendor without a permit. At times, the cops would give him a fine or take away his modest merchandise. But on that day, December 17, 2010, Mohammed refused to let the police officer, Fedya Hamdi, seize his produce. In the ensuing scuffles the policewoman together with other male officers put him on the ground and took away his merchandise and scale. Helpless and humiliated, the twenty-six-year-old Mo-hammed sought recourse in the local municipality, hoping to recover his belongings, but the officials refused to see him. Only then did he bring paint fuel to pour onto his body, setting himself on fire in front of the very municipal office that had denied him justice. Such a symbolic act by Mohammed Bouazizi sparked the stunning uprisings that spread like a wildfire from Tunisia to Egypt and on to the entire Arab region.

A remarkable 16 percent of the population in Tunisia and 8 percent in Egypt took to the streets, according to the Arab Barometer (compared to 2 percent in the French Revolution and 1 percent in the anticommunist revolution in the Soviet Union). Most participants in both countries were young (fifteen to twenty-nine years of age), male, and middle class. Whereas in Tunisia youth participation was highest, in Egypt middle-aged people seemed to make up the core participants.[1] The typical protestor looked "single, educated, relatively young (below 44), middle class, urban, and male."[2] It seemed that young "middle-class poor" occupied a central place in the revolutionary protests. Yet the participation of diverse—older (in Egypt 6 percent and in Tunisia 5 percent above sixties), better-off or poor, and especially female—constituencies was instrumental in bringing the protests into the social mainstream.

Here, I want to tell the story of how the subaltern groups got involved in the uprisings—how their individual practices in the nonmovements assumed collective form, and how their close-knit *shillas* served as vehicles for collective thinking, planning, and acting. Focusing primarily on youth, the poor, and women, I discuss what their participation meant in exceptional revolutionary moments. Although the young protagonists played a decisive role in initiating and pushing through the uprisings, it was largely the active presence of the ordinary people, women, the poor, elderly, and children that generated revolutionary breakthroughs. Whereas in normal times, the subaltern groups struggle separately to enhance their sectoral interests (e.g., collective consumption, gender claims, youthfulness, or recognition), they now focused on broader concerns of the general citizenry (freedom, dignity, social justice) united in a singular nationwide uprising. This marked the emergence of *revolution as movement* or revolutionary uprisings, distinguishing them from the routine acts of claim making and sporadic protests. It signaled the moment of breakthrough wherein the particular followed the general, and the ordinary turned extraordinary.

## TUNISIA RISING

The story of Bouazizi resonated with millions of Tunisians who strove to live a dignified life in the nation's urbanizing rural settings, like Sidi Bouzid, where the inhabitants had to grapple with rural necessities of land, irrigation water, or bank loans, and the urban needs of wage work and cash, and of paying for water, electricity, and other services.[3] Grown up in such a setting, Mohammed did not attend university, nor could he finish high school because he had to work full time to support the siblings, including his sister who managed to go to college, own a personal computer, and use the internet. Such households were not uncommon in communities like Sidi Bouzid where dispossession, poverty, and joblessness went hand in hand with higher education and college graduates versed in social media and the global consumer products. Indeed, the youths of such subaltern households played a decisive part in opening and sustaining the 2010–2011 uprisings by way of protesting, mobilizing, communicating, and spreading the news online or through phones and friends.

Not long after Mohammed Bouazizi's blistered body fell on the ground, hundreds of relatives, friends, and local youths descended on the scene demanding truth from the officials. Many had already known Bouazizi from his Hamama tribe and from his participation in the earlier local protests. The indignant youth—among them Bouazizi's distant cousin, a law school graduate now working in a grocery shop—took photos and videos uploading the news of the events in the social media to bring them to national attention. As the sporadic protests and clashes with the police continued, Sidi Bouzid did not sleep the night. Things escalated the day after with mass demonstrations breaking out in the neighboring provinces with the chants "Work Is Right, Oh Band of Thieves." Rights activists and local trade unionists of the UGTT were quick to deploy their organizational skills to initiate and coordinate the protests. In Sidi Bouzid, the Commission of Citizenship and

Defending Victims of Marginalization quickly emerged to relay information about the events to cyberactivists who would then circulate via social media. Two UGTT members, the schoolteacher Silman Lousi and an employee of the Architectural Institute BouAziz, played a key role in organizing events and disseminating information.

Meanwhile, in the capital, Tunis, the student activist Malek, from the provincial town of Tal'a, had already received phone calls from his friends in Sidi Bouzid reporting the happenings on the spot.[4] Malek and his *shilla* began to think of ways to escalate the protests in Tunis. Deploying their skill and activism in the General Union of Tunisian Students, they set up on December 26 a Facebook page, "Tunisian Street Protest News Agency," in Arabic, French, and English to report the events widely. A dozen male and female students came together to produce and manage a bulletin they called "Resistance Diaries." At night, young protestors went around in the neighborhoods to inscribe slogans on the walls such as "Employment is a right, you gang of thieves!" or "Sleep easy, martyr, we will continue the fight," and many more. Some students returned to their native towns to work closely with friends and *shillas* to enhance the protests, as Malek did in the impoverished southern town of Tal'a. In the popular neighborhoods, the boys fought the police forces and reestablished security after the police left their neighborhood in January 2011. Their active presence in the uprising earned them the status of *rigal* (men) and *thuwwar* (revolutionaries) by the residents.[5] Once students returned from the winter break, university campuses became the site of unprecedented discussion circles, open meetings, and bloody clashes with the security forces. "Every day, we had sit-ins and demonstrations in the university," recalled the student Elyssa.[6]

Feeling alarmed, the regime desperately sought to control the situation, dispatching missions to Sidi Bouzid, Salyaneh, al-Kaf, Jendouba, and others for reconciliation, but to no avail. If anything, the mass unrest intensified and in the course of four weeks extended from Sidi

Bouzid to Meknassy, Menzel Bouzaine, Regueb, and then to Mezzouna, Sidi Ali Ben Aoun, Jilma, Kasserine, and others moving northward to the capital, Tunis, in mid-January. The largest demonstrations took place in Tunis. With no central coordinating center, each town and locality developed its own system of agitating, organizing, and coordinating mostly by the local youth and labor union activists. In Tunis, for instance, "the protests were not organized at all," recalled Elyssa; "we as friends would see each other in the bars or cafés to talk about the events, and then I would see familiar faces in the street demonstrations." The operation of kinship ties, cliques, and nonmovements seemed to be crucial in the formation of the collective protests. Fuming about the last speech of President Zein al-Abedine Ben Ali, a resident of Sidi Bouzid illustrated how dispersed individuals turned collective: "We all listened to this horrible speech. We told ourselves, 'It's not possible; people can't possibly believe this stuff.' We heard the RCD's [ruling party] boats and the surveillance planes, honking in the streets, and then I told myself, 'It's over. The people have been tricked; we are fucked.' Then I pulled myself together. I told myself that whatever, I would go outside and see what happens.... So I went into the street and headed toward the main avenue and there ... [pause, he sobs] there ... I found myself surrounded by people who had thought the same things as me and come to the same conclusion. We found each other, in disbelief, in front of all the others [RCD activists], and thank God, there were a thousand times more of us."[7]

As police repression under Ben Ali had confined student activities to college campuses, the youth *shillas*, street corner associations, and fraternities emerged to serve as mobilizing bodies of collective dissent during the uprising. In Sidi Bouzid, for instance, local youth from different neighborhoods, such as Al-Nour, Awlad Bilhadi, al-Fra'idiyya, and al-Khdra, would assemble in the city's cafés not only to socialize, vent, or discuss things as in the past but also to coordinate and organize the course of action—that is, how to carry on the protests, where to go, what to target, or what slogans to chant.[8] In one of them, the high school student Bilal and his seven close friends discussed how to bring the protests from the main streets into their poor neighborhood, al-Noor Algharbi. To maintain anonymity in their own locality, they operated at nighttime, fighting the intransigent police and its tear gas with rocks and Molotov cocktails.[9] Radicals in the UGTT, notably the teachers union, had formed their own cliques connected to the underground Communist Workers Party where they organized protests in places like Kasserine and neighboring areas. In turn, the cliques associated with the Islamic al-Nahda surfaced from underground by initiating protests in Sidi Bouzid and Kasserine. In the capital, Tunis, *shillas* allied with the leftist student Saghiri met in cafés to discuss how to extend the uprising into the working-class neighborhood of Tadamon. As a result of their initiative, the neighborhood rose up, with residents overwhelming the violent police with an onslaught of rocks and gravel.[10]

### The Poor in Battlefield

Clearly, then, the marginalized youth played a leading part in the Tunisian uprising. An astonishing 28 percent of the young population (fifteen to twenty-nine years) including 36 percent of student body took part in the nationwide protests.[11] Conversations about the some 500,000 "educated unemployed," the middle-class poor, as a major challenge to the regime reverberated in the public and media. At the time of the uprising, the middle-class poor connected the activism of students and educated youth to the lifeworld of the poor and deprived, those masses of people whose presence and claims injected a radical impulse to the uprisings. The poor militants provided vital human ammunition for the continuation of the protests. When activists in Sidi Bouzid, for instance, felt that protests were waning after a few days, an unemployed young man, Hussain Naji in Rfala, electrocuted himself in public by climbing on an electrical pole. His act of sacrifice instigated yet a new wave of mass outrage and insurgency. This was followed by a spate of self-immolations by young unemployed in Kasserine's al-Zohour poor area, Gafsa, Ariana, and other areas causing mass riots and battles with the security forces. Protestors attacked police stations and other government buildings including the offices of Ben Ali's ruling party.[12] The researcher Mohammed Yaghi reports that out of twenty people killed in Kasserine between January 8 and 10, 2011, fourteen were from the very poor district of al-Zohour. Here, the residents burned down the police station and drove the police out.[13]

In the capital, Tunis, residents in the poor neighborhoods of Tadamon, Sijoumi, Kabareih, Rahrouni, Halq alwad, al-Mahamadiah, and Karam attacked buildings and symbols representing the state, setting banks on fire on January 12. Tadamon, the largest working-class area in the capital and the site of cost-of-living mass unrest in the 1980s, had its own educated unemployed, or middle-class poor, who linked the area to college activism. In the area 105 there occurred a stiff standoff between the residents and the police who had warned protestors to disperse. When the residents refused, the police fired tear gas. In the intense battles in the maze of curvy and narrow alleyways, the police received a hail of rocks and rubbles coming from all sides. People "liberated" the neighborhood from police presence.[14]

The dismantling of police stations undermined state control; it broke down people's fear and contributed to the regime's downfall. It also caused a sense of insecurity and anxiety over crimes as the institutions of public order themselves were under assault. Even after the ousting of Ben Ali, when the police chief in Monastir called on 220 policemen on January 15 to return to their duties, only 30 conscripts showed up.[15] In truth, more than any other social groups, it was the poor who made sacrifices. Of the 125 total victims during the uprising in Tunisia, 95 were day laborers, manual workers, or jobless. Others included students (fifteen), taxi drivers, technicians, hairdressers, and teachers. Some 88 percent of those killed in greater Tunis came from a lower-class background.[16]

The poor paid a high price in the uprising. But what galvanized their grievances and brought to the surface their hidden politics were the local catalysts of the better-off UGTT members, in particular the leftist teachers union, which had become an asylum for scores of political and social dissenters who had been "exiled" by the Ben Ali regime from their original institutional positions.[17] As members of a national union that predated the regime itself, these activists brought their passion and organizational skill into the uprising from years of rehearsal in such occasions as the Gafsa miners' intifada in 2008 or in the street protests against Israel's assaults on Gaza in 2009.[18] Acts of self-immolation by the poor and the unemployed had indeed taken place before, as in Monastir in March and August 2010 and in Bousalem and Metlaoui in the summer. But none followed mass protests. Mohammed Bouaziz's drama proved different because the local people, youth, trade unionists, and professionals moved into an uncoordinated coalition that turned that individual drama into a nationwide collective uprising.

*Women Join*

Of course, many of these protestors were women—subjects of poverty, discrimination, and police brutality; mothers, sisters, or partners of male protagonists who braved the repressive police, or otherwise those well-to-do who longed for a free and just Tunisia. Countless images of street demonstrations, blogs, and Facebook pages left little doubt about the visible presence of women in the uprising. Some 7 percent of all Tunisian women took part in the revolution, according to the Arab Barometer data. They included young and elderly, secular and religious, college students, lawyers, trade unionists, as well as rural dwellers such as those in Sidi Bouzid and Kasserine. "They went to the streets and were carried on shoulders like heroes, something that never happened before or in other countries," remembered the activist Rasha proudly.[19] Some, like the well-to-do young woman Elyssa, were drawn into the revolution through social media. But on the streets, Elyssa said, "I felt fearless, even though people were getting killed. . . . And yet, no one would care [in taking the risk of protesting]."[20]

From the very outset, female relatives of those killed or beaten by the police came out to join the protests, as did thousands of others whose relatives were spending time in Ben Ali's unforgiving prisons. Mothers who lost their loved ones in the uprising voiced their grief and grievance out loud in public, describing the young victims as the children of the nation. Women associated with the Islamic trend al-Nahda, including 30,000 prisoners, were as visible as others in the public arena. They shared much with the secular women on the importance of women's public role, personal status, and on the idea that the revolution was for the freedom of all Tunisians. There were also many marginalized women from the interior provinces who joined their male participants in the demonstrations for which some paid a heavy price: they were beaten and sexually assaulted or raped by the security police, as reported in the villages around Kasserine.

Not just in the streets, many women worked hard in cyberspace—sending news, publishing articles, communicating, and mobilizing. Fadwa, a college student "took part in the uprising via Facebook, by posting articles and videos about the events that took place; I wrote about the repressive policy and about protests in Tunisia's interior provinces." She was proud to have "joined in the first demonstrations at the beginning of the revolution."[21] Several female bloggers such as Lina Ben Mhenni, Emna Jemaa, and Neila Kilani gained public recognition for their relentless cyberactivism during the momentous days of the revolt. Nuwress, a female law school student in Tunis "learned about the uprising from my close circle. We were in the group of more informed people," she remarked. "So we began to get the news that there were uprisings and social movements in the interior regions. We began to discuss." But more news came "from the cyberactivists about whom we did not know.[22] So we began to learn and get documents in the internet about the revolution." She later set up an educational tent in Kasbah

Square in Tunis to educate ordinary citizens about the meaning of the regime change and its legal and political implications. It was here that Nuwress, like so many other well-to-do participants, experienced a transformation. For the first time, she came out of her "bubble," encountered families afflicted with poverty and misfortune but full of dreams and hope. "I saw young people with high college degrees and no jobs; I saw people had turned to crime to make ends meet. I felt guilty. And so, I wanted to do something good for this huge change."[23] Nuwress then became an activist. Qamar, a mother of three children, felt similar transformation in her daughters. "After Bouazizi's self-immolation, my daughter told me *'Je sui Decembre'* [I am December, the month of revolution]. . . . I saw my children in another world," Qamar recounted.[24] "When I saw them in the revolution, I understood that I was living through a big thing. . . . This experience of seeing and living in new, this for me meant revolution."

## EGYPT FOLLOWS

As Tunisians began to feel the taste of a new order, youth activists in Egypt were already planning for a street rally to highlight the police torture of the young Khaled Said on charges of drug dealing. The unexpected downfall of the Tunisian dictator Ben Ali on January 14, 2011, brought the idea of "revolution" and its possibility to the Egyptians. Young activists who had called for a day of protest against police brutality on January 25 began to utter the word *thawra*, revolution.[25] The group We Are All Khaled Said met physically and secretly to coordinate with eleven others, including the youth of the Muslim Brotherhood, the young supporters of the popular opposition figure Muhamed Baradei, and the well-organized April 6th Movement. Once the date was set, the youth groups made relentless efforts to bring protestors on to the streets. On the advice of a retired police officer, the activists planned to begin demonstrations simultaneously in twenty different Cairo neighborhoods. They mobilized in the social media, sprayed slogans on walls, printed tracts, and distributed them in the popular neighborhoods such as Imbaba, Boulaq, and Dar al-Salam. The protest calls by the Facebook page We Are All Khaled Said alone received 300,000 supporters. The video appeal of the young female Asma Mahfouz passionately daring men to "be men" to come out on January 25 remains one of the hallmarks of youth activism in Egypt's revolution. When three men attempted self-immolation in the image of the Tunisian Mohammed Bouazizi, activists stated that they would rather see police stations be set on fire, not people.

Their remarkable campaign paid off. Crowds of tens of thousands gushed into the main streets from every direction like an uncontainable flood. In the teeming squares, Tahrir in particular, activists organized mass rallies, set up banners and stages, and built makeshift tents to spend the nights and stay on until President Hosni Mubarak left. Before long, they organized medical teams, cleaning crews, food supply, and security groups, virtually turning the square into a liberated urban zone. Multiple leaders, male and female, discussed strategies, assigned tasks, and allocated resources. The young activist Abdelrahman coordinated communication with different groups on the ground and took charge of organizing the cleanup of the square.[26] At the outset, organizers expressed unease about possible sexual pestering as boys and girls were to stay overnight in the occupied square. But against expectations, those in the square exhibited an extraordinary discipline and respect for gender equality.[27] "The female vanished to be replaced by the human woman," as the campaigner Nehad Abou El-Komsan observed. Social and religious divisions also seemed to disappear. Indeed, the very experience of the uprising altered the subjectivity and behavior of many participants.

The key preoccupation, however, was how to deter the security forces, consolidate the occupation, and above all, force Mubarak to step down. With multiple leaders and amorphous centers, the organization of the uprising remained horizontal. The spread of the protests beyond Cairo into Alexandria, Suez, Mahalla, Port Said, Ismailiyya, Tanta, Aswan, and others rendered a unified leadership even more remote. Certainly, horizontalism made decision making more inclusive and police crackdown more challenging, but it left the movement susceptible to internal discord and the manipulation of the regime. Feeling endangered, the youth groups affiliated with the political forces (April 6th Movement, Islamist Muslim Brothers, nationalist Karama, leftist Justice and Freedom and Tagamu' Party, and supporters of the liberal Baradei) came together on February 8, 2011 to forge the Coalition of Revolutionary Youth (CRY). CRY became a party to negotiate with the regime over transition to a new government. Some of these young activists showed impressive ability to make coalitions overriding the prevalent political divides. On January 30, when the aged leaders of the traditional political forces—all in their sixties and seventies—met to discuss how to move forward, six young activists in their twenties joined in. These unassuming youths spoke of their ideas and the path ahead with such conviction that it put their audience in deep restraint and reflection. "Whatever you want from us, we'll do," responded the old men after a long pause.[28]

Such attempts notwithstanding, the real thrust for mobilization of the uprising came from local leadership and built on trust and charisma in the networks of family, friends, and collectives, which had already developed in the neighborhoods, schools, colleges, workplaces, or street corner associations. "My involvement in politics was not only because I believed a different world was possible," recalled an activist. "It was because I had dreamed up a world with my friends, with my family and loved ones, and we had taken to the streets, to organizing, to writing, to creativity in order to achieve it."[29] In Cairo's poor neighborhood Imbaba, youth had developed circles of friendship and common interests, which they would deploy in everyday interactions. Imbaba's soccer fans, the Ultras, had formed strong local networks within which they met, associated, hung out, and exchanged news in their localities and beyond. Neighborhood activists like the leftist Amr Abu-Tawil had directed some of these local energies into a network to upgrade local resources such as garbage, water, roads, and the like. Later, the Baradei campaign became an important vehicle that brought such youth non-movements to its organizing ambit. Once the uprising broke out, local activists formed the Popular Committee to Defend the Revolution. Members of the Ultras informed one another to join the protests in Tahrir on January 28 to fight off the security forces, which they despised for their everyday pestering. In the meantime, local mosques and churches became important locations to assemble, discuss, and plan for action—in particular on Fridays and after the prayer times when demonstrations were usually organized.[30]

From local networks, some figures surfaced onto the wider public through social media, where they mustered larger followings during the uprising. Activists such as Abdelrahman Yousef from Kifaya, Islamic liberal Mustafa Ibrahim, liberal Shadi al-Ghazali Harb, Marxist Hossam al-Hamalawi, April 6 leader Ahmed Maher, blogger Mona Seif, and cyberactivists Abdelrahman Mansour and Wael Ghoneim became national characters. Among them, Ala'a Abdel-Fattah would become the iconic persona of the revolution. Through a persistent mobilization, Egyptian youth led a mass uprising, backed by millions of ordinary people, that eventually forced President Mubarak to step down on February 12, 2011. Mubarak transferred power to a Supreme Council of Armed Forces (SCAF) to oversee the transition to a new government. Egyptians celebrated the end of Mubarak with an ecstatic jubilation throughout the country. The CRY called on protesters to end the protests and return to "normal life." But it warned that "if we don't like how things progress, the 20 million people who protested won't fail to protest again."[31]

The role of the young people in spearheading the uprising was so prominent that the episode came to be dubbed the "revolution of youth," *al-thawra al-shabab.* Some 12 percent of the Egyptian youth took part in the uprising.[32] For their leadership, youth received respect and recognition from the elders. On February 12, hours after Mubarak stepped down, a female activist tweeted, "My dad hugged me after the news and said, 'Ur generation did what ours could only dream of. I am sorry we didn't try hard enough.'"[33] The novelist Ahdaf Soueif could not conceal her deep admiration for these youths. "We the old revolutionaries have been trying since '72 to take Tahrir. They are doing it," she commented. "They are going to change the world. We follow them."[34]

However spectacular youth leadership and activism might have been, the uprising could not succeed without the involvement of the ordinary people: the poor, middle layers, women, children, or elderly. For only these diverse constituencies could "normalize" the uprising, giving it a popular character. As in Tunisia, key players among these constituencies were the poor and working people whose world had been organically connected to youth activism through the mediation of the "middle-class poor," those educated but economically deprived who traversed between the world of education, cyberspace, and activism of the main street to the world of backstreet slums and squatter settlements of their dispossessed parents, relatives, and neighbors.

### The Underdog
The poor neighborhoods supplied a major source of the rebellion. On the very first day of the protests on January 25, 2011, poor Cairo residents from al-Waraq, al-Mu'tamadiya, Bulaq El-Daqrour, Imbaba, Dar al-Salam, and other districts in Giza marched to Tahrir square. Some 200 activists in the slum community of Naheyan mobilized up to 20,000 demonstrators over the issues of police brutality and the price of bread.[35] Likewise, the massive informal community of Imbaba in the heart of Cairo, known for its Islamist history, joined the uprising in earnest. Following a meeting by some thirty leftist and nationalist activists in front of al-Azra church, a small protest quickly swelled into hundreds

and then thousands as they marched through the deprived Sekka al-Hadid and the maze of narrow backstreets.[36] More dramatic events were to follow on the historic Day of Anger, January 28, 2011, when an animated group of activists met in a local mosque just after the Friday prayer to organize a demonstration.[37] Their initial march of fifty people, half of them children, rapidly grew into a mass demonstration of which "one could not see the beginning and the end." With the incursion of the riot police, the area turned into a battle zone, with people shouting, barricading, fighting, throwing rocks and Molotov cocktails, or holding wooden shields to break through the police cordons.[38] Imbaba made its first martyr by the fall of the young Muhamed Sayed Abdul-Latif to the police shotguns.[39] But the crowd marched on, then joining the streams of similar marches that flooded from other neighborhoods. The protestors called for the downfall of the regime, invited others to join in, battled with the riot police for hours until forcing their way toward Tahrir Square.[40]

Imbaba was known for its "Islamist" past when in the early 1990s, hundreds of radical Islamists had penetrated this opaque space of narrow alleyways that had no maps, street names, or home numbers, creating an "Islamist state within the state."[41] But by the time of the revolution, things had changed. "The last thing youth are talking about is religion," said Ahmed Metwalli, a son of an ex-Islamist just after Mubarak's fall. "It is the last thing that comes up. They need money, they need to get married, a car. . . . They will elect whoever delivers that."[42] The poor of Imbaba had risen up because of their outrage at their denigration, having to bribe the police to go to the hospital or get ID cards. "This isn't the January 25th revolution; this is a revolution of dignity," said a resident named Samih Ahmed. "We don't need prayers, sheikhs, and beards; we have had enough of the clerics." In the meantime, artistic youths inscribed the symbolic images of the revolution, the numerous murals, slogans, and images of martyrs of the revolution on the walls of these underdog neighborhoods.

In Cairo's Dar al-Salam, the Day of Anger began with a demonstration of no more than 20 people but expanded to over 5,000 as they walked through the streets of this squatter settlement.[43] By the time the demonstration reached the old Cairo, there were 30,000 protesters. The crowd astonished the organizers by what they were chanting— "People Want the Downfall of the Regime," "Death to Mubarak." When they reached the old Cairo, a few attempted to storm the police station but faced a heavy police barrier. The crowd continued their march toward the city center, engaging in violent clashes with the riot police along the way. The protesters eventually arrived in Tahrir Square with a sense of relief as if they had entered a liberated space of safety and solidarity. "Despite our tremendous anger and exhaustion, we felt like we had reached our home," recounted Gamal, a local lawyer and activist. Back in Dar al-Salam, in the meantime, people had captured the police station, putting the officers to flight.

Indeed, this was a moment of liberation for the subaltern, notably the poor young male, who were the object of everyday police brutality. In Cairo's Gamaliyya, Ataba, and Moski areas, people fought off the heavy-handed central security soldiers with their bare hands. The poor residents of Bulaq abul-Alaa, close to Tahrir Square, deployed their experience of fighting the riot police to shelter the revolutionaries from attacks and detention. While most young activists assembled in Tahrir Square, the poor of the slums and *ashwaiyyat*—such as Imbaba, Helwan, Dar al-Salam, Bab al-Shar'iyya, Bulaq El-Daqrour, and Matariyya— waged unrelenting battles against police stations and detention centers. On the Day of Anger, the journalist Khalil Abu-Shadi saw a remarkable fight between the people and the police in Maidan Matariyya. As the flurry of fire from the riot police vehicles mixed with the echoes of booms and blasts, the shaken crowd ran around the streets littered with rocks, rubble, and the wreckage of burned cars. "There is no government; we are the government," the crowd was shouting. Hundreds stormed into the security headquarter by breaking its iron door, then looting the building throwing stacks of documents out of the windows. "These marginalized Cairenes," reported the journalist, "defeated the security forces by a relentless hurling of rocks and Molotov cocktails—a weapon the young poor and the unemployed mostly deployed."[44] Some called for the killing of the security soldiers, whereas others protected them with the chants, "Leave alone the soldiers; they are poor like us."

In the first few days of the uprising, the protesters set some 100 police stations on fire. In total, one-half of all police stations in the country were attacked.[45] This alone questioned the established binary of "violent" and "nonviolent" revolutions that is so present in the accounts of "civil resistance."[46] The police vanished from the public scene by the evening of January 28, when the Interior Ministry pulled 1.5 million security personnel off the streets while letting criminals out of prisons to cause chaos and insecurity. For the poor and the oppressed, freedom from the police was a genuine victory, which they paid for with their lives. During the uprising, 837 protestors (and 49 police officers) perished. Of the 290 victims who can be identified by their profession, 169 were workers, day laborers, taxi drivers, or unemployed, while 121 held college degrees or were corporate employees, engineers, lawyers, or university students.[47]

Of course, not everyone joined the revolutionary protests.[48] Expectedly, the rural migrants and the very poor of the older groups preferred to stay away from such large-scale movements. A study confirmed that the poorest income had the lowest rate of participation in both Egypt and Tunisia, indicating not the "absolute" but "relative deprivation" as a cause of dissent.[49] Yet, the heterogeneity of the informal neighborhoods where residents held diverse educational backgrounds tended to facilitate the link between the parochial and the cosmopolitan. *Ashwaiyyat* communities like Imbaba housed not merely the rural, illiterate, and abject poor but also industrial workers and segments of the "middle-class poor"—government employees, newly married and educated couples, as well as professionals such as lawyers or teachers who could not afford to secure housing in the formal market.

Despite the claim by Ahmed Maher, a leader of the April 6 Movement, that the "workers did not play a role in the revolution," there were at least sixty strikes by workers in the days just before Mubarak's ouster.[50] Indeed, as the days passed, factory workers and government employees took more industrial actions. Workers in telecommunication, oil, military production plants, and industries in the city of Suez stopped work, while the employees of state-run newspapers and some 3,000 university professors, among many others, marched in support of the revolution. Workers had initiated some 1,700 protests and strikes in the year before the revolution and continued with even greater intensity after.[51]

Beyond joining mass demonstrations in city centers, the poor also staged their own "mini-revolutions" in their localities. In Cairo's Manshiat Naser, where hill rocks had demolished several homes, residents attacked and set fire on the Neighborhood Council (Majlis al-Mahaliyat) and the police station, which they deemed responsible for corruption and evictions.[52] Indeed, when the police retreated and disappeared from the public arenas on January 28, "revolution was over for the poor," as if an insurmountable victory had been achieved.[53] With the police and the fear of police gone, the poor pushed for their claims more aggressively. Thus, hundreds of poor families occupied some 510 apartments in the Wahayed public housing in Duweiqa. They reasoned that "these apartments were for us, for the families from the Duweiqa slums." To secure their occupancy, they reported to the municipality and visited the Ministry of Defense, which permitted them to stay.[54] Things, however, were to change soon after the uprising when SCAF moved to evict the squatters with an offer of alternative housing. At this juncture, the illegal construction of homes and informal additions went on unheeded throughout the country. Half-built vacant apartments were taken over, and public lands in the periphery of cities were occupied to construct dwellings. The sudden rise in the price of cement pointed to the widespread illegal constructions during the revolution. And street vendors who would otherwise get chased away by the police took over prime spots in city centers to market their merchandize. Struggles of this sort were to assume an unmatched momentum in the immediate postrevolution.

## Mothers, Daughters, Wives

In many ways, the backstreet lifeworld in the poor neighborhoods was the domain of women. The actual merging of private and public, through the extension of home life into the outdoor *hara*, meant that women (mostly married and middle aged) were visible out there in public—in balconies, rooftops, alleyways, or local markets. The working women, especially those from the 3.3 million female heads of families, spent even more time out of the home. When the uprising came, women of the poor neighborhoods did not retreat indoors. Rather, they engaged. Some joined families who claimed unfinished apartments and illegal constructions; others gave support to the street protesters or joined them. Demonstrating through the streets of Imbaba on January 28, the novelist Ahdaf Soueif could not miss observing women who gathered in the balconies "smiling, waving, dandling babies to the tune of the chants." Old women called, "God be with you. God give you victory," she recounted.[55]

Not just the poor but women from all walks of life, some 4 percent of all female population (compared to 13 percent of all men) joined the street protests.[56] "There were hundreds, if not thousands, of women involved in organizing supplies, medication, banners, marches, international contacts, and general mobilization for this movement," related an eyewitness.[57] "There were veiled women who covered their face, or just their hair or appeared unveiled. There were women alone, with children, young and the elderly all standing in solidarity together." Women of the Muslim Brothers stayed over in apartments near the Goethe Institute and Tahrir overnight to be present in the square during the daytime.

Activist and professional women involved in "human rights" were of the first to join the uprising. Many of them brought their earlier experience of activism during the Kifaya movement of 2005 and labor strikes of 2008 and 2010 to something more spectacular than they could imagine. When the lawyer activist Nehad Abou El-Komsan marched to Tahrir, despite the suffocating tear gas covering the air, "I was engulfed by a form of happiness that I had never known before in my life. . . . I wanted to stay in the square and never leave it." But she had to exit periodically to send the news outside and tend to her children, terrified by the rumor of crime and insecurity that the regime had spread across the country.[58] It was then that the well-known Asma Mahfouz called for the formation of popular committees to protect the people in Tahrir Square and beyond.

Lesser known women organized food deliveries, supplied blankets, staged rallies, and secured medical assistance on the ground. These included women like Isra'a Abdul Fatah, political activist of April 6 and media coordinator; Wedad el-Demerdash, factory worker and activist; Asma'a Ali, organizer in popular neighborhoods; Nada Aziz from al-Mahrousa radio; Basma Abdul-Aziz, anti-torture activist.[59] Asma'a Ali worked in rationing committees, security, advocacy, cleaning, broadcasting, guarding the square inlets. "I joined the organizing committee in making the groups chant one slogan and in wandering everywhere in the square to share and exchange ideas to reach an agreement."[60] Nadia al-Halabi encouraged many people to spend the night in the square and bring food to the in-sitters. Outraged over her college-educated brother being without a decent job, friends in their thirties unmarried, and protestors beaten up, teacher Nada Ta'ema was there to make a difference.

In fact, most women, perhaps similar to men, had little experience in contentious politics before. But they were endowed with profound affect that fashioned their participation in the uprising. College graduate Asmaa was enraged by the "police officer beating a man on the street" but was not initially allowed by her father to partake in protests. Things changed, however, when she saw Asma Mahfouz challenging men to go to the streets. She saw "this girl not fearing arrest, murder, or disappearance" and decided that she "must participate in the revolution."[61]

With friends and family, she prayed in the mosque and joined the march toward Tahrir. On the way, they were attacked by the riot police with tear gas and ran away in every direction in fear and fury. When she found her father in the midst of confusion, she hugged him and cried hard. From then on, Amaa stayed in Tahrir, day and night, only rushing home periodically to rest, wash, and pick up food, blankets, and first aid. Tahrir transformed Asmaa, bringing her out of domestic innocence into a brave new world. Her experience was similar to so many ordinary women like Alaa, who was so taken by the Tahrir moment that she said, "I was most depressed after the eighteen days were over. . . . I felt that we had done the best thing ever."[62]

Networks of friendship and *shillas* were crucial in women's participation in the uprising. Women joined the protests as part of doing things together with friends, family, and relatives. "We would stay at the square for three days, and we would get back home to take showers and change clothes before we head to the square again with food."[63] Alaa, a young female, would pick up neighbors or anyone on the way from Masr Gadidah to the Tahrir protests. She spent the night on the day of the Battle of Camels with a group of friends. For the dentistry graduate Ghouson, "January 26 was my first time participating [in a protest]."[64] She went to the demonstrations together with friends, many of whom volunteered in Resala. She had worked as a medical student to teach the poor children remedial lessons and in the process had seen poverty, inequality, corruption, and "no social justice." When Mubarak left, Mona felt there was something wrong. "Was it a frenzy that was over? Do we have a role to play?" she wondered. That would pave the way for her to become a labor activist after the revolution.

Ordinary women often hesitated to join when they needed male support or still could not make sense of things. They would "wait to see what was going to happen," as the fifty-five-year-old medical doctor Mona did.[65] But many were eventually drawn in through neighbors, friends, distant networks, and sheer empathy. Hoda, in her fifties from

Haram, watched clashes on TV and saw people demonstrating and even attacking the police stations. On January 29, she went to Tahrir and set up the Haram Group tent where she stayed with others until the end of the uprising.[66] Hesitant Mona went so far as becoming a revolutionary, protesting and posting news and comments online. For her, the Tahrir moment represented a "model for the Egypt we want, which includes everything and everyone regardless of any differences—Christians, Muslims, Salafists, socialists, communists, liberals, nonpolitical people, and those who don't belong to any thought camp at all."

Unlike men, hesitation for women came with an understanding of certain gendered constraints that were prompted paradoxically by the very power women's public presence espoused. There was something threatening about women's public contention in a society and politics overburdened by patriarchy. Ironically, the nonthreatening ordinary women—hijab-wearing women, mothers holding children, the elderly—posed a greater threat to the authorities and brought anxiety to mainstream men. Consequently, unlike men, women had to manage two potential dangers to be publicly active during the uprising. First, the physical and sexual violence of the security forces and regime thugs, and second, the deeper repression of family and community, what Nehad Abou El-Komsan called a "social culture [rule] that always dealt with women as the weaker person in need of protection."[67] Of course, there was the memory of the hideous sexual assault of National Democratic Party thugs against the protesting women during the Kifaya episode in May 2005. And precisely for such defiant visibility, some had to pay a double price. The victims went through painful divorce, social rejection, forced veiling, or a slap on the face by parents. No wonder that during the uprising, many women like Radwa faced "some sort of curfew at home. We were not allowed to leave home [for fear of sexual assault]."[68]

Indeed, any act of violence, including those committed by the revolutionaries, would disenchant women.[69] The Egyptian revolution was relatively "peaceful," but beatings, attacks against the police stations, injuries, and killings did take place. This drove many women away from the streets. "I didn't know that there would be violence, burning, killing," remembered Ghouson. "So I had a major shock, and I stopped participating for a while and started to become against the revolution."[70] Consequently, many women gravitated toward activities in safer spaces—posting on social media, helping with logistical supplies, or, like Ghouson, treating the injured in field hospitals.

This, however, did not mean that women remained in the background of the uprising. Some used their comparative advantage, skills, and networks to lead in the foreground. Basma Abdullah, for instance, "assisted in training fifty male and female youth on techniques for raising political awareness on the internet, each and every one of whom trained another ten people." She encouraged many youths to "spend the night in the square, to continue exercising pressure on the authority to fulfill our demands."[71] This did not even include women artists, journalists, writers, lawyers, and bloggers who were at the forefront in various ways, giving speeches to the crowds or feeding the in-sitters. When, on January 28, the regime shut down the internet and mobile phones, it was young females in their twenties like Mona who relocated from their homes into an undisclosed location to work with male comrades to hack into the system to reestablish communication and send news to the outside world.[72]

In Egypt as in Tunisia, women participants in the revolutions clearly went beyond their particularistic claims regarding gender equality, despite its significance. They focused on the broader concerns of ending repression and establishing justice. The protesting women, religious and secular alike, were fighting for the freedom not just of women but of all citizens.[73] Only after the downfall of the dictators did they return, with relentless campaigns, to their concerns for gender justice.

## A Social Minority

Somewhat similar was the experience of the social minorities. Already underground and constantly at risk, many queer individuals poured into the streets protesting, carrying banners, helping out with supplies, attending to the injured, mobilizing online, and getting arrested. In Egypt, Tahrir became the central locus for queer people to meet and connect. "I was holding a sign saying 'Secular,'" said a gay participant. His friends "were holding similar signs and we all were chanting that this protest is for the people and not for any party or religion."[74] He wished LGBT rights would be recognized, but this was possible only "when Egypt becomes a real secular country," where individuals would "accept people who are sexually different than they are." Queer claims were clearly eclipsed behind the overarching demand for "freedom, social justice, and democracy" that other protestors also shared. "I loved how diverse yet finally united Egypt is." This sentiment of unity and oneness was expressed more vividly by another gay man. He remembered a time in Tahrir Square when a prostitute joined in the gatherings. "But people over there never treated her as a whore," he stated. "It was amazing. . . . We all suddenly became one people." Even though Tahrir had become a space of freedom, even sexual freedom, "my sexuality was not the issue at the time. What I was thinking was my Egypt, the Egyptians, whom I trusted then 100 percent—the men, women, neighbors," he emphasized. "My sexuality at that time dropped to the bottom of my concerns."[75]

## SUBALTERN AND REVOLUTION

Clearly, the youth, notably young males, were instrumental in initiating and pushing forward the uprisings in Tunisia and Egypt. Youth affordance—that is, strategic agility, endurance, and "structural irresponsibility" (relative freedom from dependence on and responsibility for others)—offered them comparative advantage to act more daringly on the stage of street politics. In this drama, the poor and lower-class male youth, those President Ben Ali called masked bandits, played a critical role. Young rebels braved the police, bullets, and tear gas; they built Molotov cocktails, threw rocks, and attacked police stations. They ran, returned, and sang songs to appease the security forces. They carried the injured, buried the dead, and fell victims to the violence of the regime agents. During the eighteen-day uprising in Egypt, out of 866 protesters killed, 200 were students and minors.[76] Those with an experience of involvement in the student, labor, women, or human rights organizations brought their skill of activism to mobilize and push the revolution forward. But for most of the young participants, *shillas*, the intimate cliques and collectives built on trust and loyalty, served as the structure of collective deliberation, decision making, and mobilization at the local level. As the passive networks of the nonmovements were activated at these contentious times, individual youths and their local collectives were linked to one another in the vast connective grids operating both online and on the ground. Meanwhile, the post-ideological sensibilities of the young protagonists—transcending religious, political, and gender divides—yielded remarkable success in forging coalitions and ensuring unity.

The episode of the uprisings signaled a shift in youth politics. "Youth politics" (and not simply "youth *in* politics") is about claiming or reclaiming youthfulness; it is articulated usually in terms of cultural politics—pursuing a particular lifestyle, seeking autonomy, and preparing for adult life.[77] But in the uprisings, the young went beyond their exclusive youthful claims, focusing instead on the broader concerns of the citizenry. No wonder, then, that their remarkable role in the uprisings earned them such admiration and respect. Perhaps in no other period of their recent history have the Arab societies witnessed so much attention to youths, whether by the general public, media, or expert communities.[78]

No matter how spectacular their activism might be, however, youth on their own can never create a breakthrough in the revolutionary mobilization. The breakthrough comes only when the ordinary people turn to becoming extraordinary—when the elderly and adolescents, mothers and grandfathers, small sisters or brothers, the poor and the better-off join in to bring such extraordinary acts of rebellion into wider social spectrum, and when these diverse constituencies transcend their sectoral claims in favor of broader claims of all citizens united in a singular movement. Extraordinary acts, even though spectacular and surprising, are by definition exceptional, isolated and thus susceptible to official control and crackdown. But the involvement of the ordinary people brings the extraordinary yet fringe acts into the ordinary and popular by giving the contenders a broader societal representation. This signifies a power of ordinariness, and in this, women and the poor have important but complex parts to play.

*Gender in Revolution*

Women constituted a significant component of the ordinary force that broadened the basis of the revolutionary uprising. But a number of questions were raised about them specifically. First, to what extent were women actually present in the uprisings, and what was their significance? Second, how much, if at all, did they participate *as women,* as voices of women's rights? And third, how did gender matter in the idea and practice of revolution? Clearly, women of diverse types and backgrounds were visible in the streets of the discontent, not just in the urban centers of Tunisia and Egypt but also in the "tribal" political economies of Yemen and Libya. Strikingly, the Arab uprisings produced more iconic women than men. In Tunisia, Amel Mathlouthi emerged as the "anthemic voice" of the revolution when she stood up to sing "Kelmti Horra" (My Word Is Free) to a sea of protesters who had filled the entire Bourguiba Avenue on the momentous day of January 14 before Ben Ali fled the country.[79] In Egypt, Asma Mahfouz became a "leader of the revolution" after she posted an extraordinary video challenging men to "act like men" to join the protests. "Whoever says women shouldn't go to the protests because they will get beaten, let them have some honor and manhood, and come with me on January 25," she pleaded in a paradoxical language that put the patriarchy to test. "If you have honor and dignity as a man, come and protect me, and other girls in the protest." In Bahrain, activist Munira Fakhro along with a few women with children inaugurated the uprising from the iconic Pearl Square. Zainab al-Khawaja went on a hunger strike to protest the beating and arrest of her father and her husband. And in Yemen, it was the young Tavakkol Karman who first led a protest to spearhead the Yemeni revolution, a role that earned him the Nobel Prize in 2011. However remarkable these female personae, they pale before the extraordinary presence of ordinary women in the streets of the uprisings. The idea did not escape the *Guardian* journalist who saw "black-robed and angry, a sea of female faces in the capitals of north Africa, the Arabian Peninsula, the Syrian hinterland, marching for regime change, an end to repression, the release of loved ones. Or else delivering speeches to the crowds, treating the injured, feeding the sit-ins of Cairo and Manama and the makeshift army of eastern Libya."[80] At least fifteen women were killed during the January and February uprising in Egypt.

However, the significance of women's participation lies not just in their sheer numbers or body counts but rather in the fact that women's mere presence substantially alters the dynamics of contention. In a patriarchal society where women are expected to mind their domestic business in managing the home and raising children, their powerful march in the streets, side by side with men, would itself signal a turning point of equality. It empowers the uprising and enrages the moral and political authority who may in response inflict moral charge, body abuse, and sexual violence. In Yemen, President Ali Saleh charged the protesting women with "immoral" acts of "mixing with men," to which women responded by ridiculing the president's hypocrisy. In Egypt, authorities perpetrated gang rape and the infamous virginity test in 2011. However, this exposure of women's bodies to male abuse, this feebleness, can ironically be empowering when the female body assumes an ethical meaning, a sacred entity whose violation would impair the moral standing of the perpetrators. After all, how can one abuse a woman / mother in public in a culture where she is perceived as the "mother of the nation," as the source of nourishment, as the embodiment of purity and honor?[81] Such advantage, together with maternal impunity—the power of mothers and elderly women seen as protectors of the weak and vulnerable—offers women the kind of comparative latitude that by definition is denied to men. So when in Bahrain male protesters became the subject of police brutality, women felt free and kept coming out to demonstrate in the streets, and in doing so gave new life to the uprising.[82] In Egypt, the sexual violence galvanized the largest women's protest in the nation's history, bringing the issue of women's safety in public onto the national agenda. Once on the stage of contention, these women, in addition, tend inadvertently to feminize and "civilize" the acts of dissent. For there is an inescapable truism that women in general, whether driven by nature or nurture, tend to eschew violent tactics and embrace peaceful struggles. And this is notwithstanding the images of "Jihadi women" or female guerillas holding Kalashnikovs or the more recent Kurdish female fighters who, according to some, represent a "new Middle Eastern femininity" shaped by the interaction of local, international, religious, and war forces.[83] In these cultures, women, mothers, and the elderly usually exude male respect and civility. Clearly, then, the very presence of women markedly influenced the dynamics of the revolutions: it helped normalize, civilize, compensate for male absence, and ultimately enhance the success of the uprisings.

If revolutions are gendered and women played a significant part in the Arab uprisings, we should take seriously some crucial questions posed by many women in the aftermath. Were women given sufficient space to play leadership roles? After all, during the uprising in Egypt, the "wise men," the elderly politicians from the traditional political organizations negotiating with the government, did not include any women. What happened to the issues of women's rights and gender equality? When were such claims to be made? Were women supposed to partake in the revolutions first and only bring up gender matters in the aftermath?[84] Such questions resonated well with the Iranian feminists who, having experienced the misogynist attitudes of the religious leaders of the 1979 Islamic revolution, expressed genuine worries about the status of Arab women after the uprisings.

In truth, both in Tunisia and Egypt, women participants seemed overwhelmingly to relinquish claims for women's rights in favor of the broader calls for dignity, democracy, and justice. Women like Norhan, then twenty-four years old, joined the Egyptian uprising fervently because of the "flagrant corruption, forging elections and all this." She saw her participation "as a very natural response." "We saw that nothing would have happened if we had not kept demonstrating; for us, it was a moment we had to capture," she recounted.[85] Women seemed to join the revolutions not simply as women with particular gender claims but as citizens concerned with a better life for everyone. Writing on Tunisia, Andrea Khalil discovered that the "women interviewed emphasized their common, collective goals beyond particularistic gender identities."[86] Indeed, very similar sentiments were expressed by women in Egypt. According to Nermin Allam's study, gender claims and language were clearly missing in the uprising, because women were preoccupied with the broader issues of national unity.[87] In fact, the women's position in the uprising, according to Khalil, reflected a "rarified moment of gender equality in which women's rights were secondary to the primordial concern for collective equality and freedom for all citizens."[88] "No one sees you as a woman here; no one sees you as a man. We are all united in our desire for democracy and freedom," stated an Egyptian feminist, Mozn Hassan.[89] It was not until after the downfall of Mubarak that feminists like Nahed Abou El-Komsan would wonder, "Will Tahrir Square remain a synonym to 'freedom, justice, and equality,' or will the revolution sacrifice its children and, chief among them, the women?!"[90]

This quandary points precisely to a key paradox in the revolutionary movements. On the one hand, the logic of revolution implies an affective and strategic urge for equality and unity: when people think and feel not in terms of "me" or "my group" but in terms of Tunisia, Egypt, or the entirety of the nation, and when the particularistic claims of the subaltern (women, youth, or the social minorities) are eclipsed behind the larger struggle for freedom and justice. But at the same time, a unified language of revolution would likely conceal variations in people's perceptions about change and images of alternative order; diversity gets screened, conflicts belittled, and a dominant voice speaks for all. The suppression of difference by the dominant voice usually works against the discourse of the subaltern, the powerless, the poor, minorities, and women.

This is crucial to tackle. For what ensures revolutionary unity is not just the affective impulse to transcend particular interests and identities. There is also something subtler at work: a tendency among participants to read and imagine their particular claims in the general ideals of "freedom" or "justice." In this *imagined solidarity*, unity is achieved, but the particularistic claims and group divisions remain, only to reemerge after the downfall of the dictators when unity is no longer urged.[91] Perhaps one needs the ingenuity of the Lebanese women activists who in their own October Revolution in 2019 could come up with the banner Tali'a Tasqat Nizam (I am coming like a bride to overthrow the system) to inscribe a feminist signifier on to a universal claim. Otherwise, activists everywhere have grappled with how to reconcile the particular claims of the subaltern with the general ideals of unity and greater good. Feminists remained wary of attempts to marry Marxism and feminism because such attempts tended to "subsume the feminist struggle into the 'larger' struggle against capital."[92] So did Marxists with respect to the marriage of nationalism and class politics or the workers' struggle.[93] And the Arab revolutions brought forward once again the question of how to merge the subaltern desire for self-realization with the revolutionary urge for unity and the greater good.[94]

## The Poor

The status of the poor in revolution is even more complex. Their participation in the revolutionary uprising is highly contingent. In the Iranian revolution of 1979, for instance, the poor mostly stayed away from street protests, focusing instead on quiet or aggressive encroachments, such as seizing land to farm or property to shelter.[95] But the Arab revolutions witnessed, as we saw, an undeniable presence of the poor in the streets of the uprisings. This was so primarily because the social texture of the poor had changed over the past decades. Not only had the spread of education, technology, media, and satellite TV brought the urban and rural poor closer to national politics, but also the "middle-class poor"—very prominent in the Arab societies—facilitated the engagement of poor families, friends, and neighbors with the organization and political imaginary of the uprising. In the Arab revolutions, the poor and working classes had lost their potential (Marxist) allies as there were no such parties anymore but had found new "organic intellectuals" among the "middle-class poor": deprived teachers, lawyers, state employees, and other college graduates, who brought oppositional politics into their sprawling neighborhoods. The post-ideological bent of the middle-class poor found a productive affinity with the ideological pragmatism of the urban poor, who were preoccupied primarily with their immediate concerns.[96] These "organic intellectuals" were crucial in connecting the poor to the larger world of the uprising.

While women, youth, and social minorities, instead of voicing their own particular claims, seemed to focus on the wider concerns for unity, justice, and freedom, the poor displayed a more complex position. Some waited to see what would transpire, others took advantage of the situation to realize their claims through direct action, and many joined the protests in earnest, fighting the police and making sacrifices. Broadly speaking, the recently arrived rural migrants and the very poor, those whose knowledge of the events remains limited, often show reluctance to spearhead public protests of such magnitude and nature.[97] Many of them are not clear about the dynamics, the aims, and outcome of such political upheavals, so they prefer to wait and see what transpires. For most of the illiterate and very poor, revolutions remain events too abstract to be incorporated into their precarious daily lives. They tend to get involved in the more concrete and local struggles, those that are meaningful and manageable for them.[98]

Periods of insurrection are also when the poor make widespread encroachments. Taking advantage of the collapse of police control, they aggressively pursue appropriating lands for shelter or farming, illegal construction, squatting homes or hotels, and spreading business in the streets and squares, in off-limit locations and spots. For many poor people, the disappearance of the police from the streets alone becomes a momentous victory, given that police repression carries an undeniable class prejudice. For some, avenging the police with violence becomes a kind of Fanonian "cathartic release," a way to retrieve respect, exert power, and cleanse the stains of their everyday humiliation. But beyond the extraordinary political opportunity, the very nature of poor people's claims, unlike that of, say, women or youths, makes them realizable. Simply put, it is not feasible for women to achieve, for instance, equal rights in child custody during the uprising, however powerful such a demand may be advanced. But it is indeed practical for the poor to acquire shelter by seizing land or occupying empty apartments. Women have to wait until after the insurrection, when the institutional order is back in place. But the poor are able to make their gains at such time precisely because the institutional order is disrupted.

Do the aggressive encroachments by the poor not echo Hernando De Soto's claim about the Arab Spring as the revolution of the class-conscious underclass, the "aspiring businessmen," for a free market?[99] De Soto suggests that the likes of Bouazizi were the victims of the institutional constraints that disrupted the flourishing capitalist enterprise in which they could gain property rights and prosper. In short, they aspired to a true market economy.[100] This conclusion, however, is an oversimplification. In truth, Bouazizi's dispossession was not due to the absence of property law but rather the legal behavior of the police who deemed Bouazizi's operation unlawful. The history of dispossession faced by Bouazizi's family, as we saw earlier, actually shows how the logic of the capitalist market—the banks possessing the family's lands due to default in debt payment—violated the moral economy and ethics of fairness within which poor people like Bouazizi usually operate. The aggressive encroachments of the poor during the uprisings seemed to echo their desire not for a lawful free market but rather for a "parallel revolution," to realize their "future in the present" in their immediate environs, to restore a moral economy grounded on the ethics of fairness and justice.

Revolutions always involve a large number of varied groups, and subaltern subjects in particular, who give the movement wider national representation.[101] The magic of the revolutionary movement lies precisely in the participation of diverse societal constituencies with different interests and expectations, who nevertheless imagine themselves and act as one singular equal entity. This distinguishes a revolutionary movement from such widespread protests as the French Yellow Vests in December 2018, or the nonstop ten-day, nationwide protests of Iranians in over eighty-five cities and towns in late December 2017. For, even though these protests were linked to one another loosely and virtually through social media, the diverse participating groups were concerned with their own particularistic claims.[102] As such, theirs was not a singular movement but merely had the appearance of singularity.

By contrast, in a revolutionary movement, the sectoral interests merge into broader claims for "freedom" and "justice"; diverse groups with different interests and claims act as one; workers, youth, the poor, students, minorities appear and act as "the people"; and, in short, the ordinary becomes extraordinary.[103] Whether a product of the primordial urge for unity and collective equality, or of an imagined solidarity of participants who project their particular concerns into the overarching calls for freedom and justice, what emerges signifies an "event" in the parlance of Alain Badiou. As if it were "a time out of time," the "event" represents a rupture, a finite historical happening that may open up infinite possibilities.[104] Seen in this light, the story of revolution is thus not just about regime change, however significant that may be. It is also about what happened in the underside, among the grassroots, in the everyday. It is about what the revolution meant to the ordinary people and how they partook in revolutionary dynamics.

*Chapter 4*

# The Poor and Plebeian

REVOLUTIONARY DYNAMICS shift radically the day after the dictators abdicate. The unity and equality that once marked the insurrections quickly dissolve and in their place come certain usual paradoxes that in turn shape the postrevolutionary moment. Ordinary people who not long before had risen to dissent and disfigure the status quo for the sake of the revolution now bear the brunt of their own creative disruption—one that is intended to help bring a new order. The extraordinary rise in popular expectations occurs ironically in conditions where even the minimum resources to fulfill them diminish. So, even though the subaltern expects to be unusually better off, they instead end up getting worse off. Having gone through a period of hardship and sacrifice for the sake of revolution (street battles, labor strikes, altruism), they emerge with high hopes but suddenly face disrupted states, dysfunctional institutions, and tattered economies for which their own struggles have contributed. Working people who had gone on strike to cripple the economy, students who caused disorder in colleges, and citizens who remained vigilant day and night to dismantle the old order find on the morrow of the revolution their wages unpaid, jobs lost, public services undelivered, and security diminished. In this critical rupture, an early disenchantment with the revolution is coupled with an extraordinary escalation of grassroots activism driven by a combination of general "disorder," disruption in police control, and a new sense of empowerment and entitlement, altogether pushing the citizens to take the matters into their own hands.

How did the urban and rural poor in Tunisia and Egypt figure in such revolutionary dynamics? How did they leave their mark on the revolutions and how did the revolutions change their lives? Scholarly works on the Arab Spring have largely ignored the role of the marginal poor. The very few that have tried have mostly misread the nature of poor people's politics. Thus, in a somewhat Arendtian sentiment, political sociologist Hazem Kandil seems fearful of the "sinister" character of the poor in impairing the revolution. But "fortunately, this menacing human mass," says Kandil, were "entirely absent from the revolt," with the result that the revolution in Egypt assumed a "civilized and peaceful character."[1] The poor were in fact present at the revolt as we saw in the previous chapter, and the revolt was quite bellicose. After all, half of all police stations in Cairo, 60 percent in Alexandria, and 84 percent throughout the country were attacked or set on fire. But the more important point here is that such a perspective cannot tell us how the poor mattered and became an important player in the theater of the revolution.[2] On the opposite side, Hernando de Soto asserts that the Arab Spring represented *the* revolution of the underclass, including poor people like Mohammed Bouazizi, whose motive was to gain property rights and operate in a truly capitalist free market.[3] As I will show in this chapter, things were more intricate than what de Soto suggests. This chapter tells the story of what the urban and rural poor were doing and thinking in these paradoxical times, and how their struggles figured in the complex postrevolutionary dynamics. Going beyond merely individual acts of survival and resistance, the poor aggressively encroached on power and property to organize solidarity networks, pursue redistribution, and take collective actions to defend and sustain their gains. They were not simply seeking a truly capitalist market in which to thrive; they were trying to remedy the harm neoliberal capitalism had done to their well-being. At this time, the poor moved to create a new order of things as a way both to respond to their immediate needs and to reorganize local life. In the process, they placed the "social question" on the political agenda and strived to realize the revolutionary demand for "social justice" on their own terms.

## HAPPY AND HARD TIMES

In Tunisia, the departure of President Zein al-Abedine Ben Ali brought an ecstatic euphoria to the dissenting populace, many of whom had suffered poverty, neglect, and repression. They had done the unthinkable by driving out a dictator who had presided over a police state for some three decades. Citizens could now speak out, lash out on the authorities, organize, exude hope, and imagine a different future. Many in exile and diaspora returned to live in a free Tunisia. Overnight, the tone and tenor in the media, workplaces, and communities changed. Schools, labor unions, social media, neighborhoods, and the streets gained extraordinary vitality and vigor as if they were heralding something new in the making.

Yet this early jubilation was mixed with a deep anxiety and anger over the unsettled current circumstance and uncharted future. Popular anger erupted at the new "provisional government" for including not only the opposition but also officials of the old regime, notably the prime minister, Muhammed Ghannouchi. Street protests continued until the parliamentary elections in October when the Islamic al-Nahda Party won most of the seats. A coalition of al-Nahda and two nonreligious parties, Ettakatol and the Congress for the Republic, formed the government. But the success al-Nahda triggered new political tensions and a deep anxiety among the secular constituencies who feared an "Islamist takeover." With the assassination of two secular activists by the jihadi Islamists in 2013, Tunisia plunged into a civil strife. Only when al-Nahda ceded power to an interim government did some political calm return. Although the presidency of human rights activist Muncef Marzouki from 2011 to 2014 exuded some optimism, real power rested with the government, whose factions, Islamic or secular, offered no substantial alternative to the previous regime in social and economic policies. Indifferent to "social justice," their platforms broadly echoed the prerevolutionary "neoclassical and neoliberal economics."[4]

In the first year of the revolution, tourism waned, unemployment rose, and foreign investment declined by 25 percent. The gross national product growth rate plunged from 3 percent in 2010 to –1.9 percent in 2011, according to the World Bank. The number of jobless would reach 700,000 by July 2011 (up to 19 percent from the 14 percent previous year) including 160,000 college graduates.[5] The crisis in neighboring Libya sent 35,000 Tunisian workers back home. Even journalists did not remain immune, as hundreds lost work when news agencies, foreign correspondences, and political parties closed down.[6] Some 10,000 workers were already on strike threatening more closures and layoffs. Things worsened for the educated unemployed, the middle-class poor. Many of them opted for cleaning homes, waitering in restaurants, peddling in the streets, working in construction sites, or simply leaving the country. For Fatiha, cleaning homes was tolerable "so long as I am doing an honorable work that helps me secure a living respectfully." "I prefer to work at the café than to sit idle at home," another said.[7] Qeis, who returned home from Germany for the revolution, left again before long, for the meagre monthly salary of 325 dinars could not sustain him. In fact, some 47 percent of Tunisians spent their monthly earnings within the first two weeks.[8]

High rent was already part of the problem, but it worsened with the rise in real estate prices. In popular neighborhoods in Tunis, two rooms went for 300 dinars or $150 per month, according to a report in *Sharq al-Awsat*. High demand and a price hike in construction materials created a trend of daily or weekly rents—with as much as 40–60 dinars per week in the poor and 80–120 dinars in posh neighborhoods. The flooding of some half-million Libyans to Tunisia contributed to the crisis. Related to this was a rise in homelessness. The Dar Tounes Association registered some 500 homeless in Tunis, half of them coming from the interior areas and some becoming beggars. A survey led by the political scientist Ellen Lust revealed that some 10 percent of Tunisians, mostly children under eighteen, asked for money in the streets.[9] Reportedly, poverty forced some 100,000 students to drop out of school in the early 2010s.[10] Although unemployment and high prices seemed to loom large in people's anxieties, security concerns about terrorism and ISIS came to occupy the first place, according to a survey.[11] In these uncertain times, disenchantment and cynicism gripped popular sentiments. Many poor people saw themselves worse off after the revolution.[12] Once again, a spate of self-immolations overtook the country. On February 19, 2011, the young Ayman Mahfouz set his body aflame in front of the police station in Qirwan, dying the day after.[13] Within days, some 180 youths attempted a collective self-immolation in the heart of Tunis but were prevented by the security forces.[14] In May, the three victims of suicide in the town of Hijib al-Uyoun were hospitalized for injuries.[15]

## PUSHING THE BOUNDARIES

But alongside such desperate acts of self-annihilation came extraordinary rebirth and regeneration. Besides disruption and disenchantment, the revolution brought a powerful sense of liberation and a new ethics of entitlement. With the state control shattered and the urge for better life intensified, the poor moved to expand the horizon of their imagination and extend their reach to life chances. In the densely populated neighborhood of Tadamon in Tunis, the inhabitants, led by the unemployed youths, were the first to attack the police, driving them out of the area. Some burned industrial sites and others looted stores, reinforcing the already tainted image of the poor as uncivil subjects. But on the morrow of Ben Ali's expulsion, the network of local youths took the initiative to establish order, security, and sociability in the neighborhoods by creating Popular Committees (Lijan al-Sha'biya).[16] Feeling empowered and secure, many residents took on illegal peddling in the streets or turned their rooms into small shops to earn an income. Alarmed by the scale of the encroachments, the Ministry of Interior banned the practice in September 2011 but to no avail. If anything, street trade expanded in a measure never seen before. The Sidi Boumendil market in Tunis expanded to be the largest informal market in the country, accounting for about half of the $20.91 billion volume traded in the urban parallel market.[17] Such vendors brought almost everything the lower-class Tunisians consumed—from Chinese clothes, shoes, toys, and utensils, to food, furniture, spices, and animals as if to display the nation's entire material culture in one space. The cross-border smuggling from Libya and Algeria made the petty trade flourish, with goods ranging from furniture, electronic devices, to medicine, and domestic appliances in the amount of some 467 million dinars.[18]

Those without permits took over the sidewalks of the central districts of the cities to create vibrant markets. The fact that Bouazizi, the hero of the Tunisian revolution, was a street vendor gave the trade much legitimacy and immunity, which the poor utilized to enhance their lots. In the capital, Tunis, they centered on metro stations, al-Jumhuriya, Hurriya, Abdel-Naser, and most streets around the medina, as I observed in April 2011.[19] Children ventured on the main streets to sell goods or clean car windows, while others peddled on roadsides, petrol stations, mosque entrances, and beaches. Those with permits, including the 450 weekly markets, protested and refused to pay tax. In the Oued Mliz market, southwest of Tunisia, the vendors mocked the tax collector, hurling things at him to drive him out of the area.[20]

Even though the elites and the media saw street trade as a way to make a living, they lashed out on what they called the "republic of chaos" and "incurable disease" that infected law and order and harmed the "legitimate" commerce.[21] Some peddlers felt remorse about their practice but refused to cease their venture. In fact, in mid-2013, they began to organize, forming a union to collectively bargain with the authorities. But this did not put an end to clashes with the pestering police. When, on May 28, 2013, the municipality sent bulldozers to dismantle kiosks and remove peddlers, the entire commercial district in Bizerte became united to deliver a fierce fight in which one man lost his life.[22] Even though the poor considered their doings as no more than *khubsi* (bread and butter) or "nonpolitical," they seemed to be aware of their political meaning. As the anthropologist Larry Michalak reported, when just after the revolution a street vendor saw the police at the gate of the medina in Tunis, he refused to run away as he ordinarily would. Instead, he poured a bottle of gasoline on his body threatening to set himself on fire if they did not go away.[23]

If the urban poor pursued mass protest and aggressive encroachment, the rural poor took advantage of the broken state control to subvert the neoliberal policies that had privatized state farms, diminished farm subsidies and credits, liberalized prices, caused food insecurity, and violated the regime's tacit social contract. Just days after Ben Ali's departure, organized small farmers attacked and caused much disruption in over 100 large farms that had been transferred to private investors.[24] Several farms were occupied by small farmers and peasants. On January 24, agricultural workers seized a large farm near the city of Beja that had been usurped by a relative of Ben Ali. Protestors asked for the lands to be returned to their original owners. Days later, groups of farmers occupied private and state lands, including those managed by the Association of Agricultural Development. Others went on to disrupt the operation of some 10,000 hectares of farmlands (e.g., preventing plowing or sowing) that belonged to rich landowners. The measure perplexed the transitional government as to how to manage such rebellious radicalism.[25] Indeed, the rural poor began to question the wisdom behind the state ownership demanding agrarian reform and land redistribution. Many claimed the ownership of lands that they believed belonged to their ancestors but had been taken away by the French colonists and then nationalized after independence.[26]

One such claim emerged in the last days of the uprising. On January 12, 2011, two days before Ben Ali fled the country, dozens of residents of the Jemna oasis—a date-growing community of 12,000 inhabitants in the governorate of Kebili—collectively appropriated some 185 hectares of farmland that the regime had given to two of Ben Ali's crony investors. The farmers, who believed the land belonged to their ancestors, settled in and began to work. To manage the property and production, they established the Association of the Protection of Jemna Oasis, composed of 129 workers, farmers, and security guards, with four supervisors that oversaw administration and finance.[27] Within four years, they tripled the output; but unlike in the past, the revenue went back to laborers and local development. The association built a marketplace and sport facilities, purchased a new ambulance, improved cemeteries and schools, supported charity organizations, assisted the sick and children, and offered 120 jobs to the youth. This represented a radical move to redistribute property from private capital to collective labor and community, a struggle in which teachers and leftist lawyers such as Taher Taheri played leading roles.

The claims to land was one thing, but access to irrigation water was another. In this quest, farmers (in Testour and Medjez el-Bab) went ahead "stealing" water and refusing to pay electricity bills to the company (electricity and gas) that supplied energy to pump irrigation water. Only the government intervention to waive half of their electricity debt brought some peace between the parties. Broadly, protests over irregular water supply, power cuts, and debt grew throughout Tunisia after the revolution.[28] Small farmers called for removing price liberalization and abolishing debt payment. Others staged sit-ins demanding an official increase in the price of their products such as tomatoes, milk, and fodder. Through such protests and practices, poor farmers were fighting the neoliberal policies that had brought them debt and precarity. Even though their widespread sit-ins, lootings, and roadblocks forced the government to authorize debt relief, their perpetual anxiety over bank loans lingered. Banks were only quick to sequester and dispossess the farmers once defaulted. Farmers needed a more concerted and organized mobilization, unions, to address the challenge.

## REORGANIZING

Unions did exist, but their leaders were corrupt and complicit with Ben Ali's regime. Within weeks of the uprising, hundreds of farmers and fishermen traveled to Tunis to demand the reorganization of the farmers union, UTAP. Others opted to create the new Farmers Union of Tunisia, to organize diverse layers of farmers and negotiate on water supply, product pricing, and cost of production.[29] The struggle to reform the unions reflected a perennial tension that marked the Tunisian labor movement for years. The UGTT acted as the most organized force to enhance the welfare of its members and provide a home for oppositional politics under autocracy. But its leadership was part of the state bureaucracy, which the rank and file defied to join the revolution. Now with a new leadership, the UGTT gained formidable power as both a labor organization and political broker.[30] On May Day 2011, it organized an elaborate festival of labor, which the artistic and literary dignitaries attended, including the Egyptian poet Ahmed Fouad Najm whose evocative qasida eulogized the Tunisian revolution.[31] In these uncertain yet hopeful moments, the UGTT affirmed its commitment to the "revolution of youth" and transition to democracy. In 2014, it brokered a historic agreement between the old illiberal elites and the Islamic al-Nahda to push for a democratic transition, an endeavor that yielded the 2015 Nobel Peace Prize. But this political role seemed to overshadow the struggle for social rights of the marginalized labor. Although the

UGTT continued to fight for better pay and conditions, it did not detract from the broad frame of neoliberal policies that had caused much strain to the working poor.[32] The leadership and rank and file seemed to pursue different strategies at a time when, in the early weeks of the postrevolutionary period, labor unrest overwhelmed the nation. Whereas the UGTT limited itself to negotiating a general pay rise, the militant rank and file called for radical reforms to the labor laws and agreements.[33] Continuing the pressure on the government, the rank and file struggles placed the plight of the educated unemployed—with 10,000 organized in the Union of Degree Holders—on the political agenda.[34]

The government of Prime Minister Ghannouchi responded to labor unrest with a plan in late February 2011 to train 50,000 college graduates for specific jobs while paying them 200 dinars ($100) per month for a year. Another 40,000 were to receive vocational training with an 80-dinar monthly payment. Others were to work in public services.[35] Once announced, the employment offices were flooded by young people rushing to claim unemployment benefits. In Tunis, over 2,100 jobless submitted applications on the first day alone.[36] An early gesture of support to Sidi Bouzid, the birthplace of the revolution, came from a few private companies including the dairy plant Délice Danone to open a new branch with 300 jobs.[37] But in general, the old elites remained defiant, vying to criminalize popular protests by resorting to propaganda campaign in the media that they continued to control.

## COLLECTIVE OUTRAGE

Neither the government response nor the intervention of the UGTT or the private sector lip service could quench the mass thirst for radical change. The political and economic elites continued with the past economic policies, and the UGTT carried on its structure of representing the better-off state employees and professional labor. Thus, the subaltern groups, marginal laborers, and unemployed college graduates had to resort to street politics. Just days after Ben Ali's departure on February 8, an angry crowd protesting the appointment of old elites to the new government surrounded the headquarter of the Tunis governorate, sending the politicians to flight. Soon after, larger crowds, youths, elders, and women staged sit-ins and demonstrations that stretched well into the main boulevard blocking the traffic. The demonstrators demanded jobs for youths and financial aid for the needy.[38] When the rumor of an impending strike in petrol stations spread, cities fell into traffic frenzy as people rushed to fill their vehicle tanks before it was too late.[39] Then came the taxi drivers going on strike in large numbers, marching toward key official buildings in the capital to convey their message.[40] Before long, on February 3, the strike of metro workers in Tunis brought the transport system to a standstill. Demanding higher pay and benefits, they refused to heed the prime minister's plea to resume work. In response, workers put forward sixteen demands wrapped in a threat of general strike. The move angered commuters who charged the strikers for chaos and disregard of public interest.[41]

These everyday protests alerted well-to-do Tunisians to the impending disruption of civic sphere and working life if other sectors joined in to claim their violated rights after years of repression. And join in they did. Within weeks, workers in customs, security, municipalities, finance, and education, among others, would cease work and launch public demonstrations of extraordinary scale. Customs employees poured into the streets in early March 2011, demanding the reopening of shut-down institutions and a return to work. Joined by taxi drivers, travel agents, and farmers, they marched through Muhammed Khamis Street in downtown Tunis.[42] Almost at the same time, the strike of TRANSTU workers halted transportation in parts of the city. Protesters demanded the dismissal of the CEO and investigation into its "financial embezzlement."[43] Even security guards did not hesitate to organize protests in May, pleading with the prime minister to improve their pay and work conditions.[44] Then the indignant workers of handling companies, bookkeepers of the Finance Ministry, and Tunisian airline workers all halted work.[45] But these paled in comparison to the mass walkout of municipality employees throughout the country over pay and the drafting of new bylaws for local authorities. In a massive disruption, clients waited in anguish behind closed doors, services remained undelivered, and garbage piled up, infesting the urban quarters.[46] The teachers' strikes would display even more powerfully the popular quest to realize revolutionary expectation for meaningful change. More than 90,000 teachers in secondary education would go on general strike in January 2015 to realize their demands for welfare benefits. They succeeded when parliament brokered a deal.[47] Within three months, 63,000 teachers, this time in primary schools, organized a national strike to push for pay rise and benefits. As teachers' protests continued, college professors were already busy organizing their own stoppage over professional claims.[48]

Clearly, public protestation of this sort had become an everyday business for millions of Tunisians at the same time as a genuine desire for a return to normalcy. While economists advocated ending the strikes and "normalizing" the economy in order to consolidate the revolution, activists urged citizens to understand the spirit of the time, the precious moment of freedom when, after years of injustice and repression, resistance was the key to meaningful change.[49] In the midst of this, the poor were caught between the desire for calm and stability on the one hand, and the urge to push the boundaries, to seek justice and a better future, on the other hand. Such conflicting views, echoing the very paradoxes of the postrevolutionary moment, highlighted the question of the representation of the protests before public eyes. Many protesters felt that the media distorted their grievance; some attacked journalists for their "bias reporting." In response, journalists staged protests at a Sfax municipality in April 2011 to demand safety in carrying out their professional duties.[50] While journalists sought safety, the employees of the governorates (as in Qafsa) went on an open-ended strike to seek protection. Symbolizing state authority, these employees and their head-quarters had become the target of abuse and assault by protesters throwing rocks, burning car tires, and occupying the buildings.[51]

The irony of frustrated employees protesting against the protests of others exemplified the recurrent tensions in the politics of the ordinary in the immediate postrevolution times. The frustration marked not just the journalists or the employees of the governorates but also the protesters themselves. Having made sacrifices for the revolution, people had developed extraordinary expectations for a better life but would end up becoming worse off. Their "creative disruptions" meant to dismantle the oppressive order also harmed their own well-being and that of their fellow citizens. Clearly, the political class, interim government, and state administrators—many from the old regime—were unable to handle the radical demands of the subaltern. In fact, they showed scant interest, let alone vision, in initiating structural change. Losing confidence in the political class (secular, leftist, or Islamic alike), the poor rested on collective disruption as a key weapon to win concessions. Thus, the phosphate workers in Gafsa resorted to industrial action because "not much had changed," as one activist put it.[52] Even though the company, responding to the local anger, doubled its workforce, the protests continued, which in turn caused a sharp drop in output. In the meantime, agricultural workers moved to stop the transfer of phosphate from the processing sites as a way to pressure the government to make their contracts permanent. "We are asking for our rights," one said. "I have been doing a job planting trees for fifteen years without a contract or any security. I am sixty-three and I have six children."[53] The fasting month of Ramadan brought an extraordinary wave of collective disruptions by the poor claiming charitable food items from the government. They took to the streets throughout the country, hindering traffic within cities and between them, until the government responded with cash to 5,000 and food items to thousands of others.[54] By 2013, Tunisians had broken the world record in labor strikes and social protests—some 45,000 annually.

## MEANWHILE IN EGYPT

By this time, Egypt had captured the world's attention with the global echo of its Tahrir moment and the relentless street politics that followed and increasingly turned bloody. The revolution's happy times were quickly marred by continuing struggles between the key political players—the military or SCAF which now held power; the Muslim Brothers and Salafis, who were gaining more ground; the non-Islamist, liberal, secular, and nationalist parties in disarray; and finally, the "revolutionaries" (those protagonists who initiated and carried the uprising through), many of whom carried on street protests to influence the new governance. Anti-SCAF clashes were to continue ceaselessly until the Brotherhood candidate Mohammed Morsi was elected president in 2012. Morsi's own short tenure faced even wider opposition from the ordinary people, liberal secular forces, and the "deep state" before his ouster by General Abdel Fattah al-Sisi in July 2013. But in truth, the street had changed. For the ordinary people, the revolutionary moment—that episode of primordial urge for unity and equality— came to an end once the dictator abdicated and new government took hold. Now the ordinary people wished to go home, work, live, and harvest the fruits of their sacrifices, "freedom, dignity, social justice." Although it was short-lived, they had a taste of freedom and the scent of dignity when the autocrat fell, the police floundered, the intelligence offices were looted, they were able to speak their minds aloud. But the road to "social justice" proved treacherous. In the first three years after the revolution, the economy experienced a sharp decline. The growth rate dropped from 5 percent in 2010 to 1.2 percent in 2013, and tourism from 11 million visitors to fewer than 2 million. Between January 2012 and April 2013, some 4,600 factories were shut down, 15 percent of Egyptians lost their jobs, and the unemployment rate jumped to 30 percent. Some 62 percent of Egyptians said they were worse off than before.[55] Water shortage and food insecurity—already the subject of protests before the uprising—continued, while the increasing debt (85 percent of the gross domestic product [GDP]) and the $18.3 billion balance of payment deficit placed the future of "social justice" at the whims of the International Monetary Fund and the Arab oil autocrats.[56]

But the poor did not wait. Feeling empowered, they moved to enhance their lots in an aggressive fashion. Squatting, land grabbing, illegal construction, and informal renovation went on in earnest. In about a dozen cities and towns, poor people occupied empty apartments in subsidized housing projects. A researcher identified twenty-one cases of squatting throughout the country. The squatters included both poor people who came from the urban slums and provincial migrants, single mothers among them. In one township alone, Cairo's Madinat al-Nahda, some 11,000 units were reportedly taken over. They called the area Elmouhtalla, the occupied territory, giving different names to local neighborhoods.[57] In the occupied units, the squatters organized a collective life; they pooled together money and resources and worked to connect their neighborhoods to water, electricity, and sewage systems, defend their new communities, and legalize their occupancy. "During the first eighteen days of the revolution, I came here with some friends and we took over a whole building," said a squatter. "The situation was dangerous. We used to hear many fire bullets sounds around. Many of them couldn't stay longer, but I had no other option. When the situation was better, I moved to another apartment, and I am currently legalized." In this fashion, Zaher became a homeowner.[58]

Meanwhile, within the first six months into the revolution, some 110,000 hectares of mostly agricultural land were taken over illegally for construction, mostly of homes. By June 2013, the Awqaf authorities would speak of 9,335 encroachments, or 2.5 million square meters on Awqaf lands, of which half were in agriculture.[59] A government report recounted 1.2 million cases of encroachments on some 47,000 feddans of agricultural lands in the first three years after the revolution.[60] In the meantime, informal innovations and vertical encroachments (adding floors, balcony, or rooms) increased 2.5 times by mid-2012, from 2,471 per year before the revolution to 6,331 in Alexandria alone.[61] Alarmed by the incessant encroachment, the government of Kamal Ghanzouri promised to halt the advances, demolishing 180 installations along the Nile in April 2012. The government used aerial photos for monitoring and proposed establishing a "new corniche" along the Nile from Aswan to the northern coast to protect the waterway from encroachments.[62] In April 2014, the government revealed it had demolished 120,000 unlicensed buildings on 7,000 feddans since the revolution. It imposed hefty fines and even seizure of building equipment on violators.[63]

Most of the encroachments were carried out by the needy (but also by opportunist developers) at times in violent clashes with the security forces. In the coastal town of al-Arish, families seized lands (from the military property) claiming they belonged to their ancestors for hundreds of years.[64] In Qursaya Island in Giza hundreds of residents battled with the military over 500-feddan land rights, which the army had claimed since 2007. Soldiers fired gunshots while residents fought back fiercely, succeeding in overturning the eviction. Then activists, artists, and intellectuals gathered to celebrate the people's victory.[65] The well-known Moqattam area in Cairo where the Zabaleen, garbage collectors, lived and operated saw dramatic squatting. Relying on powerful local clans and the ambiguity in ownership status, organized squatters acquired some 50,000 meters of land in the surrounding areas through forceful appropriation or payment far below the market price.[66]

Beyond land acquisition and illegal construction, thousands campaigned for state housing, fought gentrification, and contested rent increases.[67] The poor residents of Duweiqa, who had been relocated from their unsafe shelters, joined forces with poor residents from other areas to demand ownership of the homes that the government had temporarily given them. Backed by the activist-initiated campaign Living Only in Name (Ehya' Bel-Esm Faqat), they organized angry sit-ins, roadblocks, and clashes with the police, threatening to launch "the revolution of the *ashwaiyyat*."[68] Tent residents whose dwellings had been

demolished went on hunger strike at the district court to demand government apartments.[69] Demand for public / state housing spread to Alexandria, Ismailiyya, Damanhour, and Port Said in varied ways.[70] Poor
families were faced with threats of eviction from their unsafe dwellings and refused to relocate unless they were given public housing.[71]
Those who were to receive public housing, as in Damanhour Ab'adiya
Project in 2012, pushed for a reduction in down payments.[72] And the
ones who had already acquired low-priced, or Awqaf, housing in Ma-
tariya unlawfully sublet the apartments for much higher rent. These
campaigns typically involved hunger strikes, street showdowns, disruptions, and fierce clashes with the police, treating housing as a violated
right. Thus, when in 2012, the Ministry of Awqaf's agents raided Ma-
tariya to force heavy fines or evict the tenants, residents displayed a stiff
resistance. "Where is the housing right?" asked in outrage the tenant
Amr Khalifa, a blind father of two living on an EGP180 monthly welfare. "We have corrupt billionaires in this country . . . and they chose
to take from the poor."[73] But nothing compared to the city of Port Said
where, in a highly dramatic show of force, some 6,000 people from families eligible for the National Project of Mubarak housing, and angered by the authorities' failure to clarify the conditions of occupancy,
descended upon the Suez Canal to halt the flow of ships. Ferries ceased
operating as hundreds of cars waited on both sides of the canal, while
a giant 190-kilometer line of waiting ships revealed the extraordinary
impact of the protest.[74]

## COLLECTIVE CLAIMS

While some segments of the poor were engaged in aggressive encroachment, others collectively resisted the claims made by the authorities on
their gains. This became evident immediately with respect to the gentrification policies, in particular the Cairo2050, a massive project from
Mubarak times that would overhaul central Cairo leading to the relo-

cation of hundreds of thousands of poor families into the desert towns.[75] Even though the project was tabled after the revolution, parts of it were nevertheless attempted. Thus, when the developer Sawiris offered to buy off the dwellings of some 600 families in the Ramlet Boulaq squatter settlement adjacent to the luxurious Nile City, most residents refused to sell, at least not for EGP3,000–4,000 per meter when the real value hovered around EGP30,000.[76] Resisting relocation to the desert town of Medina al-Nahda, people looked out for one another to form a solidarity network. "We are like fish; this is our water. If you take us out of here, we will die," an elderly man stated.[77] The neighborhood exploded when a fight between a resident and his employer in the towers over pay led to one death and twenty-two injuries by the security forces. Residents smashed windows, set cars on fire, and blocked the main Corniche Avenue.[78] Following a number of arrests, activist lawyers became involved in assisting the residents to defend their right to stay.[79] Residents organized a march from Ramlet Boulaq to Maspero on April 7, 2013 to bring their grievances to broader public attention. The sight of the elderly and women with their traditional black attires and headscarves marching through the main streets of the city reminded one of how much the revolution enabled the poor to go beyond their usual quiet encroachment. The group Ahyaa Bel Esm Faqat organized campaigns for the release of the detainees and media events to assert the residents' right to remain. In the meantime, the Popular Committee (Al-ligna Al shabiyya) weighed in to represent the residents before the authorities and bring unity and order to the otherwise multiple voices.[80]

When I visited the area in June 2012, the case was still in court and the mood was tense. Yet life seemed to go on as vibrant as ever in the neighborhood, with people feeling a new sense of empowerment from the revolution and their own cultural capital. As a colleague and I walked through the narrow alleyways that linked lines of feeble dwellings, people surrounding us invited us into their homes. Unlike the shabby and makeshift exterior makeups, the interiors were a different world, full of life, energy, and hope. Family members navigated between the tiny kitchen and small but clean and orderly rooms decorated with religious symbols and family photos. They brought drinks, chatted, cracked jokes, watched TV, and discussed politics. Friends and neighbors joined in, and the young showed off their baggy pants, gelled hair, and mobile phones. But beneath this hazy world of hope, humor, and humanity, there was also a deep-seated anxiety about the fate of their habitat. Yet intimidations, beatings at night, and petrol bombing by the Nile City agents notwithstanding, the families stood firm in their determination not to give in.[81] In truth, beyond all the turmoil and turbulence, the revolution had brought a fresh mood, a renewed sense of solidarity to this locality. Neighbors got together to improve their community; they paved roads, planted trees, and shared amenities. Men still gathered in the makeshift cafés to play *tawla*, women socialized by the doors of their dwellings in the alleyways, and youth strived in their poverty to claim and act out their youthfulness. These poor people's resilience to insist on their claims paid off; they won their case in court in August 2013.[82]

The quiet encroachment had over the years resulted in major gains in collective provisions (energy, piped water, sewage system, paved roads, garbage collection, and security), which once formalized turned into entitlements. But when those gains were threatened or taken away, the poor went on rampage. Postrevolutionary Egypt saw remarkable social protests when basic urban services such as electricity, water, or sewage system faced disruption. The daily power cuts caused by enhanced consumption, mismanagement, or discriminatory blackouts against the low-income neighborhoods brought millions into the streets in the cities and urbanizing villages.[83] Residents of villages in Luxor gathered in front of the power stations to express outrage, while dozens in Kafr el-Sheikh warned to set the power station ablaze.[84] The government subsidy could not prevent Imbaba activist to organize in August 2012 the campaign We Won't Pay to combat power cut.[85] On the other hand, water shortage had continued intermittently since the late 2010s, prompting protests that came to be known as the "thirst revolution." With the rising demand and disruption in provision, dissent reached a new height after the revolution. The summer 2013, the last months of President Morsi, saw an extraordinary escalation of social protests as tens of thousands poured into the urban streets and villages, blocking highways, occupying power stations, battling the police, and refusing to pay their bills in Cairo, Giza, Alexandria, Qalyoubiyya, Doqliyya, Sharqiyya, Tanta, Luxor, Qina, Qalyoubiyya, Kafr al-Sheikh, Aswan, Fayyoum, Minya, and other governorates.[86] The strategic value of power cuts has made them a weapon to undermine political foes. Just as the US government used this weapon against President Nicolás Maduro of Venezuela in 2019, so did the Egyptian military in 2013 against President Morsi.[87]

Protestation of this sort reflected an aspect of broader developmental deficits that had gripped subaltern life. For instance, only 24.7 percent of the rural population in 2011 (compared to 88 percent of urban) were connected to the sewage system, according to CAPMAS. Indeed, claims for social provisions echoed a de facto call for the return of the social contract that the post-Nasser governments had violated. From the villages of Luxor and Aswan to the popular districts of Alexandria, Port Said, and Minya, the poor expressed public rage over "terrible services," sewage breakdown, poor schooling, flawed waste management, and bad roads.[88] Many joined activists from the April 6th and Kifaya movements in mocking Morsi's el-Nahda project, which was supposed to tackle such social ills.[89] Villages like Tahsin in Beni Obeid with 3,000 residents asked for better schools, paved roads, and health units; they refused to pay governmental dues and disallowed officials to enter the village unless their demands were met. "Before the revolution, we were oppressed, and after the revolution, we are forgotten," their banner read.[90] Some, like villagers of al-Shaqib in Aswan, cut off railroads to demand authorities to install proper rail crossings, the lack of which had caused fatal accidents,[91] while others, such as the deaf and mute in Minya, stopped trains from running because city authorities had neglected them.[92] Then came the pensioners who erupted en masse, with some going on hunger strike in central Cairo to demand an increase of 25 percent in their bonus (*alaavah al-ijtimaiyya*). Siding with the Tamarrod movement to impeach President Morsi, one protester stated how after thirty-seven years of work, he received only EGP340 per month.[93] During 2012, Egyptians held 500 sit-ins, 581 local protests, 414 labor strikes (up from 335 during 2011), and 558 street demonstrations.[94] The following year, during Morsi's presidency, there were a staggering 7,709 local protests and 5,821 street demonstrations and clashes.[95]

## PERIPHERIES

Most of the unrest took place in the urban areas, but a good number of protests happened in Upper Egypt and many in the villages. This partly reflected the growing "urbanization" of rural communities enjoying electricity, piped water, communication, education, and nonagricultural occupations.[96] Indeed, the combination of "urban" expectations and opportunities with rural / agricultural concerns (over land, irrigation water, credit, pesticide, or seeds) had pushed the rural social world closer to the urban universe.[97] Thus, in the upper Egyptian village of Abu-Rish in Aswan, for instance, local activists including an accountant and a social worker (linked to Cairo's Hisham Mubarak Law Center) would work with the villagers and associations to improve such "urban" provisions in the village as piped water. This was a time in the country when "we felt we could speak, and people would listen to us," as one activist said.[98] Villagers advanced clear demands, negotiated with officials, organized street protests, and formed a Popular Committee to coordinate the campaign that involved lawyers, engineers, farmers, and others. Villagers were particularly adamant to get a soccer field for their youths. For this, they organized loud demonstrations and sit-ins to force the authorities to grant the necessary land.[99]

Social struggles of this sort came largely from small farmers (90 percent of all landholders) who owned or rented less than five feddans and relied on family labor. Yet to secure an adequate subsistence, some 80 percent of them had to work in jobs outside agriculture.[100] The small farmers had already faced increasing cuts in subsidies and liberalization of agricultural input, such as seeds and pesticides. Tenancy law 96 (passed in 1997) struck a new blow when it increased the rent and then left prices to the whims of the market. Some 900,000 tenants were consequently dispossessed. Even though their stiff defiance entailed violent clashes with security forces in 100 villages that left dozens dead and thousands arrested, small farmers saw an opportunity in the 2011 revolution.[101] A good number seemed to join the uprising (5 percent, according to Arab Barometer), but they did more in the immediate post-Mubarak era. They campaigned for agrarian reform, land to the tillers, and supply of water and fertilizer by organizing 150 protests, 74 sit-ins, and 84 mass demonstrations in 2011, according to the Land Center. Over seventy protests, largely on shortage of irrigation water, were reported for 2013.[102] Some occupied what they considered to be their rightful land and pursued legal means to repossess it. At least fifty villages experienced land seizure. Once occupied, the farmers began to develop the lands and felt entitled, like the registered farmers, to receive agricultural inputs such as pesticides at a special price.[103] According to the Egyptian anthropologist Yasmine Ahmed, the small farmers justified the claim over land not on the popular notion of President Nasser's "gift" but on the idea that they were entitled to the land because their labor had developed it. For them, the lands were their "legitimate right" that merited official recognition.[104]

Radical agrarian reform and legal battles demanded a powerful collective voice. That voice came with the revolution. The forceful demand by the workers for "independent unions" during the uprising seemed to prompt the minister of manpower and immigration, Ahmed Hassan al-Borai, to decree the formation of labor unions just after the uprising. The decree eased the bureaucratic hurdles, reduced state surveillance, and legalized independent syndicates. As a result, some 900 syndicates including those of the small farmers came to life. Helped by political parties and advocacy groups such as the Land Center for Human Rights, four farmers unions and federations with an estimated membership of 700,000 emerged within the first six months after Mubarak.[105] The unions covered mostly evicted farmers or those in debt to banks from such governorates as Fayyoum, Kafr el-Sheikh, Mansourah, Ismailiyya, and Giza. Through these unions, the farmers hoped to negotiate with state officials to secure access to land and agricultural inputs, health care, representation in parliament, and the like. But access to land and security of tenure remained the prime objectives. Small farmers who had seized lands wished to acquire government "cheap pesticide" but were refused due to the illegal status of their occupancy.[106] The question of legality of the expropriated lands, therefore, remained a bottleneck.

How much leverage did the small farmers really hold to realize their claims? Even though most of them worked outside agriculture, as farmers they lacked the kind of institutional power that, say, factory workers enjoyed. Individual and family-based farmers were self-employed, similar to street vendors. But unlike street vendors who could extralegally occupy spots in desirable locations to do business, small farmers had serious limitations accessing land, irrigation water, or cheap fertilizer, as these resources were linked to and protected by powerful interests in the structures of power and property, capitalist state and economy. So long as these structures remained unchallenged and union pleas unheeded, in order to secure those resources the farmers would have little choice but to resort to disruptive repertoires: blocking roads and interrupting traffic, the most audible yet hazardous tools of street politics.

## URBAN STREETS

Street politics took on broader meaning in cities, and workers played an integral role in this. Once the uprising erupted and the dictator abdicated, Egypt experienced a spectacular growth of estimated 1.5 to 5 million street and market vendors spread in key spots of cities.[107] In Cairo, Tahrir Square, the Nile corniche, downtown streets, and Ramses Square saw the largest concentration of stalls, kiosks, and mobile vendors. Street rallies offered a lucrative market to boost vendors' businesses. Tahrir Square, where epic gatherings and demonstrations continued for months, became at times a surreal space of contention and commerce. While the revolutionaries battled the police, built barricades, and dodged tear gas canisters, the square vendors carried on with their routine of trading hot tea, cold drinks, food, flags, and badges. The vendors became an integral element in Tahrir's spatiopolitical fabric, selling watermelons carved with slogans such as "Down with Military Rule" or drinks with names such as "January 25 Tea" and "Tahrir Licorice Juice."[108] They catered to visitors and protestors alike who spent months protesting in the square. While new vendors entered the business, the old-timers began to consolidate their positions, build fences around their stalls, and establish permanent structures. Some named their places the Revolution Shop (al-Mahal al-Thawra). Meanwhile, they mobilized to defend their gains in anticipation of hostile municipality agents.[109]

Vendors had their own stories. Sayed Atef set up his cold-drink stall around Tahrir a month after the uprising. "The traffic in this area was exceptionally dense at that time, so I thought about selling some drinks since most families that came to visit the square enjoyed a nice drink here," he said.[110] Nagwa, a female seller, left her abusive husband to come to Tahrir and support her children. Many men had lost their previous jobs, and others had just entered the job market. They did not pay tax and enjoyed a good degree of autonomy and flexibility but often felt vulnerable and had to dispense bribes of up to EGP70–250 for their unlawful practices.[111] Yet, as part of a vast informal economy that produced 40 percent of the GDP, they all were seizing these moments to better their lives, even though their plebeian livelihood invited the fury of local merchants, the disdain of the elites, and the hostility of the state. Local merchants complained that they could not compete with the cheap offerings of the vendors. The elites whined about "backward" image, public sanitation, and "sexual harassment." And the authorities expressed concern over traffic congestion, illicit trade, and public disorder. For this, both SCAF and President Morsi moved to crack down on street trade. In fact, little had changed in the official policy of criminalizing the unauthorized vendors since 1957 (law 33). Under Mubarak, unlawful hawkers received three-month prison sentences and fines up to EGP1000. The Islamist Morsi increased the penalties to six months of prison and an EGP5,000 fine. Meanwhile, ministries joint forces to "cleanse" the central districts of Cairo, Giza, Doqliyya, Mansourah, and Alexandria from the "parasitic street vendors"—a measure that the prerevolution governments had failed to achieve.[112] Thus, in September 2014, when the Cairo governor deployed heavy police force with armored control vehicles to move some 1,000 street vendors from the city center and al-Ataba to a Targoman market, vendors seemed to comply. But once their negotiations with the authorities failed, they planned to return. An official reported that vendors began to organize, held meetings with leaders in each street, and once the police withdrew, resumed their operation in the streets again. They threatened to bring their families to fight the police if necessary.[113]

Through an everyday war of attrition, street subsistence workers simply resisted, briefly retreating and then returning and regrouping. It was a war that continued relentlessly thanks to the persistence of vendors, the complicity of the police, and bribing. The removal of street booksellers in Alexandria's famous cultural hub of al-Nabi Danial Street brought out not only the vendors but also intellectuals and left liberal political parties to protest against what they considered the Islamist Morsi's war on culture and enlightenment.[114] And when in October 2012, a twelve-year-old fruit seller working in Tahrir Square was shot dead by a sniper, thousands of vendors staged a powerful demonstration from Tahrir to the supreme court. The striking scenes of marching vendors with pushcarts and mobile stalls through the main streets of Cairo remain one of the most evocative hallmarks in Egypt's street politics.

This act of solidarity served as a prelude to serious attempts to organize the street vendors in a national syndicate.[115] Now proliferated and visible, street vendors felt the need to unite to deter eviction threats and insecurity. By December 2012, active hawkers led by Ramadan al-Sawy had collected 4,000 colleagues' signatures to set up a union. They soon established an office in Cairo and obtained support from counterparts in Helwan, Giza, Suez, Alexandria, and Asyut. Assisted by lawyers from the Egyptian Initiative for Personal Rights (EIPR), they set out to obtain legal recognition. They fought to change the "laws and procedures surrounding the usage of public space in cities, to ensure financial security, and to redefine their relationship with authority."[116] Their struggle for urban citizenship was coming to life. "Just give me a reasonably priced and strategic spot that I can rent, even if it is only one meter, then I will happily pay rent and taxes," as stated a vendor.[117]

Indeed, building organizations had at this juncture become a common feature of poor people's politics after years of restriction. Thus, following Mubarak's downfall, a citywide association of *ashwaiyyat* (informal settlements) was formed in Cairo to work toward securing and upgrading slum communities and calling for the dismissal of corrupt local officials. From the start, the association lashed out at the Cairo2050 project and urged the residents to resist relocation.[118] Numerous Popular Committees (Lijan al-Sha'biya), which had initially formed to protect neighborhoods, turned into local associations for development. The Zabaleen demanded the new government to secure and systematize their work and dismiss the international contractor that covered 40 percent of waste collection.[119] Then came a group among 400,000 domestic workers that succeeded in establishing their first independent syndicate (Niqabat al-Amilat Bilajir al-Shahri). These efforts pointed to the desire of the wider marginalized groups—day laborers, street traders, fishermen, or brick layers—to empower themselves through organizing.[120]

Activists, notably those from the middle-class poor, played an important part in these collective endeavors. Among them stood out the subaltern, notably "community lawyers." As the educated children of these very poor neighborhoods, their efforts included not only defending activists against the security state, but more importantly, they represented their subaltern communities—whether it was the squatters of Ramlet Boulaq, the poor farmers of al-Waraq Island, the villagers of the delta, or the fishermen of the Manzala Lake—against the claims of the government, the military, and developers. When in 2017, al-Waraq Island in Cairo faced the threat of eviction for redevelopment, the farming residents organized a collective resistance led by local lawyers. These activist lawyers mediated between the poor and the state and navigated both street politics and the legal battle. When street politics became perilous, they would bring the fight into the courtrooms.[121]

Just as lawyers assisted street vendors, slum dwellers, or fishermen, the youth activists of the campaign We Live Only in Name (Ehya' Bel-Esm Faqat) mobilized to bring basic services to the poor.[122] Others organized the We Want to Live campaign to help remedy poor people's livelihood at a time when the persistence of neoliberal policies had made public provisions such as trains, hospitals, or drinking water less affordable. The We Will Not Pay campaign advocated for poor residents not to pay their electricity bills unless a clear schedule and fair distribution of power cuts were guaranteed. Beginning first in Giza's Saft al-Laban, the campaign moved to towns and villages in the delta and Upper Egypt and was adopted by the leftist Popular Alliance Party.[123] Reminiscent of *Masakhane* in post-apartheid South Africa and the Chilean slum dwellers' "refusal to pay" campaigns in 1990s, these reflected a struggle for leveling, a struggle for equality in what a city can or cannot offer to its citizens.

## INSURGENT CITIZENS

Poor people's struggle for (urban) citizenship was truly remarkable in the Arab revolutions. Reinforced by a strong "entitlement ethics," it embodied attempts to secure a shelter, claim state housing, battle eviction, contest high rents, demand collective provision, and realize leveling. Urban citizenship also meant that the poor wished to be an integral part of the city, not only the *ashwaiyyat* they inhabited, and to have freedom of mobility and physical appearance. They disdained policies and people that rendered them as "outsiders" or "intruders." They wished to extend their horizon of the city beyond their backstreet localities by forging access to the larger urban universe. Thus, in Cairo, the informal communities located around the inaccessible Ring Road took the matter in their own hands to construct access ways and ramps to the highway. Small tuk-tuks or micro-taxis could then bring people from the nearby settlements to these "transfer points" from which they could move to the rest of the city. Many activities then developed around these new pathways of mobility. Tea stands served them with respite, car repairs shops offered service, and minibuses carried people to the city. Meanwhile, the inhabitants volunteered to establish exit ramps to facilitate car access onto the highways. These costly initiatives would involve collective efforts in which the community members offered labor, cash, materials, and tools.[124] In one settlement, the residents paved the roads, opened a police station, produced a CD about the initiative, and invited the governor to officially inaugurate their access ramp. In a similar fashion, residents of the poor neighborhoods divided by rail tracks built crossings to connect the divided community. Frustrated by these initiatives, the government agencies would close 1,650 of such illegal crossings by May 2015.[125] Still others in the Ard el-Liwa informal community thought of mapping their neighborhood. A local tailor drew an elaborate sketch of streets, alleyways, slopes, bridges, and homes, giving their community a life on paper, a recognition that had officially been denied.[126]

Building and bolstering communities was part of a broader quest for a kind of de facto citizenship. There was a sense among the poor that they belonged and shared the nation with all its sufferings and offerings. Now was the time to practice it. In the informal community of Ezbet Khayrallah with 650,000 inhabitants, residents who had joined the uprising in their thousands began to organize and recuperate their lives. Young lawyers and activists established the Ezbet Khayrallah Lawyers Association for Rights and Liberties in 2011 to push for public interests and defend the claims of the locals.[127] Others moved to upgrade the residential buildings. Together with the Paint Cairo initiative and later the Catholic Relief Services, they renovated and cleaned up a number of buildings on the Ring Road.[128] In the neighboring Dar al-Salam, local *shillas* and activists initiated multiple projects concerning social, educational, and cultural developments in the area. The Karama libraries were launched in several localities on May 14, 2012. The initiative aimed to engage the local youth, develop the culture of reading, and teach literacy to elders. The community lawyer and rights activist Gamal Eid dedicated his German Roland Berger award money to cover costs while local volunteers implemented the initiative.[129] The Karama libraries opted to connect to and cooperate with the community organizations and the local newspaper *Sawt el-Salam*. They also sought collaboration with the Ministry of Culture. But the officials, fearing the people's independent initiatives, sought to undermine the initiative by pointing to its "foreign" source of funding. Yet the initiative endured, altering the cultural mode of the neighborhood. For the first time, children and youths had a reading home to go to anytime. The library also served as a place for cultural activities, journalism, and photography. In 2014, it exhibited the photo productions of the local children about their neighborhood. Its cultural sister, the local paper *Sawt el-Salam*, had become an institution of its own, offering a new image of this otherwise underdog *ashwaii* community. Developed by the local youths, the paper wished to reflect the news, views, and concerns of the Dar al-Salam residents and serve as a venue for artistic and creative activities of the young residents.[130]

How did the elite respond to poor people's claims, clamors, and encroachments? The elite's attitude toward the poor seemed astonishingly familiar—a mix of charity, neglect, and hostility—as if they hardly internalized the fact that their societies were experiencing a popular revolution. An early charitable overture in Egypt came from TV presenter Amr El-Leithy with the Billion Campaign to Develop Slums. Other celebrities joined in, but the rhetoric went nowhere. Then emerged the army in late 2012 with a generous message to build 600,000 housing units for the poor of slums within six months.[131] The message aimed at courting the poor to dislodge the Islamist president Morsi. But the message faded before long. The government's position was in flux, moving from "development" to demolition, neglect, and resettlement. In the 1990s, the fear of Islamist militancy promoted the government to "develop" the opaque informal neighborhoods, but the Duweiqa earthquake in 2008 shifted the policy to demolishing "unsafe" settlements, relocating inhabitants to the desert settlements, and ignoring the rest. After the revolution, the Morsi government came up with a forty-year project to build forty-four new cities in the desert, despite the fact that such "ghost cities" had absorbed only 20 percent

(800,000 people) of the target population.[132] Following the coup, the military initially stepped in to cooperate with the government to "develop the *ashwaiyyat*."[133] But under the minister of housing, Mustapha Madbouli, an architect of Cairo2050, the government favored "desert development" at the cost of neglecting 2.3 million poor families without safe water and half of all Egyptians deprived of a decent sewage system.[134]

Policies, whether in Tunisia or Egypt, had much to do with how the elites perceived the poor and the revolution. In a conversation with an elite group in Tunis just after the revolution, I sensed how much disdain they held for what they called the revolution of the street people. They largely avoided the poor and their spaces, practically opening the opportunity for the Salafi Islamists to fill the vacuum.[135] In the neighborhood of Sayidah al-Menoubiya, "no one comes to see us, not even the police," complained a resident.[136] "Revolutionaries never come here. They are afraid of us and think that we are wild animals. . . . They are not better than Ben Ali," others stated.[137] In Egypt, the *ashwaiyyat* remained the nation's internal "other," defined by *ashwaii* culture and people. Top officials continued to view the nonconformist poor young men as *baltagi* or thugs, and the *ashwaiyyat* as an urban pathology that produced thuggery, crime, and 95 percent of "child prisoners," never mind that those very neighborhoods housed 63 percent of Cairo's population in 2015.[138] The rich despised the poor for being part of the revolution, and the poor disliked the political class for excluding them.[139] This striking contradiction signaled how much the revolutionary alliances had shifted from the uprising times. The result was that the revolution failed to secure the poor with reliable allies at the top among those in governmental power. They had to rely on themselves.

The poor felt the elites' disdain and neglect, and their response was pragmatic. Even if they voted, the poor invested slight loyalty in any particular government or ideology. The poor could not afford to be ideological. They were preoccupied more with the immediate concerns of survival and furthering their lots. By the time Morsi was elected president, they had lost confidence in SCAF. "I am a poor Egyptian. . . . I am from the *ashwaiyyat*," said Hosniya el-Sayyid from Cairo's Imbaba. "It is not important for me who is president, Morsi or anyone else. And if there is a second revolution, I will take part in it."[140] In Imbaba, many like the law student Muhamed had voted for the Muslim Brothers and President Morsi after trying Prime Minister Ahmed Shafiq. But their enchantment vanished soon.[141] Clearly, this was a different Imbaba from its 1990s version as the hotbed of radical Islamism. Just days after Mubarak's ouster, Ahmed Mutwalli, a college graduate whose parents were Islamists, echoed how Egyptian revolution had nothing to do with religion, with Islam. "Bread, social justice, and freedom," that is what the revolution is about, Mutwalli said.[142] "The last thing youth are thinking about is religion. . . . They need money, they need to get married, buy a car. . . . They'll elect whoever can deliver that." But perhaps nothing was more telling about subaltern speech vis-à-vis the ruling elites than the public castigation of President Sisi by a poor female food vendor in Cairo's Sayyid Nafisah captured on video:

> Now Egypt is at its worst, Egypt cannot find food, the populace is hungry, no one can wear clothes, or buy things or get educated. No health either and nothing at all. He [Sisi] is just continuously bringing in loans from outside, and he says he's working and doing things. What is he doing? He's not doing anything. Nothing has been done. He tells you I'm building roads and bridges. But the *muwazzafeen* are now overburdened. . . . Their social security payments have increased, the prices have gone up; everywhere is expensive, expensive, expensive. He hasn't looked at these people seeking livelihoods; no one has looked at them; he hasn't looked at those who collect garbage to eat as food. The government sitting on the armchairs, making tons of money every day. Just took 22 million at the expense of all

these poor people. I say God is enough for us and is our advocate against them. Where are the responsible officials? The one
responsible for us is our God; he's feeding this population.
He's feeding the poor. That's it. There is nothing here [in the
market]; no selling, no buying. Who can afford to eat here, let
alone buy and sell? No one is buying anything. He [Sisi] is good
at only one thing: "Terrorism, terrorism"! What terrorism?
How terrorism? You've been fighting terrorism for six years; if
you had been fighting terrorism around the world, you would
have wiped it out. What are you fighting? You said the [Muslim]
Brotherhood, and you took them away and detained them. You
said Morsi, and you've detained him. So what terrorism? If you
aren't up to [fighting] terrorism, don't be in charge. If you're not
up to this country, don't be in charge. That's all.[143]

REFLECTING ON THE FRENCH REVOLUTION, Hannah Arendt pro-
claimed, "No revolution, no matter how wide it opened its gates to
the masses and the downtrodden . . . was ever started by them."[144]
Aside from the fact that the Tunisian revolution owes its eruption to the
downtrodden Mohammed Bouazizi, the Arendtian condescension
toward the poor as an actor of revolution seems to miss the intricacy
of popular politics and the revolutionary dynamics within which it op-
erates. The rage, daring, and feeling of self-determination expressed
by the poor woman peddler in Cairo's Sayyid Nafisah are a common
feature of immediate postrevolutionary times when the people, freed
from political tyranny, take initiatives to assert their will. Feeling like
"free citizens," or "owners of their country," and yet facing disruptions
to their state and economy, they move to exercise varied forms of self-
rule in farms, factories, schools, workplaces, and neighborhoods. Such
radical politics have a long history in most revolutions, including in the
Middle East. In the aftermath of the Iranian revolution of 1979, workers
occupied hundreds of factories to run them through *shuras* or factory

committees.[145] Farmers took over agribusiness. The urban poor grabbed lands to build homes, occupied apartments and hotels, acquired urban services, and demanded security of tenure. For a while, spatial hierarchies crumbled, replaced by scenes of managers and workers dining together in the nation's workplaces. The poor were further empowered by the intense competition between various left and Islamist groups to secure their support. And their radical measures were backed, at least for some time, by the idioms of equality, social justice, and socialism that held currency in most of the twentieth-century revolutions.[146] Despite the authoritarianism of the Islamist regime, these grassroots initiatives followed some significant policy change expressed in land reform, nationalization, and democratic representation through workplace, local, and city councils.

But as I suggested earlier, the refolutions in Tunisia and Egypt failed to bring a fundamental transformation of the states' ideologies and socioeconomic visions. The new regimes continued to adopt much of the old social and economic policies. Indeed, the social world of the new elites could not sit well with a genuine pursuit of social justice, a fundamental claim of the revolutionary subaltern. This was the case not only in autocratic Egypt but also in democratic Tunisia. It is true that the establishment of procedural democracy in Tunisia, which owed much to the struggle of its labor movement,[147] allowed for more effective struggles for social justice; in fact, democratic Tunisia fared better in terms of "equality" and "human development" indicators than Ben Ali's time and autocratic Egypt, according to the United Nations Development Programme index.[148] Nevertheless, the absence of allies in the government meant that the subaltern groups had to rely primarily on their own social networks and cultural capital to take up the cause, as described in this chapter. So while these revolutions embodied *in practice* radical initiatives on the part of the subaltern, no serious *ideological* frame, intellectual support, or social movement advocacy anchored them. If anything, the "commonsense" thinking among the new political class (secular and Islamist alike) dismissed such radical practices as "out of place," "extremist," "utopian," and above all, "unlawful." In Egypt, workers did take over their factories but only in twelve plants whose owners had left, given up, or had gone bankrupt. The media, politicians, and even the unions dismissed such practices as "unlawful," ones that violated the principle of property ownership.[149] Small farmers who had seized land remained unsecure and their ownership undermined because the lands were deemed "illegal." For example, even in democratic Tunisia, the government refused for years to back the remarkable experience of self-management in the Jemna oasis on legal grounds.[150]

I can see why the Egyptian novelist Ahmed Khaled Tawfiq would be enraged by such legalism that subverts the spirit of revolution. "The revolution is a woman carrying its children and standing at the gates of the courtroom awaiting its rights," he wrote. "Lost in the corridors of law and the games of lawyers . . . she should not have resorted to the law from the beginning."[151] Most of these subaltern acts were certainly illegal, but were they necessarily illegitimate? After all, the very act of revolution was by definition "illegal," and it yet enjoyed a wide popular legitimacy. Whereas the political class drew on the prerevolution legal standards to judge the legitimacy of subaltern acts, the subaltern groups saw the "revolution" as the source of a new legitimacy that justified their radical acts and initiatives. By challenging the property norms, claiming redistribution, and practicing self-rule, the poor placed the "social question" on the political agenda. Structural obstacles and class disdain notwithstanding, the poor people's remarkable struggles enhanced their life chances, seriously questioned those neoliberal policies that had caused marginalization and inequality, and instilled a radical spirit into these otherwise nonradical revolutions.

*Chapter 5*

# Mothers, Daughters, and the Gender Paradox

WOMEN'S PRESENCE in the Arab Spring protests was so strong that few could deny the key part they played in the uprisings. This was the case not just in Tunisia and Egypt but also in Yemen, Bahrain, Libya, and later Algeria, Lebanon, and Sudan, where reportedly women made up some 70 percent of demonstrators at some of the 2019 protests.[1] The significance of women's participation in the uprisings lay not simply in their numbers or body counts, even though this was crucial; it lay more in their inherent capacity to "feminize" and "civilize"— that is, to turn the otherwise narrow, masculine, and potentially violent protests into a broad-based societal upheaval. Extraordinary acts, even though spectacular and surprising, are by definition singular, exceptional, and thus susceptible to ridicule or repression. The sheer participation of women (together with the elderly and children) widened the constituency of the opposition and rendered police violence more difficult, while their unequivocal urge for unity greatly enhanced the success of the uprisings in ousting the autocrats.[2]

Yet two puzzles marked the story of women in the revolutions. First, although women took part in large numbers in the uprisings, they rarely raised any explicit demands for women's rights; the language of gender was simply absent in these spectacular political happenings. This underlines what is considered the revolutions' "gender paradox."[3] Second, despite their crucial role in the success of the uprisings, women's rights experienced a serious setback on the morrow of the revolutions—and this ironically at the time when the dictators had fallen and space had been cleared for a pluralist democracy. Some observers have named this puzzle the "democracy dilemma".[4] By addressing these overlapping puzzles, I want to discuss what happened to women, what they thought, and what they did after the uprisings when people began to get back to their normal lives. The aim is to dig deeper into understanding how gender works in the Middle Eastern revolutions broadly. Scholars have already examined the important issue of feminist, patriarchal, or religious ideologies of the revolutionary leadership.[5] What I wish to scrutinize is the actual dynamics of women's involvement in the revolutions and the response that it elicited from the patriarchy across class lines.

Women, like other identity groups, partake in revolutionary uprising not simply as women concerned with gender demands but as part of "the people," focusing on unity, equality, justice, and freedom. As women's particularistic calls dissipate in favor of universal claims, their dispersed collectives and disparate nonmovements merge into a nationwide movement we call the uprising. The simultaneity of these two incidents signals the transformation of the collective protests into a revolutionary uprising, or revolution as movement. But the day after the dictators abdicate and normal life begins to set in, women go through two contradictory trajectories. On the one hand, they are immensely empowered by having experienced during the uprising an exceptional episode of equality, unity, and a "personal revolution." At the very same time, however, they fast realize that their rights as women receive an immediate onslaught both in the streets and the institutions of the new (democratic) governance, primarily because the patriarchy, wounded by women's extraordinary public presence and cross-gender challenge, attempts to regain its control unleashing an unbridled masculinity.

This coincidence of both empowerment and onslaught renders women exceedingly outraged, pushing them to embark on a remarkable remobilization. Even those in the provincial and rural areas who previously remained in the seclusion of domesticity move into the public sphere. With the halt in political surveillance, women tend to activate their passive networks in nonmovements by building new collectives or joining social movements. At this time, elitist "state feminism" diminishes before the flourishing grassroots groups forged by ordinary women who bring subaltern concerns to gender debates. This episode represents the honeymoon of new women's movements before the new regimes attempt to co-opt or consume the new energy, prompting many to pursue their claims in the practice of everyday life.

Although excited about the heavy engagement of women in the Arab uprisings, some observers seem to be perplexed, even frustrated, by the absence of gender language in the uprisings as if women would necessarily mobilize for gender equality. Feminist groups like Nazra activists in Egypt, for instance, insisted that gender claims were indeed part of the discourse of the uprisings because the demands for dignity, freedom, and justice also included women's rights.[6] Others maintained rather defensively but correctly that even though the language of gender did not matter during the uprisings, it dominated the public debate that immediately ensued. On the other hand, for the scholar Nicola Pratt, there was in fact no gender paradox because Egyptian women (like men) were concerned not with gender matters per se but primarily with the "social reproduction"—that is, the welfare and security of all members of the albeit patriarchal family—that had been undermined by Egypt's neoliberal policies. But even though women in general adhered to prevailing gender norms and expectations, they were actually challenging those norms simply by leaving home along with the men to participate in street protests.[7] This important point raises some questions. First, was the absence of gender language not specific to Egypt? The answer is no; it involved all Arab uprisings including the latest in Sudan.[8]

Second, were women the only ones to avoid particularistic demands? And third, if gender rights were not a central issue in women's lives, why did they become one immediately after the uprisings?

As we saw in Chapter 3, social groups participate in political uprisings like the Arab Spring not as women, youths, queer, or Christians but as part of wider category of "the people"; instead of pursuing their particularistic claims, they follow such broader calls as justice, freedom, or dignity. This is not because the "liberation of women necessitates the liberation of all human beings," as Sheila Rowbotham argued in her discussion of gender and revolution.[9] Instead, generality, ambiguity, and unity are fundamental elements of the "revolution as movement," where participants move to speak not in terms of "me" or "my group" but of the "nation" and where the particularistic concerns of diverse groups are eclipsed behind the affective and strategic desire for unity, equality, and greater good.[10] This is certainly a contradictory yet necessary political happening. The challenge of how to materialize the subaltern desire for self-realization and universal claims would come only later. It came quickly after the revolution when the consequences of this contradiction in their revolutionary mobilization were expressed in protracted conflicts, deep outrage, and intense remobilization.

The paradox then lies not in the absence of gender discourse during the uprising but in the fact that their visible and vocal public presence in the revolution led women and their rights to face serious challenges just after the dictators were toppled and the prospect of pluralist democracy loomed. Women were now tormented by extensive sexual violence, assault, and gang rape or more generally restrained by the new conservative regimes and sidelined from playing meaningful parts in state institutions.


## PATRIARCHAL BACKLASH

For months after the ouster of President Hosni Mubarak, Egyptian women in the streets became the target of individual and collective, impulsive and organized violence. Whether young or old, veiled or unveiled, they endured terrifying agony to appear in public rallies only weeks after they had helped topple a dictator. The first signs of assault came from the religious right. In the volatile postuprising days when state control had been tattered, conservative clerics found more space to broadcast their moralizing and often belligerent callings. Their misogynistic sermons sounded as though they were heralding a new moral order—a mood that reminded me of the postrevolutionary Iran of the 1980s. The hefty surge of conservative Salafis onto the public sphere, with their male vigilante groups roaming around the streets of Cairo or Tunis to enforce "modesty" in society, terrified many women who felt some of their hard-won rights had come under severe assault.

Then came the state, including the police and military under the Supreme Council of Armed Forces (SCAF), which inflicted extraordinary sexual violence. In March 2011, when the military police violently dispersed those in Tahrir Square demanding civilian rule, a number of women including the twenty-four-year-old veiled Samira Ibrahim were arrested, beaten, given electric shocks, strip-searched, and forced into a "virginity test." Ibrahim brought a lawsuit against the officer in a highly publicized trial in which she exposed how SCAF violated female bodies and presented women activists as impure and immoral social outcasts who had brought shame to their families and communities.[11] But none of the starkness of the state violence against women matched what befell a victim known as the "blue bra woman." On December 17, 2011, when the security forces descended on Tahrir Square to clear the sit-in, a group of soldiers grabbed this woman, whose identity remains unknown, kicking her on the stomach and dragging her unconscious body on the ground, while her removed abaya exposed her blue bra.[12] The video clip of the incident went viral. It instigated an extraordinary public uproar against sexual violence and a public debate centered on the dignity and purity of the female body. To strip the protesting women of any moral virtue and protection, SCAF's Major Adel Emara described them not as virtuous women "like your daughter or mine" but as disgraceful deviants who dishonored their families by spending days and nights with men in the streets of contention. In this manner, the military patriarchs greenlit, if they did not outright organize, "fellow citizens" or gangs to intervene by spreading terror among women in public arenas.

In a rather horrifying pattern, dozens of men would encircle the victims in the midst of swelling crowds. Then tens of hands would pull the victim in different directions, touch her body all over, strip her, rape her with fingers and objects even knives, while tens of others would watch. A few would say, "Don't be afraid; I'm protecting you," leaving the victim in a state of shock and confusion.[13] These gangs terrorized not only activists but also ordinary women simply for being there. Sexual aggression was not new in Egypt.[14] A survey conducted in Cairo just before the uprising showed that 83 percent of Egyptian women (and 93 percent of foreign women) had experienced sexual harassment in one form or another.[15] But the post-Mubarak wave was different. Even the well-publicized police and gang violation of the female protestors in 2005 in Cairo (which a policeman reportedly justified by proclaiming to some women it was to stop them from taking part in demonstrations again) could not match the extent and intent of the postrevolution violence. The assaults continued for months, contaminating most political rallies in Tahrir and beyond. The first systematic assault on International Women's Day, March 8, 2011, effectively told women to "go back home where you belong." Gang rapes increased on the second anniversary of the revolution when nineteen cases of public rape and sexual assaults were documented.[16] The summer of 2013 alone saw 186 cases of mob attacks.[17] But out of hundreds of perpetrators, only seven were arrested and five sentenced to life imprisonment.

Why such a shocking wave of sexual violence at a postrevolutionary time when people expected to feel free and festive? To begin with, the unremitting protests after Mubarak against the military rule were disrupting the quiet reconstitution of power by the wounded counterrevolution (the army, police, intelligence, judiciary, and others) that SCAF practically represented. The participation of women—as virtuous bodies, mothers of the nation, and endowed with maternal latitude—was "feminizing" the street opposition against the military rule. SCAF needed women to return home so that it could tackle the restless young men with greater impunity. The pattern was not limited to Egypt. The Sudanese rulers would eight years later follow their Egyptian brothers to drive women out of the street protests through the notorious Janjaweed forces—by targeting and detaining women, removing their scarves, cutting their hair, and raping them.[18] In the Syrian revolution, the regime of Bashar al-Asad had already deployed female bodies, detaining, abducting, and raping women at roadblocks, detention centers, or at home in front of their family members. Violence against women became a weapon of war, a strategy to humiliate men and masculinize the opposition.[19]

But in Egypt, there was something more subtle at work, which had little to do with how "provocatively" women were dressed, or if they were "violating men's modesty" (as the Muslim Brotherhood female deputies claimed),[20] or whether they were "whores," as a SCAF member stated in a CNN interview. The distinct presence of women in the streets of the uprising had not only challenged the patriarchal sensibilities of the moral-political authority, but it had also caused a profound anxiety among ordinary conservative men. Particularly susceptible were those young men, demeaned by economic misfortune and disdained by class snobbery, who felt as though they had nothing to hold on to but their valorized masculinity, which they undertook to assert against unknown women in the anonymity of the urban crowd. Their violent performance often assumed some kind of collective fun, an "entertainment," as the historian Hanan Hammad observed.[21] Perhaps it is in this sense that the prominent scholar Denniz Kandiyoti views such extraordinary violence not simply in terms of patriarchy, but of "masculinist restoration"—one that comes into play precisely "when the taken-for-granted, naturalized character of patriarchy is called into question."[22]

Like in Egypt, unemployment and the precarity of life in Tunisia had demeaned many men and undermined their patriarchal responsibilities to provide for the family. But Tunisia did not experience the same kind of organized or spontaneous sexual violence as Egypt, even though everyday harassment increased after the revolution. Men stared at young women, followed them, yelled at them, and touched them on the streets or public transportation.[23] A survey of 3,000 women in 2016 showed that 53.5 percent of Tunisian women suffered from some form of violence (and 41 percent physical violence) in public between 2011 and 2015.[24] Yet there was no evidence of systematic violence to push women out of public space and into their homes. For unlike Egypt, the military in Tunis remained in the barracks and allowed for the transition to electoral democracy, where the first elections in October 2011 brought the Islamic al-Nahda to power and the second, in October 2014, the secular Nidaa Tounes. The gender paradox in Tunisia then took a different form, best expressed in what Valentine Moghadam calls the "democracy dilemma." Women who join uprisings for democracy may suffer consequences because democracy allows the emergence of all sorts of ideas and forces, including patriarchal conservatives who, once in power, may curtail the rights women have already achieved.[25] Post-socialist Eastern Europe is a testimony to this dilemma, and so are post–Arab Spring Tunisia and Egypt.

Thus, while unity and equality reigned during the uprisings, old institutional habits and hierarchies returned soon to marginalize women, if not to discard the rights they had gained through the years. In Tunisia, men continued to consider public office their prerogative. Even though political parties were required to field equal numbers of men and women in their electoral tickets, all except for one leftist party placed men at the top of the list. Only three women served in the first transition government, and two of them quickly resigned in protest. Women remained virtually absent from public debate in the media— only 10 percent of those appeared on the radio and TV and 2 percent in the print media were women.[26] Veiled women were particularly excluded from the mainstream media. Even the new revolutionary commissions, such as the National Commission for the Establishment of Facts about Corruption, barely had female members. In the old tradition of "state feminism," women were to be at the center of "nation building" (according to the trope of nation as mother) while men retained the prerogative of "state building," thus keeping the most and major positions of the state institutions under their control.[27] Rather than a subject of emancipation, women were to serve as an object of modernization.[28]

Things were even grimmer in Egypt. Women made up less than 2 percent of delegates in both houses of the first parliament after Mubarak, and they had only three members (out of twenty-six) in the 2012 Ministerial Council. The Islamist winners, the Muslim Brothers' Freedom and Justice Party and the Salafi al-Nour Party, expressed little support for women's rights. If anything, they vigorously lobbied against the *khulʿ* (that allowed some leeway for women to initiate divorce) and rejected women's right to travel without the consent of a male guardian. They opposed the criminalization of female genital mutilation (FGM), women's custody of children below the age of fifteen, and the legal age of marriage being eighteen. Even the female deputies in the Islamist camp lent no support for the United Nations Convention on the Elimination of All Forms of Discrimination against Women (CEDAW). The conservatives in general drew on the patriarchal social structure and norms to oppose women's public presence. No wonder an Egyptian woman in Tahrir Square would express in dismay how the "men were keen for me to be here when we were demanding that Mubarak should go. But now that he has gone, they want me to go home."[29]

## FEELING EMPOWERED

The irony of all this is that such patriarchal backlash occurred at a time when many women undertook a tremendous transformation in their subjectivities. The revolutions had fashioned a wholly new experience of both selfhood and publicness. Women were becoming more self-reflexive, more vocal, and more entitled. It was as though a "new woman" was emerging from the terror and triumph of the uprisings. "At the stepping down of Mubarak," said the young Radwa, "it was a moment I felt like everything could be possible in this country. . . . Everything was possible."[30] That moment transformed her. "The person who I was before January 25 [2011] is totally different person now." Radwa went from being aloof from public engagement just a few weeks earlier to joining the campaign No Military Trial for Civilians right after Mubarak's removal. She left her advertising job in the corporate sector to work in civil society and human rights, using her expertise in art to campaign against smoking and FGM. "Before, I never knew that Egypt had that much of an LGBTQ population, and that many nonreligious people, atheists, and others . . . were born and raised here." And she removed her hijab.

Ghouson, a young female graduate had studied dentistry because her parents wanted her to keep the medical tradition in the family, but she was not happy with it. Before the revolution, she remembered, "I was not that strong to make a decision about things that had to do with me." But "the revolution was a turning point in my life."[31] "I told myself, I don't want to play this game anymore. . . . My thoughts were being formed in a human rights way, in a way that I really wanted to do something [good for society]." Against the will of the family, she gave up on being a dentist and pursued a human rights career. "I experienced a total shift in my life, in the circles of friends, in my thoughts, everything," she recalled.

For Sara, participating in the uprising meant breaking free from the overbearing discipline of the patriarchy, marrying the boy she loved and not being "sold" by her conservative father "to the one who pays more."[32] Somaya, who married at nineteen and then divorced while supporting her children, took part in the revolution because "I suffered from corruption; after my divorce, my children and I receive only EGP125 monthly alimony although my ex-husband's income is in the thousands," she explained. In the process, Somaya gained a new vision and daring: "[The] revolution changed me; I became stronger. Now I can defend my rights, and I will not relinquish them," she recounted. "I will sue my ex-husband again, and I will fight for the rights of my children with appropriate alimony."[33] On the other hand, Asma, a college graduate, moved from a sheltered life in the seclusion of home to the battlefield Tahrir where she spent the nights. She saw beatings, tear gas, injuries, death, and then victory. "The revolution changed my life," described Asma with passion. She became "completely different" from who she was before.[34] Her parents acknowledged that she developed "a mind of her own now." After years of commitment, she took off her hijab and married a human rights advocate.

Somewhat similar processes occurred in Tunisia. Despite disruption, conservative backlash, and continuing conflicts, many women sensed a new energy and optimism. "Tunisia was set free," remarked Rasha, an activist in her late twenties. "I used to write on the internet because we were not allowed to publish articles in the newspapers. . . . A few years ago, people did not know me; it is different now," she recounted. "We had only one political party; now we have one hundred. We have built organizations and networks. I am the leader of one organization and a member in another one. Before, it was impossible," she remembered proudly.[35] Qamar, an academic in her fifties, believed "we have a revolution going on in practice," and "women are the path of change. . . . They are enacting the revolution in their lives, in their talks, their acts and practices."[36] The "society has a complex against women," and men and the elderly often resist change, she acknowledged, "but women are continuing. In a few years, we will be over this."

Countless stories of this type reveal how much ordinary women's subjectivities—in relation to state, politics, religion, morality, and their bodies—had changed. "This newly found power of ownership of one's space, one's body, and one's language," according to the scholar Samia Mehrez, was "in and of itself a revolution."[37] Women seemed to experience some sort of "human revolution," a liberation in mind and imagination. Perhaps nothing stirred more emotion in this human revolution than the rebellious act of Alia El-Mahdi, a twenty-year-old Egyptian, who exposed her nude self-portrait online for a society in which covering one's body, sometimes from head to toe, had become a norm. For the young Alia, taking off her clothes was not for the male gaze but "a way of revolution," "to protest oppression" and claim "freedom."[38] This act that shocked many in the Arab world followed an unprecedented media exposure and debate, leading to her exile in Sweden, where she joined the radical feminist group FEMEN International. FEMEN had already found support in Tunisia where a high school student, Amina Sboui, posted a topless photo of herself on Facebook; it included a caption that read, "My body is my own and not the source of anyone's honor."

Some considered these female rebels among historic insurgents who "have struggled for freedom and dignity first and foremost through their bodies." Their doings may appear like madness "but in madness, sometimes there is a lot, a lot of reason," argued the media scholar Marwan Kraidy.[39] Supporters of Amina called April 4, 2013 the International Day for Topless Jihad. Some emulated her, posing topless on social media, and the FEMEN activists in Europe, Algeria, and Morocco held events to publicize their cause. A few Tunisian associations and the Ministry for Human Rights supported Amina's freedom of expression, if not her rebellious deed. While Amina's father saw her as a "victim of a failed society," others questioned if such highly individualized feminism held any purchase in mainstream Arab societies. The feminist scholar Sherine Hafez, for instance, criticized Alia and Amina for associating body covering with backwardness and misogyny, because that association would effectively "appropriate the choice of millions of women who find empowerment in covering."[40] Muslim feminists decried these female insurgents, and a number of religious radicals made harassing threats. The Tunisian Adel Almi, a vegetable merchant-turned-preacher, called for 100 lashes or otherwise a "psychological treatment" for Amina. Harsh reactions notwithstanding, the bold acts of Alia and Amina, nevertheless, generated quiet sympathies among groups of individual women who in their public lives chose to remain discreet rather than vocal for fear of conservative reprisal. Yet in truth, the quiet revolution that the ordinary and unassuming women experienced intellectually and behaviorally seemed more far-reaching and consequential than the highly mediatized tales of the female rebels.

## RAGING DEBATE

The conservative backlash against Alia and Amina suggested that liberal individual feminism was only a small part of the emerging sensibilities. In fact, on the opposite pole of ultraliberal FEMEN had grown Islamic Jihadi women, mostly young, educated, and middle class, like the twenty-one-year old Henda Saidi, a bright law student from La Marsa in Tunis, who one day disappeared to join an ISIS group after the Syrian civil war only to be found dead in her cell along with five other female comrades in a police raid.[41] Yet despite the headlines, both the ultraliberal ideas and Jihadi conservatism remained marginal. The mainstream trends, whether religious or secular, campaigned for women's rights often in negotiation with and recognition of the prevailing sensibilities.

In Tunisia, Islamic women activists mostly associated with al-Nahda drew largely on Islamic tenets regarding equity, focused more on social justice for women, and remained critical of the elitist "state feminism." For them, the revolution was a "beautiful dream" that offered them a free space wherein they could intensely mobilize and engage in public life. The "revolution has given us our freedom and injected into our political work a new spirit," stated a female al-Nahda activist from Ghabes.[42] After all, an estimated 300 to 1,500 of them had been detained and tortured under Zein al-Abedine Ben Ali on charges of "terrorism" or membership in al-Nahda, even though many of them were barely political but wore hijab or were married to men with long prison sentences.[43] The Islamic women activists in Tunisia enjoyed institutional power through representation in al-Nahda. Among forty-nine women who were elected to the assembly, forty-two were affiliated with al-Nahda. Religious women activists were not "extremists," but at times they took conservative positions on gender issues. For instance, on the debate on the new draft of the constitution, they pressed for "complementarity" instead of "equality" between men and women, which the constitution eventually adopted. They were hesitant to change sharia-based inheritance law, which allowed women to receive only half of what men do. "Islam is the religion of the state; therefore, we cannot play with inheritance laws," argued Fattoum Lassoued, an al-Nahda Party member of parliament. "It touches upon the very nature of the Tunisian society. Inheritance laws are a red line."[44]

Secular feminists were alarmed. Immediately after Ben Ali, they staged relentless protests against the Islamist trends including al-Nahda on the wake of Rachid Ghannoushi's return from the exile. They were concerned that religious politics would push back women's achievements and reinstate gender inequality. "As women we are scared to lose our rights, such as being forced to wear the hijab and losing our jobs," stated an office secretary to Reuters.[45] In November 2014, Kalthoum Kannou, a judge and mother of three children, became the first female candidate to run for president of Tunisia. In her campaign, she emphasized consolidating civil state and gender equality.[46] The persistent campaign of these women reinstated gender equality in the constitution, which the conservative deputies had opposed.[47] Secular activists in Tunisia followed the universal ideals of gender parity. For some of them, the very hijab and habitus of religious women was at odds with the modernist project and therefore suspect. Although the rift between secular and Islamic activists remained, they often shared common values on gender discrimination. More importantly, a new generation of younger feminists strived to transcend the divide, focusing instead on debating such issues as privacy, sexuality, and police brutality.[48] It was very different in Egypt. Except perhaps for such feminists as Alia el-Mahdi, hijab and habitus, religious belief, and rituals were seldom a matter of dispute. In fact, most women's rights activists in Egypt adhered to religious belief, praying and fasting even if they did not wear hijab. Yet they vehemently opposed extremism and religious rule, which they thought would subjugate women's well-being. Women's rights activists decried the Salafis and the Muslim Brothers for their obstructive positions on civil and individual liberties, in particular women's personal status. Here, the key division was not between "secular" and "religious" constituencies, for these categories bore little meaning in Egypt. It was between "Islamists" and "non-Islamists."

There was a concern that the predominant gender debate reflected the fixations of mostly educated, urban, middle-class, and prosperous areas. In Tunisia, for instance, women of the marginalized, southern and rural regions seemed to disdain the kind of individualism that secular liberal feminists espoused. "Women in the north can do everything, drive, divorce, work, etc. But in the south, they just stay home and work with the children," stated a woman from Tataween.[49] It seemed that the Islamic idea of collectivity bore greater resonance than the more individualist tenets of secular feminism. In addition, a qualitative study appeared to confirm that the *language* of traditional gender norms—on gender roles, male superiority, public male versus private female, and the like—remained prominent.[50] Yet it is a mistake to assume that rural women were oblivious to gender justice. Rather, they experienced discrimination, expressed dissent, and claimed redress differently. For instance, although thousands of rural women worked on land as men do, they rarely owned what they tilled.[51] Many rural women felt that the lack of adequate infrastructure in their community affected them adversely more than men. The forty-year-old Rafika and fellow women in her community were stuck in their village because the lack of paved roads limited rapid transportation. Rafika had suffered twenty-four hours of agony before reaching a maternity hospital in the neighboring town. These women now wanted better roads and infrastructure to enjoy mobility, access, and travel to the nearby towns. Rafika expressed that she was no longer afraid of men after the revolution, not even her husband.[52]

In Egypt, the feminization of poverty had left over 13.4 percent households fed by mostly poor women. These women often defied the police to operate in the street subsistence economy. Some, like the street vendor Nesma, a divorcée and mother of three children, resorted to working inside the underground stations. "The government should find me an alternative if they want me to leave my place here." Others operated inside trains, often ran away, hid, or changed locations when the police arrived. A few went online to publicize their homemade merchandize such as food or leather products and discussed market strategies and production initiatives.[53] Ordinary women often invoked and uphold gender equality through the religious lens, with the basic understanding that gender equality should not contradict the rather malleable notion of "religious edicts." "The Islamic sharia treats all human beings equally; we don't need any laws," one stated.[54] Yet others lashed out against Islamists for opposing gender equality in inheritance on the basis of sharia. "I bring my money to the family and I spend as much as my husband spends," a forty-one-year-old teacher complained. "Are we equal in duties, but not in rights?"[55]

The revolutions in Tunisia and Egypt shifted the language of women's rights from the elites, regime, and state feminism to grassroots activists of diverse backgrounds who proceeded to build a bottom-up feminism. Numerous independent groups sprang up not only to claim personal rights but also to highlight what rural and subaltern women desired. In Tunisia, several associations joined forces to initiate projects like Manich Manich to provide rural women with social skills to speak out to the public officials or make claims for health and infrastructure. A few trainees traveled to Tunis in March 2017 to discuss their concerns with the minister of women affairs.[56] Just like Tunisia, in Egypt the revolutionary mood penetrated into the rural areas including Upper Egypt, where poverty had remained the primary concern for women. "Before the revolution, most of the women were ignorant about anything that was happening in the country," explained Israa Said Thabet, a mother of two children from the city of Asyut. "After January 2011 they increasingly started to follow the news and to express their political views."[57] For rural women, change seemed to occur primarily in the private realm, the households, where they challenged some of the discriminatory social conventions affecting their lives. "We are witnessing a revolution against every traditional aspect," according to Israa.[58] It was perhaps in this logic that a young woman like Doaa, a twenty-three-year-old mother from Qalyoubiyya governorate would break free from her troubled marriage, because she no longer accepted "the cultural impositions and the routine imposed on me by this society."[59]

## FROM NONMOVEMENTS TO MOVEMENTS

Women's extraordinary personal journeys revealed how far they had come, from dispersed individuals mostly in nonmovements to members of organized campaigns, once their subjectivities shifted and space became available to them. Their passive networks connecting shared concerns now found structures in a plethora of new and old clubs, collectives, associations, and online communities. From a life of isolation and passivity, Radwa joined a campaign that had already been set up by political women such as Mona Seif, Nazly Hussein, Malek Moustafa, and Leila Soeif, who were dismayed by SCAF for systematically placing civilian activists under military tribunals.[60]

Hoda, who was in her fifties and "could not make sense of the things" before the revolution, joined the new leftist Coalition Party. In the meantime, she remained "restless along with my colleagues in Haram working in the Pensioners Syndicate and the Popular Committee," she had started. "We wanted to do something."[61] Hoda attended the meetings, printed brochures, and mobilized intensely no matter how much time and work was needed. But her selfless efforts were frustrated by the condescension of the old male leaders to whom she was no longer prepared to defer. She left the coalition to establish, along with the activist Fatma Ramadan, the Syndicate of Pensioners. With Fatma, she deployed her talent in journalism to report on labor unrests, investigate workers' claims, and campaign for their rights. Hoda and Fatma moved on to leadership in the union, despite the resentment of male colleagues, but resigned when General Abdel Fattah al-Sisi took governmental power.[62]

Alaa, a university student, created a reading group with a known university professor as an adviser; many joined and read and discussed key texts such as the *Communist Manifesto*. "Reading and discussing them represented a turning point for me," Alaa said.[63] The group stopped only when the political situation deteriorated after one year. She joined the Dar el-Amad organization which offered free courses on social, political, and religious issues, including one given by a sheikh on Islamic heritage. In a striking post-ideological posture, Alaa simultaneously embraced Marx and the mosque. Then she traveled abroad to explore Jordan, Lebanon, South Africa, and the conflict zones of Yemen, Palestinian Gaza, and Syria to bring aid and moral support. "Before the revolution, my parents would not have let me travel alone," Alaa affirmed. "The revolution gave me hope and space I would have never reached before.... It eased my movement so much and made me feel like I was able to breath and do things." In the midst of repression following the coup, she took on board the dictum "Disenchantment is a luxury," continuing to generate a space where she could perform her active citizenry. She took on research work in Suez, volunteered in an economic rights nongovernmental organization (NGO), campaigned for Boycott, Divestment, and Sanctions, and connected to Black Lives Matter. After years of being veiled in a Muslim Brotherhood family, she removed her hijab.

The impulse to create collectives or join organizations derived also from the urgency of the situation when patriarchal backlash, whether from institutions, elites, or ordinary men, threatened the safety and security of women. In Tunisia, the perceived threat to the Personal Status Code (PSC) pushed women to mobilize in largely organized fashion both on social media and in formal organizations. Within days of the Islamic parties' decision to run for the Constituent Assembly, over one hundred women groups emerged on Facebook to mobilize in defense of the PSC, equality, or individual pursuits.[64] While online groups focused on education, mobilization, and transnational linkages (e.g., highlighting the experiences of women in Iran in 1979 or Saudi Arabia), the formal organizations set out to address such issues as poverty, illness, and divorce. Prison was another key topic, given that many women were imprisoned, including under Ben Ali, and suffered mental as well as physical torture.[65] The Aswat Nissa, established by the feminist Ikram Ben Said in the spring of 2011, was succeeded by the Women's Political Academy in 2012 to empower women to occupy political leadership positions.[66] Over 4,000 women ran for Parliament in 2011 and then again in 2014. But the key preoccupation for activists was both to safeguard the rights Tunisian women had achieved for decades through "state feminism" and to make this official feminism their own, through such bodies as the Tunisian Women Association, established just weeks after Ben Ali's removal in April 2011.

Thus, whether secular or Islamic, feminism in Tunisia became bottom-up and involved women of diverse social backgrounds.[67] Groups like Chouf arranged self-defense classes, frequenting lower-class male cafés, involving ordinary women, and giving space for sexual minorities; they worked against the commoditization of the female body and organized writing workshops for women to express themselves through poetry or personal prose.[68] In the same spirit, Choufthounna (Did You See Them?) prepared a feminist art festival to give women an opportunity to exhibit their arts to the broader public.[69] Other female artists asserted their presence in the male-dominated streets through their impressive murals and street art on themes that were unmistakably feminine and intimate.[70] Indeed, an explosion in women arts came to challenge both state feminism and Wahhabi Islamism. They highlighted a humanist feminism that draws on the freedom of expression and "unites personal experience, spirituality and transcultural values."[71] Artists such as Nadia Khiari, Aicha Filali, Sonia Chamekh, Nadia El Fani, and Nadia Jelassi used posters, documentary films, cartoons, photo montage, photography, and installations for women's rights. They created videos and posters urging citizens to vote and warning against the dangers of counterrevolution and misogyny.

Engaging in organized campaigns was even more pressing for Egyptian women, for they had faced a patriarchal military rule, unfathomable sexual violence, and other severe threats to their rights. Some expressed outcries in the press, on social media, and college campuses. Others fought back individually against the moralizing Salafi zealots in the streets. But many opted for organized efforts to thwart gender violence and ensure gender equality before the law. Activist groups moved to devise initiatives to protect women in public and combat sexual assault. The Operation Anti Sexual Harassment (OpAntiSH), set up in November 2012, coordinated with several other women's groups to serve as an emergency force to neutralize attacks on the streets or save women in danger. With hundreds of volunteers, gateway cars, safe houses, lawyers, and doctors, its operations included intervention, safety, and control.[72] Like the feminist group Nazra, they stressed that this was not a group of men "protecting" women but a mixed group combating sexual violence.[73] The group Tahrir Bodyguard had similar practical aims but differed ideologically. The initiative Slasel Nefsi, launched in April 2012, aimed to send a series of clear and short messages, such as, "I aspire to walk in the street without hearing immoral words" or "I want you to know that the problem is not in my way of getting dressed," carried by both women and men on the streets to raise public awareness.[74] Other groups like the Take Your Right by Your Hand campaign founded in March 2013 taught techniques of self-defense against sexual harassment. Some argued that self-defense or changing laws were not adequate to fight sexual violence. There needed to be a restructuring of police forces, who remained indifferent to or even perpetrated violence against women.

Organized efforts had already resulted in the spectacular women's march against the police and gang violence under SCAF in 2011, triggered particularly by the savage beating of the "blue bra woman." On December 20, protesters from all walks of life took to the streets of Cairo in what is now recognized as the largest women's march in Egypt's history. Activists marched with the ordinary, veiled women with unveiled, mothers with daughters, Muslims with Christians. Protesters chanted "Down with the Military Regime," "Egyptian Women Have No Fear," "She Won't Be Afraid, nor Will She Accept It." As women marched and chanted slogans, men formed a human chain to protect the protesters from assailants.[75] A month later, another spectacular march, The Street Is Ours, stretched from Sayyeda Zeinab to Tahrir Square. Over one hundred organizations and personalities issued a statement bitterly denouncing the assaults and those complicit in blaming the victims. They lashed out at the authorities for failing to protect their citizens.[76]

Building collectives was certainly the order of the day in these post-revolution times. Dozens of new women's organizations sprang up while the old ones altered their focus to forge a more bottom-up social movement. In early 2012, Ghadeer Eldamaty established digital feminist platform The Girls' Revolution, where women shared their own experiences centered mostly on sexual and domestic violence, restrictions on women's mobilities, and freedom of movement. For the groups, the notion of free choices emerged as a central concern.[77] The new feminist group Bahia Ya Masr (Cheerful Egypt) emerged in March 2012 to transcend NGO-ization in favor of building a social movement and mobilization in the streets for citizenship. It prepared a list of hundreds of women qualified to serve in amending the constitution. Its campaign "It Is My Right to Be Happy" was directed at residents of the poor neighborhoods for whom it organized iftars during Ramadan or Eid al-Fitr celebrations. In separate efforts, seven gender studies graduates established Sawa (Together) to work "toward full equality of women and men in Egypt." The Egyptian Feminist Union (EFU), originally founded by Huda Sha'rawi in 1923 and dissolved in the 1950s, was officially resurrected in November 2011 to empower women in personal and public domains, in human rights and democracy. Meanwhile, fifteen feminist groups joined forces to create the Coalition of Feminist Organizations (FO) in order to bring feminist agendas to the new constitution, a step toward gender equality.[78] Encountering new feminist militancy as well as backlash, the older organizations such as Nazra and Fouda Watch moved to adjust their missions to a greater emphasis on grassroots campaigns while maintaining their interest in bringing women to national institutions such as the parliament within the framework of modern nation building.

But there were challenges. Despite its appeal, horizontalism resulted in some degree of fragmentation, dispute, and disorientation. Horizontalism allowed for decentralized decision making, unhierarchical organization, and a network of multiple voices, but it also made incongruous demands, expectations, and working methods inevitable. A few NGOs became competitive about recruiting members rather than cooperating to build coalitions. Some leaders displayed authoritarian treatment of the new recruits or "volunteers," reflecting a generational gap in understandings of activism.[79] Thus, during the campaign against sexual violence, the younger feminists bitterly opposed the language of "protection of women by men" on the grounds that it would reinforce patriarchal discourse. Drawbacks notwithstanding, what was unfolding, however, signaled a new social movement taking shape from below, one with diverse layers of activism, degrees of commitment, domains of engagement, and perceptions of gender justice. This movement adopted new modes of mobilization and advanced new questions around the body, sexuality, and publicness, all expressed best in the women's impressive artistic works.

Feminist artists went around in urban neighborhoods, popular quarters, to imprint murals and images on the walls, while engaging in discussions with the curious onlookers. In one shocking rendition of the Egyptian flag, the eagle in the middle was replaced by a simple blue bra, referring to the brutal beating by the police of the blue bra protester. The Sitta el-Heita (Women on the Walls) project squarely confronted the notion of women's domesticity (*sitta el-beit*) by bringing the image of women into the masculine public, urban walls in cities such as Alexandria, Cairo, Mansourah, and Luxor. Do'aa el-Adl's piercing cartoons, published mostly in the daily *al-Masry al-Youm*, single-handedly took to task the underlying misogyny of the trafficking of women, underage marriage, and the practice of FGM. Her caricatures would demolish the image of patriarchal autocrats, perpetrators of sexual violence, religious misogyny, and prevailing gender norms. Perhaps nothing was more expressive of this new wave of feminist activism than those sexually violated women, dubbed as "bad women" by the police, who courageously came forward on television screens to speak out about their agonizing ordeals in public. These women, together with groups like Harassmap, Anti-OP, and others, prompted a raging debate in the media and public spaces. Events were held in universities and other institutions to raise awareness and push for change in public policy. For the first time, bodies, sexuality, and their place in public came to occupy a central place in Egypt's public debate. Protagonists called for the state to take its hands off the female body. In an extraordinary turn of events in June 2014, sexual harassment entered into the Egyptian Penal Code as a crime.

## GAINS AND GLITCHES

This was a significant victory for women in Egypt thanks to their persistent campaign. But it could not match with what women in Tunisia achieved. In Tunisia, women's associations mushroomed in astonishing numbers just in the first few months following the ouster of Ben Ali. Independent women's collectives mobilized in earnest to ensure representation in postrevolution political discourse. Even though women remained largely underrepresented in the management of state institutions, their large presence in the law-making bodies continued. Women gained 24 percent of seats in the 217-member National Constituent Assembly. They worked hard to influence the drafting of the new constitution to formally enshrine gender equality and women's rights. Adopted in January 2014, the constitution included the most progressive Personal Status Code in the Arab world. It upheld the abolition of polygamy, equal rights to divorce, and increased women's rights to custody. It guaranteed equality between men and women, representation of women in elected assemblies, equality in the work environment, and the state's commitment to eradicate violence against women. In 2016, political parties were obliged by law to ensure that not only the electoral lists but also their leadership included an equal number of men and women. Domestic violence against women was legally outlawed in 2017. The ban on Muslim women marrying non-Muslim men was scrapped in 2017. And in a landmark bill in November 2018, the cabinet called for equality of men and women in inheritance.

In Tunisia, gender equality in law was undeniably remarkable. But as critics asserted, things were quite different in real life.[80] For instance, even though the law criminalized sexual violence, it was poorly enforced when it came to the police, courts, or households. In fact, violence against women increased after the revolution. Around 70 percent of women would experience gender-based violence by 2017.[81] Some victims of domestic violence formed an online group, Chaml (Coming Together), to encourage others to publicize their stories.[82] Conservative voices called to outlaw abortion and rejected the equal inheritance share proposed by the government. Women still received lower pay than men and held a far smaller percentage of paid jobs. They made up only 4 percent of decision-making positions.[83] There was still a need for educational, institutional, and normative change. The subaltern and rural women, in particular, continued to suffer from the discriminatory gender norms. Some 40 percent of rural women remained illiterate, and over 300,000 were without the official identity cards necessary to vote.[84] Even in revolutionary Sidi Bouzid, despite general improvement to their lives, poor women endured marginalization, violation of rights, and inequality in pay.[85]

Generally in both Tunisia and Egypt, women underwent more extensive transformation on gender matters than men did. Women developed new expectations, but men mostly continued with the old ways. If anything, women's novel persona and public presence challenged masculine sensibilities leading at times to their hyperassertion. The majority in Egypt still opposed women running for president.[86] For most men (and women), the family with its unequal structure remained exceedingly powerful. In a survey conducted by the International Men and Gender Equality, some 86.8 percent of men (and 76 percent of women) in Egypt thought a woman's most important role was caring for her home and family, rather than any sort of career ambitions. And 90 percent of men (and 70.9 percent of women) believed that women should accept violence from a spouse or partner if that keeps the family together.[87] In a campaign they called the Men's Revolution (al-Thawra al-Rigal), divorced fathers strived to overturn *khulʿ* and reinstate men's exclusive right to divorce.[88] A 2017 survey showed that 63 percent of Tunisians opposed equal inheritance share.[89]

In both countries, mainstream men and women seemed to uphold conservative gender norms. As usual, it was people on the margins that revolted and disturbed the conventional sensibilities in an extraordinary fashion. Yet many women in the mainstream seemed to live a double life: in public, they adhered to the societal norms, but in private and in practice, they questioned them.[90] It appeared as though the "discursive" diverged from the "performative"—women might say one thing in public but do something else in private. This is consistent with the general pattern of operating in double spheres, open and hidden, and living a double life in politics, religion, and society as a way to secure one's standing in perilous and precarious conditions. This was the case during Mubarak and Ben Ali. It was undermined briefly during the revolutions but returned after General Sisi ascended to power in Egypt. While Tunisia's fragile democracy allowed associational life to flourish, General Sisi's Egypt reverted to what Tunisia was under Ben Ali. In a widespread crackdown, almost all independent civil society organizations were dismantled and the women's movement received a severe blow. While General Sisi brandished "women's freedom" as a selling point to his Western patrons, his regime drastically silenced independent voices and critical collectives at home. It was no surprise that many women began to return to the opaque sphere, operating in nonmovements as a venue to assert their agency.

## RETURN TO NONMOVEMENT?

A medical doctor at fifty-five, Mona was transformed by the revolution. "I was exposed to different currents and learned respecting others, listening and understanding others." She learned that "we have a strong diversity in Egypt. . . . We are not one thing [but] all of us can live as one."[91] Mona supported the post-Islamist Abdelmon'em Abulfotouh (expulsed from the Muslim Brotherhood) as someone who would embody this diversity. But she became deeply disappointed when Muhamed Morsi became president. Yet she did not give up, even after General Sisi took power. To cause change, Mona opted to work on individuals, their moral sensibilities. She believed that everyone as active citizen should work within the areas where they can assert their presence—whether in their village, neighborhood, NGO, family, or college club. Indeed, active citizenry of this sort was what Tunisian academic and mother Qamar had embraced as a way to change patriarchal norms in society. "We have 10,000 active women in society working," said Qamar proudly.[92] "They are not organized, but they are spread in society, in the quotidian, in the everyday life.... And nobody can do anything about this." Such struggles in everyday life were crucial to alter norms and establish new ones. "We can do a lot on dress, on public presence, and the like.... I am very optimistic for my daughters."

Return to nonmovements in Egypt was expressed not only by young women asserting their presence in masculine spaces, such as riding bikes in public against the social mores, but also, even more so, by scores of unmarried women, the *mustaqillat* ("independent women"), who left their families to start a life of their own. The trend defied a long-standing norm in the region. Some needed to attend school and work (*mughtaribat*), while others had to relocate to places with better jobs and educational opportunities. "I have to achieve my goals regardless of what people are saying," stated a young journalist who opted for an autonomous life. "I chose to live separately from my brother, who also lives in Cairo, to find more time for writing and reading."[93] Some had left their families in small towns to study or work in Cairo and decided not to return, while others wished to free themselves from the overbearing parental control (*haribat*). But the underlying sentiment seemed to be a desire for autonomous life, *istiqlal*—to make decisions about where to go, when to come home, or whom to see.[94] It underlined mobility, home making, autonomous space and time. "For me, *istiqlal* was a dream.... I wanted to have my own space, a room where I can close the door, a closet that no one opens, a locker where no one looks for my secrets," said one young woman.[95] Autonomous life became a debated trend prompted by the inertia of the revolution, but it presented a challenge. There were by far more women desiring to pursue such a lifestyle than actually practicing it. Only 35 percent would voice their wish to their parents out of fear.[96] Parents and relatives often deemed such a lifestyle as tarnishing the reputation of their daughters and worried about harassment and surveillance. Neighbors often talked about these single women, and landlords were reluctant to rent them rooms. In response, the girls devised ways to get around the challenges. Some chose to "be less noticeable" by living in "an apartment block where there are lots of doctors' clinics and companies," as one stated. Others convinced their parents that because of unsafe streets, it was better to live close to work or school.[97] Many formed networks, gathered together online, such as the Femi-Hub Facebook page, to exchange ideas, seek support, forge identity, and build community.[98]

Leaving home was one thing, taking off hijab quite another. In a striking move, countless women removed their veils individually or in friendship networks, *shillas*—a radical shift from the 1990s when veiling became the norm.[99] The precise scale of unveiling remained unknown, but it became visible, discussed in public, and numerous people appeared to know someone anecdotally among friends, families, or colleagues taking off their hijab. Aisha, who removed her niqab, the full face and hair cover, said ten of her friends decided to unveil after 2011. "I believe the revolution was a liberation from everything, and our notions of religion changed, especially because of the disappointment that came with the rule of Islamist groups," she stated.[100] "I simply reached a realization that I could not continue to wear it to please, in a society which categorizes women into those who wear the veil (good women) and those who don't (incomplete women who lack guidance)," stated another woman.[101] Interestingly, while Tunisian revolution opened the space for more expansive religiosity and veiling—something that Ben Ali's repressive secular regime had subdued for decades—Egypt experienced an aversion to religious display or establishment Islam. Many became deeply suspicious of religious politics, the rule of the Muslim Brothers, and its exclusivist attitudes. They were not turning away from religion per se but from its public display. "I am a Muslim and I pray, but it's not the veil that defines it. It's my relationship with God," stated one.[102] Yet they did so in a society that not long before would celebrate those putting on hijab like contestants in a beauty pageant while disparaging those who took it off as depraved. In line with the trend, after the 2013 coup a number of institutions such as TV and airlines became reluctant to employ veiled women, while certain bars, restaurants, or seaside resorts restricted those with hijab. It was no longer incredible to hear the stories of wedding parties barring female gusts with hijab from attendance. Even men, in a dramatic turn from the 1990s, began to prefer to marry unveiled women.[103] There was certainly a change in attitudes. The revolution cultivated in many women a new courage to do what they might desire doing but were fearful of its social consequences. Their venture displayed a desire for selfhood, or self-realization, which they tended to practice individually but in a social way, in local and distanced networks, in the dispersed but connective actions of a nonmovement.

PERHAPS NO WOMEN'S GROUP in the region became as concerned about the Arab revolutions as Iranian feminists. Some three decades earlier, they had participated passionately in a revolution that ended up relegating them to nearly second-class citizens. These women had voluntarily put on hijab to display unity and equality with their traditional sisters. They had relinquished their feminist claims in favor of calling for freedom and justice for all. But once the revolutionary protests ended, these women faced a religious state that took away many of their rights and made hijab-wearing mandatory. It is therefore unsurprising that Iranian feminists would caution their counterparts in Tunisia and Egypt to be weary of revolutions and their likely resurrection of patriarchal force. Yet in a powerful quest to be part of these historic transformations, women everywhere continued to pour into the streets of the uprisings in greater numbers—in Syria, Yemen, Libya, Morocco, Jordan, and later in 2019 in Algeria, Sudan, Lebanon, and Iraq.

The story of women and revolution is at once the story of pursuit, paradox, and prejudice. A standard critical view charges the patriarchy with luring women to participate in uprisings but pushing them away when all is over. This is not false, but there is more to the story. A paradox of revolutionary mobilization is that it demands unity and equality among insurgents who are otherwise structurally divided and unequal. In a genuine pursuit of equality, women passionately march and battle side by side with their unequal patriarchs—fathers, brothers, husbands, men—to establish an order that is not just for themselves but for all. But this very pursuit of equality by women destabilizes patriarchal sensibilities and hierarchies, prompting patriarchal backlash. Women respond to the backlash with unusual ferocity born out of the extraordinary empowerment they receive from the revolution. If during the uprising, women march along with their patriarchs in a common fight, in the postrevolution times, patriarchy becomes the target of their struggle.

In the Arab Spring, women's participation certainly changed the dynamics of the uprisings. By injecting feminine, motherly, and civil ethics into the otherwise narrow, masculine, and fragile rebellions, women turned them into political upheavals of far-reaching representation. Mothers and motherly impulses may, of course, prevent the young from "dangerous" revolutionary protests, but their nurturing impact is undeniable when mothers join the fight. In an urge for unity and equality, the protesting women called not simply for their own rights but the rights of all citizens. Even though gender language was absent, gender practice was not. Theirs, then, was not a feminist struggle for gender equity but a feminization of struggle that enhanced the uprisings. Feminist struggles thrived after the uprisings when women confronted unexpected sexual violence, renewed discrimination, and continued marginalization. At the time when women were expecting equality, which they had gotten a taste of during the uprisings, they encountered prejudice. And this did not come merely from the religious governments like Iran's after the "Islamic revolution" or the Muslim Brothers' in Egypt. The nonreligious, secular, nationalist, and westernized postrevolution regimes also enforced discrimination, expecting women to go "where they belong." This chapter has already detailed sexual violence in Egypt and gender prejudice in Tunisia after their revolutions. In Sudan, where women made up sometimes 60–70 percent of the demonstrators during the uprising in 2019, they were pushed aside during the negotiation between the civilian opposition, Forces of Freedom and Change, and the military. Of the dozens of negotiators, there was only one woman.[104]

But patriarchal assault and renewed prejudice is only one part of the narrative of women and revolution. The other part contains the exceptional sense of empowerment and enlightenment that women experienced precisely because of their active presence in the revolutionary mobilization. Women's presence had empowered not only the uprisings but also their own intellectual and affective selves. This coincidence of both assault and empowerment in the immediate postuprising era rendered women exceedingly outraged. It provided the ethical and affective spur for widespread activism. Activists moved to overturn "state feminism" and build a more grassroots and bottom-up feminism, before the counterrevolution strived to reinstate it. Even though ideological (Islamist versus non-Islamist) and class divides undermined women's unity, gender struggles took on different forms and idioms, often hiding in plain sight in the practice and performance of everyday life.

*Chapter 6*

# Children of Revolution

YOUTH OF DIVERSE BACKGROUNDS—MALE and female, poor and comfortable, Muslim and Christian—had shined in the arenas of the Arab Spring. A remarkable 28 percent of the young population (between fifteen and twenty-nine years old), including 36 percent of the student body in Tunisia and 12 percent in Egypt, had taken part in the uprisings. They had discussed and coordinated mostly through their cliques and collectives, on street corners and in cafés, schools, or associations. They had fought the police, braved tear gas canisters, carried the injured, and given their lives for the revolution. No longer lost, hanging, or trapped in waiting, these young people were now seen as *thuwwar*, revolutionaries. The youthfulness of the revolutions seemed to echo what Alexis de Tocqueville described the revolutionary France as "times of youth, enthusiasm, pride, generous and sincere passions."[1] Perhaps no other social group had gained as much credence in these transformative events as the youth, and in no other times in its history did Middle Eastern politics witness such attention to youth—whether as victims of exclusion or vectors of change. It was not a surprise that the uprisings came to be dubbed the revolutions of youth (*thawrat al-shabab*).[2] In this chapter, I want to show what happened to the young after the uprisings, what the revolution meant for them, and how it affected their lives. By narrating their thoughts, feelings, and actions in everyday life, I also wish to explore how the ordinary young figure in extraordinary upheavals and how we can account for the relationship between youth as a distinct social group and revolution broadly.

Scholarship on youth and the Arab uprisings has focused largely on how the indignant youth suffered from the highest rate of unemployment, how they moved from being passive subjects to active agents, or how the rising "youth movements" initiated the revolutions. The relationship between youth, digital technologies, and the revolutions has been particularly well examined.[3] While we have certainly learned more about the involvement of young people in the uprisings, much of the literature exhibits the perennial problem of treating youth as *incidental* or tangential to the core stories and analyses.[4] As such, these scholars discuss not youth politics but certain forms of contentious of politics in which the youth happen to play a key role, such that if we were to substitute youth with a different group, it would have no significant bearings on the analyses and narratives. In the studies where "youth" do take a more prominent place, there is little discussion about the specificities of youth claims and their presence in such contentions. "Youth" often appears as a term to designate an age cohort rather than a conceptual category with particular analytical implications.[5] In fact, much of the work on "youth movements" broadly are not about *youth* movements per se but about certain political organizations, parties, or networks—such as Kifaya, the Egyptian democracy movement of the mid-2000s—in which young people happen to be active. This kind of treatment is not limited to the Middle East but in fact seems to inform much of the literature on youth and politics globally.[6] This strand of scholarship then tends to examine not *youth politics* but *youth in politics*. The discussions of "youth in politics" do certainly teach us a great deal about the extent to which young people care about or get engaged in public life. But they say little about the particularities—concerns, forms, directions, pitfalls, or promises—of such political engagement. For these, we need to delve into "youth" and "youth politics."[7]

## YOUTH, YOUTH POLITICS, AND REVOLUTION

"Youth," in the sense of young persons, is in part related to a particular life stage and thus a particular location in the social structure, where the individual navigates between the world of childhood (as the time of vulnerability, innocence, and need of protection) and adulthood (the world of work and responsibility). Theoretically, a young person experiences a life of relative autonomy, a kind of "structural irresponsibility," where they neither substantially depend on other people such as parents, nor do others (e.g., family members or children) depend on them. Of course, the reality of young people's lives is more complex and may vary across cultural, class, and gender divides. For instance, many adolescents in poor families may have to seek work to earn a living instead of attending school. Girls may get married early, thus assuming the responsibility of being a parent and spouse without experiencing youthfulness. Unmarried girls, even in middle-class families, often take on domestic responsibilities of cooking, cleaning, or caring for children. Nevertheless, young individuals may not constitute collective agents unless they assume a youth habitus and an awareness about themselves as "young." Only then do young people become "youth" as a social category, acting as a collective agent.[8]

If we understand "youth" in this fashion, youth politics then takes a different form from what is commonly perceived and presented. From this lens, youth politics is not the same as "student politics," which is concerned with student rights, the cost of tuition, educational policies, or other contentions that are shaped by the school environment. The protests in Spain's universities in 2010 or those led by Camila Vallejo in Chile in 2011 concerning public spending on education and putting an end to the commercialization of schooling, exemplify what I mean by a "student movement." On the other hand, youth politics is also distinct from such things as the "youth chapters" of different political movements or organizations, be they fascist, Baathist, or leftist. Rather, youth politics, strictly speaking, is about claiming or reclaiming youthfulness; it expresses the collective challenge whose central goal consists of defending and extending the youth habitus—a set of dispositions, ways of being, feeling, and carrying oneself (e.g., a greater demand for autonomy, individuality, mobility, and preparation to transition to the adult world) that are shaped by the sociological fact of being young. Countering or curtailing this habitus is likely to generate youth dissent. A well-publicized sign in Baghdad's Tahrir Square uprising in October 2019 captures well this sense of, albeit fading, "youthfulness." "We are a generation born in your wars, spent our childhood in your terrorism, our adolescence in your sectarianism, and our youth in your corruption," the sign aimed at the ruling oligarchs read. "We are the generation of stolen dreams and premature aging."[9]

Of course, in reality, most youth are currently students, most students are young, and almost all are at the same time citizens carrying broader concerns. From this outlook, youth politics encapsulate contentions that derive from their multiple positionalities as students and citizens, filtering through class, gender, racial, and other identities. Whether the young behave according to their sheer youthful impulses or respond to the broader and shifting power structures—of class, gender, race, or age—has been widely debated, but youth political behavior cannot conceivably be understood without considering the interplay of youthful agency and societal structures, mediated by political culture and political opportunity. Youthful claims are articulated mostly at the cultural level and in the form of claims over lifestyle. But youth often get involved in both cultural politics as well as wider political struggles. Thus, to serve as transformative agents, the young would have to go beyond their exclusive youthful claims to draw on the broader concerns of citizenry. Yet, to these broad political campaigns they usually bring a good degree of youthful tastes and sensibilities displayed, for instance, in sociality, graffiti, fun, and youthful energy, as we have seen in the streets of Cairo, Tunis, Algiers, Khartoum, Beirut, or Baghdad during the 2010s uprisings.[10]

What, then, of youth and revolution? More specifically, how do we account for the place of youth in the new revolutions of our times, the refolutions—those revolutionary movements that come to compel the incumbent regimes to reform themselves instead of replacing them? How do we characterize the politics of youth in conditions where, thanks to digital technologies, youth are able to mobilize, lead and sustain popular revolutions but remain on the margins of the postrevolution governance? Given their leading role in the uprisings, are the youth revolutionary by character? We should treat with caution the current sentiments that project youth as the forerunners of democracy or redeemers of our uncertain future.[11] For there is no set political trait intrinsic to youth, be it revolutionary or conservative, active or apathetic, solemn or cynical.[12] Rather, youth political behavior tends to shift, often navigating between activism and apathy, radicalism and cynicism, passion for politics and aversion of politics. And this is not due to some "emotional instability" afflicting the young but a function of their superior potential for transformative politics but inferior position in the structures of hierarchy. Young people are endowed with certain *youth affordances*—such as agility, aversion of the status quo, structural irresponsibility, as well as intimate cliques, collectives, and communication skills—that lend themselves to a distinct capacity for revolutionary activism. They equip the young with greater capability to engage in and even lead mass uprisings. Youth emerge from such uprisings extraordinarily empowered and entitled but confront the new patronizing elites, reproducers of old order, who push the young to the sidelines, thus making them resentful of politics. These conflicts shape the young people's pathways in postrevolution times.

In both Tunisia and Egypt, youth affordance allowed the young to play a leading role in the uprisings. Like other groups, they transcended their exclusive youthful claims in favor of unity and equality to focus on the broader concerns for justice, dignity, and freedom. Youth spearheaded and carried through many aspects of the uprisings, but expectedly elders and patriarchs took charge of the postuprising regimes. Thus, they expressed a deep aversion to high politics and politicians, yet remained frustrated by their own social and political marginalization. They did not wish to be in government, yet nor to be governed. There was little interest in either leading or following. With little trust in power at the top, they moved to build alternative power in their surroundings. The reassertion of patriarchy and politics-as-usual by the new rulers caused a profound outrage. It drove the young to indulge in an intense street politics and political campaign on the one hand and despair and disenchantment on the other hand.

## AS IF A NEW NATION BORN

The downfall of the autocrats felt like a historic rupture, breaking decades of repressive politics-as-usual. For many, it felt like an unthinkable dream come true, the birth of a new consciousness, even a religious experience, that opened new horizons for imagination. "We have made history," said a Tunisian young man proudly just hours after they had toppled President Zein al-Abedine Ben Ali. "We got rid of a hated man and his hated family. Now we have the possibility of creating a new country."[13] "What we saw in Tunisia is a tsunami," according to a young woman Lamloum. "It's a milestone, it's groundbreaking. And this parenthesis which some people are eager to close will not be closed," she stressed with confidence.[14] The youth developed a powerful sense of people relying on their own collective wisdom rather than following a patriarch at the top. "We have changed, and there's no way we are going back to the worship of individuals," the young Rasha in her twenties told me in Tunis in July 2011. "Tunisian people won't worship anyone."[15] They fervently embraced the open political space as if it signaled the birth of a new nation. A focus group interview with the young in nine cities in Tunisia in March 2011 confirmed an overwhelming youth optimism for the future. The youth expressed an extraordinary excitement for political participation, including, but by no means limited to, voting in elections.[16]

In Egypt, the revolution similarly brought a tremendous feeling of elation and hope for the young who, only weeks earlier, felt deeply alienated in their own homeland. Now, in a dramatic shift, they felt a new sense of themselves and pride in the nation. "Before the revolution, we all felt like that wasn't our country, and we didn't even belong here," a university student in Alexandria recounted. "On 11th February [2011, the day President Hosni Mubarak stepped down] we felt that we are the owners of this country . . . and now we must do something for it."[17] Perhaps nothing better captured the birth of the new Egypt than the scenes, melody, and lyrics of the music video "Sout al-Hurriya" (Voice of freedom), made in the last days of the uprising. "In every street in my country, the voice of freedom is calling," it sang.[18] As if to pay their debt to these very streets that had endured their battles against the old regime, groups of youth descended upon Tahrir Square with brooms, brushes, and buckets of paint to clean and wash off the dust and debris, while a human chain protected the sidewalk curbs that were receiving a fresh coat of paint.[19] In a sense, these young people had begun to clean the nation—its streets, its schools, its institutions—to a fresh start to build it anew.

Yet, this early euphoria began to shift quickly, as the politicized youth found immediate hurdles to their urge to "do something" for their country. In Tunisia, despite or perhaps because of years of tyranny, the young began to express an early distrust of conventional politics and politicians. "I won't be voting because I don't think you can trust politicians," said the twenty-five-year-old Sadek Adouni. "I protested for revolution, for democracy. . . . But it was a lie." The subaltern youth felt as though their revolution was usurped by the middle-class elders and elite men who took charge of the government after Ben Ali. "Young people were in the forefront of this revolution, but today they have been set aside. It is the older generation that is in the government and busy creating political parties," complained Aisha, a twenty-four-year-old-woman from Nabeul.[20] This seemed expectable given that the young had neither experience nor interest in governing, but the young still felt oddly unacceptable.

Similarly, the revolutionary youth in Egypt faced elderly patriarchs in the guise of the military rulers (Supreme Council of Armed Forces, SCAF) and then the Muslim Brothers under President Muhamed Morsi who took over power after Mubarak. The paternalism of the military rulers in particular incensed the revolutionary youth who had just overthrown a dictator and gained extraordinary admiration. Ahmed Maher, the leader of the April 6 Youth Movement, recounted later how the military men, who replaced Mubarak, cheated them. "They invited us, talked to us, and said, 'You are our children; you are doing what we wanted to do,' and we trusted them." Even many Muslim Brotherhood youth who would usually obey their leadership lashed out against the rigid hierarchy, paternalism, and misogyny of their elderly male leaders.[21] Thus, the "revolutionary youth" continued their protests against the new regime throughout 2011 when the police remained conspicuously absent while SCAF's harsh response led to thousands of arrests, injuries, and slayings.[22] Roughly 940 people had been killed and over 7,000 injured since January 25, 2011, including 1,000 permanently blinded in the course of the uprising. Yet the political confrontations were to continue through Morsi's presidency until the July 2013 military coup.

## ORGANIZE LIKE EGYPTIANS

After years of absence, postrevolution Egypt saw an explosion of youth political groups. Hundreds of politically charged collectives emerged to exert pressure to change things or raise awareness.[23] The well-known

April 6th youth group had emerged on the political scene in 2008 when it organized support of the Mahalla textile strikes. Expanding after the uprising, it grew to have some 15,000 members by 2012 with offices and branches all over Egypt. In the period after the January 25 revolution, it developed an explicit political agenda—fighting SCAF in favor of a democratic government. The Coalition of Revolutionary Youth, formed in Tahrir prior to Mubarak's ouster, brought together fourteen deputies from different youth groups and political forces.[24] The leftist Cairo-based Al Rabta, formed in February 2011, linked with other groups and coalitions to work on awareness raising, popular participation in the political process, and enhancing the revolution. Al-Masry al-Horr (The Free Egyptian) consisted of human rights activists, feminists, and nongovernmental organizations (NGOs) members who pursed a largely liberal agenda. Allotus, consisting mostly of information technology specialists, campaigned to defend the revolution from the counterrevolutionary forces by raising awareness and working with neighborhood councils. The Maspero Youth Union, with 16,000 revolutionary Coptic youth, was formed in March 2011 in reaction to the destruction of the Holy Virgin Church of Sol Village. It defended Coptic identity and heritage. Revolutionary Committees for the Defense of the Revolution (*el legan el thawreyya lil difa' an el thawra*), composed of mainly left-leaning protest groups, hosted highly effective events in the urban neighborhoods. Dozens of similar groups advocated political freedoms, redistribution of wealth, and increase in civic awareness.[25] Revolutionary socialists focused on working-class aspects of the revolution, others to defend the revolution from restoration, while still others like Masrena, with well-known youth activists, helped create cooperation between various intellectual and political forces in pursuit of the goals of the revolution. A number of youth groups formed political parties, such as the El Thawra Mustamirra (The Revolution Continues) Alliance and al-Tayyar al Masry (Egyptian Current), built by the defected youth of the Muslim Brothers. Still others focused on single issues of vital im-

portance such as No to Military Trials for Civilians and the Askar Kazeboon (Military Liars) devoted to disclosing the lies of the military
rulers. El-Sahby, made up of tweens, expressed cynicism about formal
political parties, while SCAF Map drew up who was who in the military after Mubarak.[26]

Youthful politics found great expression in the political arts of graffiti, rap, poetry, calligraphy, and street performance. Earlier in January 2011, individual young artists in Egypt had come together to set
up the Revolution Artists Union to support one another and coordinate activities. Artists organized the Al-Fann Maidan (Art Is the Square)
festival in Cairo in 2011 as well as Mad Graffiti Weekend in May 2011,
a collaborative initiative that exposed censorship through the arts. Art
moved from a medium of expression into a means of political awareness. The walls of the city centers and popular neighborhoods turned
into a canvas to express ideas, disseminate dissent, expose misdeeds,
and make meaning, as if they were the wallpapers of the revolution.[27]
A Google map showed the location of major art works throughout the
city. The powerful work of Hema Alagha at the entrance of Muhammed
Mahmoud Street in Cairo depicted Egypt's "revolutionary youth" in
the image of Leonardo da Vinci's Vitruvian Man, albeit with a sharp
twist—manly and mighty but wounded, with broken arms and legs,
hands cuffed and chained together. Young artists went on to paint some
of the most memorable images of resistance on the hefty barrier walls
that the military had erected to prevent the flow of street protests. In a
way, graffiti art became a movement marked by an identity axis and collective efforts, serving as a forum for public discussion, the articulation of revolutionary ideas and mobilization. The work of these rebel
artists took a radical turn in May 2011, when a group of them stormed
the Ministry of Interior to paint the portrait of Khaled Said on the
wall of the ministry.[28]

Beyond graffiti, rap music also became a medium of youth dissent.
Earlier in the revolution, the powerful hip-hop song "Prisoner" received

hundreds of thousands of hits on the YouTube and social media at large. "To every oppressive ruler, stay in your place / The people's anger is coming to take you out," Aboul Saoud sang in a different song.[29] When the famed Ahmed Mabrouk known as "Rock" addressed the young crowd in Alexandria in April 2012 with "What do you want to hear?," the crowd roared back *kazeboon* (liars) referring to the military rulers.[30] He went on, "We say no to a lying military / Whatever they say is nothing but lies / When we refuse, we're killed or thrown in jail / Nothing's changed. Stand up, Egyptians!" His album *Waqt Al-thawrajiya* (Revolution time) had been released just days before the January 25 protests, as if foretelling the arrival of new times when the young would be poised to alter, clean up their homeland.

## IN COLLEGES, COMMUNITIES, STREETS

The desire to "clean up the nation" also meant working to transform the communities. Multiple youth initiatives sprang up in the cities to paint and beautify poor neighborhoods, their buildings, stairways, and fences, or fixing alleyways, rooftops, and green areas. Hossam, a student in Alexandra, was one such youth who wanted to "do something" for his country. He gathered friends and classmates to form the initiative Achieve Your Goal that grew to include 115 volunteers. They visited the homes of poor families to clean, decorate, bring food bags, and help the poor to "feel like revolution was made for them."[31] Hundreds of youth-led Popular Committees (Lijan al-Sha'biya), which emerged originally to protect the neighborhoods when the police disappeared, evolved later into community development initiatives. Some, like al-Ashanak ya Baladi, Nahdat al-Mahrousa, Artellewa, and Misr Be-lalwan, assumed national fame. Faculties of fine arts and architecture offered expertise and art students were eager to join in.[32] Most volunteers were students from middle- and lower-class families with little affiliations to political parties. They used social media to call for ideas of development initiatives and civic participation. Even though many of these groups disappeared before the end of the year, others like Orid, Salmiya, Min Ehyaha, Lik Dowr, and Mantiqati continued, thanks largely to the tremendous energy that the ethic of "doing something" had unleashed among the young. Omran, from a lower-class family in Benha, was only twelve when he joined the uprising. Now in a new Egypt he wanted to "do something," impatiently moving from one thing to another—fighting the military rule, joining the Life Makers but then resigning because it had "no ideas of drastic change."[33] His activism took him to the leadership in the Union of School Students. His team met with the Minister of Education to reform the fees, education quality, teachers, and the problem of exam leaks. Not getting support, students called for a general meeting but were blocked by the security forces. Their efforts to involve UNICEF in a discussion about alternative education was likewise thwarted by the ministry. But Omran and his comrades would not relent. For them, "the idea of limits ended after the revolution," meaning limits to what one could do or imagine.[34]

It was such imaginations that brought the spirit of the revolution into the schools and universities. Students led sit-ins, demonstrations, and Facebook campaigns to expose corrupt teachers and administrators. Massive protests had already called for a serious reform of the education system—of teaching, curriculum, exams, and teacher-student relations.[35] Teachers complained about "uncontrolled pupils," "chaos, disorder, and disrespect" in schools. Students were especially critical of the *thanawiyya amma* (university entrance exam) that they believed needed to change. "The process of high school exams is a purely military operation," according to Omran. The system focuses on "discipline, achievement, punctuality, and all the things that a military state is only successful at." When the school authorities in Gharbia province came up with the essay topic, "Write a letter to SCAF thanking them for supporting the revolution," students posted the prompt on social media, causing countless comments, discussion, and the mockery of the military rule.

Politics was not new to universities in Egypt or Tunisia. College campuses had been the hotbed of anti-regime, anti-imperialist, Islamist, and secular activism alike long before the revolution. In the uprising, students participated not as students with exclusive claims but as part of the "people" fighting for freedom and justice for all. But once Mubarak was gone, they campaigned for educational reform, beginning with removing intelligence agents, Mubarak appointees, college presidents, and deans from the colleges. Students of six universities demanded the dismissal of the ministers of higher education and interior for mismanagement.[36] A leaflet circulated in Tahrir called for the dismissal of "pashas and beys," the college leadership aligned with the old ruling party. Some asked for a new legislative framework for universities and others for elected administrators.[37] Students in the German University in Cairo claimed independent unions, and those in the American University demanded reduced tuition fees. Students at the national universities mobilized for and revived the National Union of Students which had been disbanded by President Anwar Sadat in the late 1970s.[38] A university president complained with humor how "everyone in the university—staff, workers, drivers, and especially students all want 'their rights.'"[39] In a significant policy change, the university presidents welcomed free student elections, elected deans, and the end of police control, all the symbols of the old regime. When I visited Cairo University in those days, the campus appeared to assume a new spirit, energy, and vitality, marked by public events, book stalls, rallies, cultural festivals, and plenty of politics. It is true, political division between the Islamists and non-Islamists certainly tainted college life and the student movement; Islamist students refused to participate in demonstrations against SCAF; and when the non-Islamist coalition won the 2013 union elections, Muslim Brotherhood students became the target of opposition. Nevertheless, it was the time of high hope and a feeling that students had reclaimed campus life. To the dismay of the traditional "elders," the youth were questioning some of the established hierarchies.[40]

If students were reclaiming schools and colleges, subaltern youths, notably the Ultras soccer fans, asserted their presence in the physical and social spaces of streets. A highly organized and combative mix of poor and educated youths, the fans had bravely fought the police and defeated the Mubarak thugs on the day of the Battle of the Camels (Muqe' al-Jamal) during the uprising. Aware of their political weight, they were now reclaiming the urban public space.[41] The Ultras' public drama displayed not only a form of subaltern masculinity but also a loud affirmation of their presence in a public arena in which the underdog felt scorned and castigated. While the elites saw them as *baltagi* (thugs), they became key players in the street politics against SCAF and Muslim Brothers rule. Indeed, as the street clashes continued, protesters became more male and younger in their twenties. Many still recalled their frequent humiliations by the police. Now with the police gone, they felt free to turn street politics into a mission, a lifestyle, and a new source of identity. There were many, like the fifteen-year-old Karim, who in their school uniforms and backpacks would show up every day in Tahrir Square in the clashes with the police. This was one way to pay back "for the sake of the revolution," as he stated.[42] Even the younger ones spent a good part of their days in Tahrir to be part of the action. When the older protestors with jobs and responsibilities went back to normal life or when parents pressed their children to come home, streets remained the preoccupation of mostly younger cohorts.

What these youngsters did was not all adventurism. Rather, it was a revolutionary impulse mixed with youthful affordance—time, energy, agility, individuality, and "structural irresponsibility." Most of them wanted to "do something," to play a role in their immediate habitat— volunteering, directing traffic, or campaigning—exhibiting an affective urge quite common in times of rupture. When an adult passerby admonished the boys as "useless kids," Karim responded in fury. "Don't say useless. You are the useless one. You're standing here while those whom you call kids go and fight," he vented. "Some of us here are trying to do something."[43] This was the fifteen-year-old Karim who would say to his parents that he was going to an internet café but in fact would return to Tahrir Square to avenge the injustice done to his friend Adel who had been shot by the police. In fact, many fans of the Ahlawy Ultras remained in the streets to take revenge of the death of seventy-two comrades who lost their lives by the violence of the rival group during the Port Said soccer match in February 2012 while the police stood by and watched.

## ELITES, ELDERS, AND DISAPPOINTMENT

Police complicity in the Port Said soccer match incident signaled how the authorities wished to portray the nonconformist youth: as unruly subjects posing a threat to themselves and to the public at large. It signified a growing mistrust between the dissenting youth on the one hand and elites and elders on the other hand. "Nothing has changed in this one year and half; nothing has changed in this country," despairingly said a young man in Alexandria in 2012.[44] He lashed out at the military for projecting the January 25 revolution as the continuation of Nasser's project, a "continuation of what has been before." As if to avenge the revolutionaries, SCAF put on trial some 12,000 young protesters, killed hundreds, and injured thousands during its sixteen-month rule. The horrifying sexual violence and virginity tests in 2011 intended to drive the female dissenters off the streets and allow the security forces to get on with the insurgent male young—those SCAF branded *baltagiyya*, thugs. The Tahrir protests in March and April 2011, Imbaba clashes in May, Maspero in October, and the Muhamed Mahmood battles where fifty protesters were killed were the height of SCAF's violence. Although a part of the Muslim Brotherhood youth stayed away from such protests, others did not; they wished to pursue a "revolutionary path" in cooperation with the non-Islamists and against their leaders who adopted a "political path" in a compromise with the military.[45] Yet most went out to support the Morsi government when it faced intense dissent from both the public and elites. Repression against youth activists took a new turn after the July 2013 coup. On the third anniversary of the revolution on January 25, 2014, reportedly sixty-two protestors were killed.[46] To quell the student unrests, soldiers were dispatched to schools to stay, in some cases, for longer terms. Even the morning drills in schools changed, including not only "Biladi Biladi" but also, in some schools, "Teslam el-Aayadi," a patriotic song that glorified the military and General Abdel Fattah al-Sisi. For the young Omran, "these were the doings of the elders." Surveillance returned to college campuses after two years of relative openness. The mounting crackdown in the universities in 2014 left 16 students dead and 3,000 arrested.[47] By the beginning of 2015, almost all student organizations with political affiliations, including the Islamist Students against the Coup and the non-Islamist Coalition of Egyptian Students (E'telef Tullab Masr), were disbanded. New private security forces began to surveil college campuses. Activist youth now had to resort to informal networks and intimate cliques to push for their claims; there remained little trust in formal politics.

None of the postrevolution governments seem to have a clear vision about what to do with the youth beyond containing their dissent. SCAF focused on maintaining discipline and order, managing the "transition," and rebuilding its legitimacy in the face of growing opposition from the political youth and women. In his turn, President Morsi faced an even bigger challenge from both the populace and the counterrevolution. His Muslim Brothers lacked any clear foresight about youth beyond attempts to keep their 200,000 young (fifteen- to thirty-five-year-old) affiliates on board—those who at times defied their leadership to work with the non-Islamist counterparts.[48] When it came to the postcoup government, Prime Minister Ibrahim Mehleb simply informed the youth, college graduates in particular, that there were no jobs in the government and that if they failed to secure work in the private sector, they would have to "drive tuk-tuk," the Indian-made auto rickshaws that serve as cheap transport in Cairo's slums. Even though the remark caused much uproar in the media, it revealed how the government imagined the future of youth. "They are responsible for their own well-being; they will succeed if they are capable," the prime minister stressed. But General Sisi wished to project himself as the president of youth—not those in the streets of contention but the well-groomed conformist youth, the frontrunners of technological advancement, the free market, and global Egypt. If the extravagant annual Youth Conference in Sharm el Sheikh was any indication, it pointed to an uncanny policy resemblance to that of ex-president Mubarak in banking on the "knowledge economy," start-ups, call centers, and the like.

Indeed, a "start-up revolution" did absorb segments of young Egyptians in the for-profit sector as well as "social enterprises" devoted to public services.[49] Some 5,000 call centers employed 200,000 in 2011.[50] But such growth could not meet the demand of the youth of whom 37 percent including 41.5 percent of high school graduates (between fifteen and twenty-four years) were out of work in 2014. Besides, the new jobs were mostly precarious, low status, low paid, and demanding, while the call centers were hard hit by the revolutionary disruptions and competition from India and Mexico. Resorting to self-help, retraining, call centers, or distractive consumption, segments of the educated youth were entrapped by the "cruel hope" of success in neoliberal economy.[51] Anger and frustration persisted. Thus, Sharif, a student who scored a grade of 92.4 percent on the university entrance exam after spending much time and money on private tutoring, would end up moving from one unstable job to the next for six years. "I wish I hadn't taken this education," he stated in rage. "I should have just worked on the street instead, trained as a mechanic, or a butcher, or a construction worker, because at least I would be able to look after my family."[52]

I perceived such angst and anger sixteen months after the revolution among the young Egyptians I knew. Their earlier energy and confidence had turned into distrust and disenchantment. They felt they had been betrayed not only by the military politicians but also by the "people," "less educated" people, who "only think of everyday life," of jobs and "stability." This youthful anger against elders displays an enduring fissure in postrevolution times that fractures families and divides parents and children. Elders often desire normalcy, stability, and getting on with work and life, while the dissenting youth wish, and can afford, to carry on with street politics to deepen the revolution. Their structural irresponsibility, in contrast to the elders' responsibility for work and family, allows the young to engage in activities that elders may call chaos. "You mistake chaos for revolution; you mistake destruction for revolution," vented the Egyptian veteran journalist Ibrahim Eissa addressing the dissenting youth. "You are an idiot who doesn't understand." In response, the young deemed the elders as the inept generation whose complicity had maintained the suffocating status quo. No wonder for the young Mina, the Tahrir episode of 2011 "was a struggle against our parents."[53] Some youths regretted how they came to the streets during the uprising without having a program or organization. "We were activists; we were not politicians," they stated.[54] Hossam, in particular, seemed very dispirited, believing that "the blood of our martyrs has been wasted." Like many others, he was thinking of leaving Egypt: "I don't want to live under these conditions." In the summer of 2013, some found hope in the popular mobilization against President Morsi to step down. But this episode tragically served the military to stage a coup, to banish President Morsi and unleash a counterrevolutionary restoration. Now under the mounting repression, beginning with the Raba's massacre of Muslim Brothers in 2014, the young activists had to seek refuge in exile, endure trauma, exit politics, or revert to hidden spheres to survive and revive.[55]

Egyptian youth had come a long way from the joyful days that marked the ouster of their autocrat. They had displayed an extraordinary optimism and energy and begun productive debates about strategy and tactics to protect and push the revolution forward. But the limitations of the refolution and the maneuverings of the counterrevolution landed them in despair and disenchantment. Surprisingly, the Tunisian youth did not feel very different from their Egyptian counterparts despite the open society and pluralist democracy that the revolution brought about in Tunisia. If anything, youth in Tunisia experienced disenchantment with the revolution, deepening distrust of government, and a greater dislike of high politics even earlier.

## TUNISIAN TRAJECTORY

The young Tunisians who had spearheaded the uprising felt sidelined immediately after Ben Ali left. For the new political elites, Ben Ali's departure meant that the revolution was over and, with it, the revolutionary role of youth. The youth were now expected to mind their own business. But in fact, little had changed in the power basis of the old regime and its institutional culture. The notorious Interior Ministry and security apparatus carried on more or less with the old ways. Pro–Ben Ali businessmen resurfaced, backing the political parties of the ancien régime. Even the politicians from Ben Ali's ruling party (RCD) remained in government while the private media continued to broadcast corrupt officials and counterrevolution propaganda. Nor was the "social question" of issues such as poverty, inequality, marginalization, and the notorious youth unemployment seriously addressed. If anything, things deteriorated. The economy shrunk due to the revolutionary disruption and declines in investment, exports, and tourism. The growth rate dropped from 3 percent in 2010 to zero at the end of 2011, and unemployment increased from 13 percent in 2010 to 19 percent in 2013. Some 44 percent of the highly skilled youth (fifteen to nineteen) and 33 percent of all college graduates remained jobless.[56] In July 2011 in Tunis, I asked a young man in Bourguiba Boulevard for direction. He volunteered to walk me to where I wanted to go. As we talked on the way, he said he had a university degree in literature but no job. At the end, when I thanked him for his assistance, he asked for money, a dinar ($0.30), for his service. He said that many of the street hustlers in the area were college graduates. Clearly, the thousands of call centers or the 284 Youth Clubs (part of the broader youth services that the Ministry of Youth and Sports provided on youth training, educational, and leadership programs) did not help much. Nor did the government's cash handouts (200 dinars per month) and social assistance. "These benefits can only be a short-term measure," stated Fatma, twenty-six years of age. "We are looking for a better solution; we want stable jobs."[57] In 2012, more than 100,000 students dropped out of schools due to poverty, long commutes, and a decline in educational quality. Even though 15,000 of them were recovered through the "back-to-school" project, dropout impact on youth unemployment was undeniable.[58] Joblessness thus remained the youth's chief source of anxiety and the main obstacle to fulfilling their dreams. The young in Tunisia could barely realize their desire for autonomy and youthfulness when 90 percent of them lived and depended on family support (compared to 50 percent on average in the rest of the Arab world).[59] No wonder the average age of marriage remained thirty-two for men and twenty-nine for women.[60] "Work is the only solution to overcome the anxiety of youths," said a twenty-nine-year-old man with a high school diploma. "Getting a job means achieving ambitions and dreams. Work means money and stability. . . . Stability means independence. When I get a job, I can do what I want, I can know new people, I can buy what I want."[61]

It wasn't only about jobs. It was also about dignity. While the people in the popular quarters described their youths as *rigal* (men) and *thuwwar* (revolutionaries), the elites viewed them with contempt. I happened to be in conversation with a group of elite family members and friends in Tunis in July 2011, who described the uprising as the revenge of the "street people," the "southern proletariat," centered on Sidi Bouzid. They said the protesters were jobless youth less interested in working than in hanging out in cafés or on street corners. Mohammed Bouazizi was no hero for them but an "unrefined scum" who committed suicide because, they claimed, he was slapped by a (police)woman. For this elite group, the uprising was a vendetta of a tribal nature. Yet strikingly, the three young persons in the group vigorously opposed their elders in support of the revolution and the youth of Sidi Bouzid—the birthplace of the revolution whose inhabitants, ironically, felt neglected by the new elites. "We went to Sidi Bouzid and people there felt like they were already forgotten," a young activist told me in July 2011.[62]

Clearly, the revolution was not over, as the political elites wished to believe. After all, a revolution may be over "when power can no longer be fundamentally questioned."[63] In Tunisia, the young, unemployed, workers, rural people, and women continued to reclaim the revolution. Social protests reached a new height in the first two years after Ben Ali. Some, like the young journalist Ghassan, got together with his *shilla* in a campaign to realize the objectives of the revolution, pushing for free media, independent justice, and against the corporate funding of political parties' campaigns.[64] Young volunteers from colleges and high schools mobilized during the afternoons or holidays to campaign for educational reform, transitional justice, and class and income equality. Through collective work, workshops, and advocacy, they aimed to renovate political parties, expose corruption, and eliminate the gender divide.[65] Schools and college campuses gained a new vitality immediately after Ben Ali. Universities pushed for more democratic governance, with students demanding change in the educational governance and administration.[66] The deans and presidents were no longer appointed but elected. The head of the Council of Universities became the minister of education. Police surveillance on college campuses ended, and networks of students and faculty took charge of campus security, though not without challenges.[67] With the secret police gone, underground student unions resurfaced, with Islamic students becoming ever more vocal and visible. The pro-Nahda union (UGTE) claimed 125 union branches in 2014 and 7,000 student members but far fewer than the secular rival, UGET, with 178,000 members.[68] In 2012, Manouba University became the site of a widespread dispute between the Salafi and secular trends over niqab or female face covering on college campuses. Even though the student movement was consumed by factional disputes, it began, as late as 2015, to pay more attention to student issues in the colleges.[69] But in my visit to the Manouba University in 2012 on the outskirts of Tunis, I surprisingly did not feel the kind of buzz and vigor I had seen in the Egyptian universities. This may partly signal a shift in the space of sociability and activism from college campuses to the social media, streets, salons, and associations.

The thriving youth-led organizations targeted political corruption and citizen education. The organization I Watch monitored Constituent Assembly activities, offered a forum for citizens (especially youth) to debate the constitution, and made a mock Constituent Assembly where 217 youths debated and made recommendations, some of which the actual Constituent Assembly took on board. The Sawti (My Voice) worked to engage youths in civil society and the electoral process. The association organized concerts with well-known entertainers to encourage youth to register to vote. The JID Tunisie, or Independent Young Democrats of Tunisia, targeted the undecided or less political youth, helping them to find a political party that fit their interests. Al-Bawsala (Compass), composed entirely of activists under thirty, publicized the profiles of the politicians running for elections in order to help young people make more informed decisions.[70] The Independent Young Democrats of Tunisia published *Ikhtar* (Choice) to educate the young on the numerous political parties and their programs.

Reportedly, 5,000 youths volunteered in Mourakiboun (Watchmen) to monitor the elections in 2014.[71]

## DISENCHANTMENT

Before long, however, the young developed a deep disenchantment and resentment with party politics, elections, and voting—a process to which their own disunity in part contributed; it prevented them from exercising much influence on the course of events. The news website Tunisia Live, created by a youth group in the aftermath of the revolution, reported that in the October 2011 national elections, only 17 percent of youth (aged eighteen to twenty-five) registered to vote. Alarmingly, out of those who did vote, 14 percent said they would not vote again.[72] In addition, youth represented only 4 percent of the National Constituent Assembly. Disenchantment with the revolution in such a short span of time was astonishing. In my random conversations with different ordinary Tunisians—hotel workers, taxi drivers, shopkeepers, young people in cafés—in January 2012, almost everyone said things were "worse off than before the revolution." They had already taken for granted that they could now speak out, organize, and protest without fear. The sentiment continued to create a deep cynicism about "politics" among the youth. Over 75 percent of the young between eighteen and thirty-four—compared to 40 percent of adults—expressed mistrust in government.[73] "I am not interested in politics.... They [politicians] are actors, are not honest," said a twenty-two-year-old college student, who nonetheless joined the Scouts in Gabes "in which I can help the poor people."[74] Before the revolution, "politics was taboo," and after the revolution, "they [politicians] want to manipulate us."[75] "I simply do not believe in politics that is party politics," said the activist Hamza Abidi. Because, according to Hamza, it is driven by "money" and "media" that enable the corrupt and elitist politicians win elections, with the result that in the end, little change on the ground.[76]

The subaltern youth felt that the new rulers had failed them. In the poor neighborhoods of Douar Hicher and Tadamon in Tunis, for instance, some 90 percent of youth in 2014 felt that their situation since the revolution had not improved or even became worse. When asked more specifically what had not improved, they cited bribery, the absence of elected local officials, and a lack of space within which they could voice their concerns. These youths continued to suffer from police abuse, with 71.5 percent of them feeling that the way the police treated them had not changed.[77] They were mostly religious—53 percent prayed and over 90 percent fasted—but they largely decried the emerging Salafis, whose visible and moralizing public presence had restricted the young females from the public arenas. Most of the young, including 30 percent with college degrees, spent their free time in the locality's bath houses (*hammams*), coffee houses, internet cafés, and mosques, but when they tried to frequent the nearby wealthy tourist areas or city centers, they often felt vulnerable to their lower-class habitus and police gaze.[78] For these young people, "work" was the most important thing in life, more than religion, and "politics" was the least important.[79] In 2013, only 8 percent of young people in Tunisia were members of an association and about 4 percent of a political organization.[80]

Disappointment with the present made many young people worry about their future. "No, I am not optimistic about the future," said a young female. "I am sure that our future is very difficult. . . . I am sure that after finishing my study, I will not find a job."[81] Given the deep uncertainty, it was no surprise that countless youths dreamed about migrating to the West in search of a better life. In fact, in the first three months after the revolution, some 25,000 people left Tunisia (mostly youth), at the same time as hundreds of thousands of Libyan refugees were entering the country. Those in the provinces would leave for work abroad, such as in Italy, but would return home to get married and form a family. Females with higher education would marry men with lower status if they took them out of Tunisia.[82] Young groups like Article 13, an association set up by a group of young women in 2012, also campaigned to pressure the government to ease freedom of movement and protect Tunisian migrants both in and out of the country.[83]

While many left their homeland for work and livelihood, some did so to pursue holy jihad. As if venturing their youthful individuality in the utopian community of *khilafa*, some 3,000 Tunisian young men and women joined ISIS in Syria and Iraq in 2014.[84] Most seemed to come from the lower-class quarters. In a survey, 80 percent of youth respondents in the Tadamon neighborhood of Tunis said in 2014 that they knew someone who joined jihad in Syria.[85] Then in July 2015, a twenty-three-year-old university student from Tunisia's interior terrorized holidaymakers in Sousse, killing thirty-nine tourists before being shot by the police. Despite its startling feel, religious radicalism remained a marginal trend. The mainstream youth espoused moderate Islam. For instance, in the lower-class quarters of Douar Hicher and Tadamon, while close to 90 percent of the youth considered religion very important, only 26.2 percent went to mosque to pray. Even though some of them expressed conservative views on polygamy, gender matters, or sharia, they overwhelmingly decried jihadi politics.[86] The focal point of youth activism in Tunisia was not religious radicalism nor electoral politics but subversive arts, grassroots movements, and civic engagement.

## DIFFERENT KIND OF POLITICS

Young Tunisians from the poor communities were already involved in subversive arts before the revolution. But the revolution gave a new boost to the genre, as if the arts, music, theater, and documentary filmmaking became the political language of indignant youth. Just as heavy metal in the early 1970s expressed the rage of the working-class youth in the deindustrializing midland Britain, rap displayed the fury of the Tunisian subaltern youth against their elites. Groups of youngsters, mostly secondary school pupils from the lower-class urban peripheries, organized artistic products and art festivals, especially rap, that at times attracted up to 7,000 spectators. They used digital technology to disseminate their work. Their music remained subversive, incensed, and highly critical of corrupt, inept, and authoritarian politicians. Weld el-Kenz's angry album *El-Boulicia Kelb* (Police are dogs) caused an uproar and received legal charge in 2013. The police union staged protests against the rapper, but he received much support from citizens for his free expression.[87] "We are apolitical, but any politician or anyone who goes astray, one day we will attack him," said the twenty-two-year-old male singer. "We are singing for the continuity of the revolution."[88] The graffiti group Ahl Elkehf considered itself an underground and oppositional entity.[89] The Zwawla (Poor Men) graffiti group warned the politicians with its slogans such as "Keep away from the poor" or "The people are fed up." The group faced arrest and indictment in December 2012 but were set free thanks to popular pressure.

Unlike the political class, these young artists were thinking in terms of revolution. "We need a new world, and we deserve it," they sang in Hamazaoui and Kafon. Unyielding to the elder artists who sneered at them as crude and crass, these youths acted like civic activists, blasting on injustice through their biting lyrics, while calling on citizens to take actions for democracy. Theirs was a youthful expression of anger at the elites and elders for stalling the revolution. Rap and graffiti were at times merged with street poetry, a project that brought many ordinary people to recite poems in public. The ISIS terrorist attacks in 2015 forced the government to restrict such public events for security reasons, but thousands of young people were already engaged in civic associations to advance their youthful and citizen claims.

In mid-March 2011, just a month after Ben Ali's ouster, a group of young Tunisians formed the Movement of Tunisian Youth (Haraka Shabab Tunis). Independent from political parties, it aimed to empower youths in employment, cultural, social, and political fields. It held public meetings in which large crowds attended and debated organizing, strategies, manifestos, and involvement of youths from the impoverished provinces. As the "voice of youths," free from any political or ideological prejudice, the movement campaigned for jobs, true citizenship, and the realization of youthful dreams.[90] Indeed, the group represented one of the countless civic associations, including 3,000 NGOs, that emerged after the revolution when restrictions on the formation and funding of associations were lifted. Most were youth-led initiatives to raise awareness about social problems, while involving the young in civic and political life after years of autocracy. Thus, the Association for the Preservation of the Medina (Kairouan) cooperated with the government to preserve the historical heritage of the old city. The Tunisian Association of Youth Hostels promoted citizenship through volunteering, tourism, and human rights. The Youth and Science Association of Tunisia encouraged young people to engage in extracurricular education of science, technology, and innovation. While Western governments and financial institutions promoted the NGO-ization of youth activism with a neoliberal bent,[91] many young Tunisians resorted to social networking websites as the key space where they debated, criticized, expressed ideas, and mobilized for social transformation.[92]

Disenchanted though they certainly were, the subaltern youth were not apolitical. Perhaps like the "waiting youth" of Niger in the *fadas*, they were "dreaming the good life in contexts where these dreams have become unrealizable."[93] But they were doing something with their lives in the more organic, grassroots, and local settings. In the cafés, they formed networks and drew strategies to cope with their subaltern conditions—to find odd jobs, smuggle, or escape to Europe.[94] Drawing on their intimate collectives, they undertook community work, engaged in theater and other arts, or ventured dangerous journeys across the Mediterranean Sea. Even in their desperation about injustice, they would say, "We need another revolution, for justice for all, because the first one failed."[95] Here, the young operated in a different moral world, what Giovanni Cordova calls subaltern moral economy—something that deviated from the dominant moral guidelines but was forged by the poor young to conduct their social transactions. They were not in tune with the modalities of high politics but tended to create their own social spaces in their local settings where they could engage and negotiate with multiple social structures to realize their youthful claims.

YOUTH POLITICS in Tunisia and Egypt during the revolutions remained remarkably volatile. Young people experienced a shifting political trajectory. Their earlier nonmovements took a more solid form to merge with the wider networks of broader citizenry to spur what came to be known as the "uprisings." Youth came out of these uprisings empowered and entitled but only to be sidelined by the new patronizing political elites. Outraged, the political youth undertook intense street politics and organized campaigns to mobilize and push for deeper change. Frustration with the elites and the stalled revolutions drove countless youth to develop a deep bitterness toward high politics and politicians. Resentful of the establishment, they reverted to the opaque sphere and nonmovements to devise ways of addressing their urgent claims, enhancing their life chances, and negotiating with the structures of power.

Of course, things were not the same for youth in Tunisia and Egypt. Young Tunisians participated in the uprising in greater number and became more disillusioned with the revolution than their Egyptian counterparts. Youth unemployment resonated much more powerfully in Tunisia while little was done to ameliorate it. Profoundly enraged, young Tunisians rapidly lost confidence in electoral politics and the state, as if the new elites and their political games differed little from the old ones. Whereas youth in Tunisia saw the new governance in the image of inept and oppressive old regime from which they tended to disengage, Egyptian youth tended to check on the new rulers. While political youth in Egypt carried their experience of activism from the

2000s to deploy more fiercely in the streets and college campuses, those in Tunisia socialized, built networks, and mobilized more in the digital media and neighborhood cafés, if not in the streets.

Yet both groups seemed to share a largely post-ideological stance and ebb and flow in political activism. The Arab Spring came at a time when none of the established ideological traditions—secular liberalism, Marxism, or Islamism—garnered hegemony. This void left the young to rest on their own experience, judgment, and experimentation to conduct social and political transactions. The mainstream youth showed an uncommon aversion to religious authorities. The popularity of slick lay preachers and household names like Amr Khaled drastically declined.[96] In Egypt, the mainstream youth were looking for a "third way"—neither Islamist nor secular but some form of post-Islamist third way or *wasatiyya*. This also included the youth of the Muslim Brotherhood who could not relate to their patronizing leaders but were seeking a more critical, open, and inclusive polity. In their turn, most young Tunisians saw the new secular elites rooted in the old regime and considered the post-Islamist al-Nahda as a fake reincarnation of Islamism. They wished to avoid both. Broadly, the young espoused an aversion to government and resented being governed. They disengaged with higher office but were frustrated by being pushed around. They seemed to want to pursue their own kind of politics—less traditional and institutional and more in tune with their personal experience and judgments. They wanted to pick and choose their slogans, their songs, their scripts. They were reluctant to follow leaders, particularly national politicians, and wished to follow their own instincts, as in pursuing political arts such as graffiti and rap music, venturing dangerous migration, or joining ISIS.

As such, theirs was not a neoliberal individualism. For it was embedded in a powerful and traditional ethos of solidarity and collectivism rooted in family, community, loyalty, friendship, and *shilla*. It was akin to what the sociologist Sari Hanafi calls reflexive individualism, one in which individuals constantly negotiate their subaltern positions in the social structure and resist its disciplinary power in pursuit of liberation.[97] Of course, gender complicated these dynamics. Female youth had a harder time enacting their individuation or negotiating their ways out in the social structure, dominant norms, and family. "I don't want to go out at night in a cab because I feel I don't want to be exposed to the police like a woman alone at 1:00 a.m. at night if something happens."[98] But there was something curiously youthful in this rather anarchist condescension toward organized power, hierarchy, and leadership—a stubborn reluctance neither to lead nor to follow. Partly a reflection of their structural irresponsibility, young people felt as though they had sufficient intellectual and logistical resources (knowledge, technology, social capital, communication skills) to depend on themselves rather than their predecessors. Thus, avoiding higher office—whether obeying or operating in the state and bureaucracy—the mainstream youth sought to create their own social spaces at the base to negotiate their subaltern predicament, advance life chances, make meaning, and generate norms. Although certainly youthful, this is not simply a matter of age; after all, young people may identify with old leaders when the latter think and act critically like them.[99] Rather, it is a matter of competing ideas about power, whether to align with the sort that is top-down, patronizing, and controlling or the sort that is built horizontally on solidarity, self-rule, affect, and local trust. Therefore, the key question is not, as frequently asked, why there are currently no charismatic leaders like there were in the old movements. The key question is why they have no followers.

*Chapter* 7

# The Social World

BY THE MID-2010s, few hesitated to describe the Arab revolutions as a failure. In truth, little had changed in the power structure of the old regimes. The intelligence apparatus, the military, state media, powerful business networks, and old elite organizations largely retained their old culture and top operators. Even in Tunisia, where an electoral democracy and freedom of expression took shape, the old mode of governance, which resulted in unjust socioeconomic policies, regional developmental disparities, and the marginalization of a large portion of the population, continued. But this was only one side of the story of the revolutions. Although not much changed in the power structure at the top of society, a great deal happened at the bottom—in farms, families, communities, schools, art scenes, and popular media. Some of the deeply entrenched attitudes altered; norms were questioned and hierarchies (men / women, elders / youths, clerics / laypeople, teachers / students, leaders / followers) challenged. Subaltern groups experienced a significant transformation in their subjectivities. Women, lower-class youths, and social minorities pushed for equality, inclusion, and recognition, while the urban and rural poor launched extraordinary efforts to reclaim dignity and enhance life chances. They challenged the logic of neoliberal policies that the political class had largely taken for

granted. Such activism by the subalterns in the social realm radical-
ized these otherwise nonradical revolutions.

Surely, these insurgent thoughts and practices faced conservative
backlash and stiff resistance from the elites and authorities. Yet there
occurred an undeniable break, a rupture, in the social realm, in that
these societies experienced new historical, cognitive, and affective conditions wherein many people came to imagine different order of things,
to figure new solutions to their problems. I see this revolutionary rupture in terms of what Alain Badiou calls the event, an abrupt and finite
historical happening that may follow infinite possibilities, a historic
condition where people come to see, feel, and do things in novel ways,
imagining different futures.[1] Here in this chapter, I wish to highlight
some of the concrete expressions of this revolutionary rupture inscribed
in the lifeworld, counternorms, and struggles around the "social question" that defied Arendtian take on the poor. Put together, they represented a revolution of the social, complicating the idea that these
revolutions were nothing but entirely failed experiments.

## DIFFERENT LIFEWORLD

Revolutionary ruptures are essentially affective moments. They are
marked by a sudden shift in the structure of feelings, when people tend
to connect, cross over the usual divides, welcome strangers, share fear,
and join in happiness. For a while, they forgo selfishness and individual
gain, embrace love, and cherish comradery. Attention to material gains
fades in favor of pride in the nation and commitment to doing something good for the community. These are not the moments of selfishness and ego but solidarity and sacrifice; not the times of experts and
specialists but poets and dreamers; not reason and rationality but daring
and "madness." "Get rid of the experts and listen to the poets—for we
are in a revolution," wrote the Egyptian revolutionary Ala'a Abdel-
Fattah on the eve of the uprising. "Ignore reason and hang on to the

dream—for we are in a revolution. Beware of caution and embrace the unknown—for we are in a revolution."[2]

If Thomas Hobbes was correct that fear is the tool of the sovereign power to rule, that fear was broken in the Arab revolutions.[3] In Tunisia, where Zein al-Abedine Ben Ali's regime had ruled with iron fist for decades, shedding fear was itself a tremendous liberation. In fact, freedom from fear remained the most salient feat of the revolution. "Tunisian revolution was not a political liberation," the historian Karima told me in Tunis in June 2017. "It was a liberation of mind—that is, liberation from fear, speaking your mind about taboo things, about politics, about religion, or homosexuality." Erosion of fear might appear an intangible and immeasurable effect—nothing like having a job or better roads or a free press—but its consequences on individual self-esteem and drive, on citizenship and cultural production, on political work and mobilization are undeniable. Shedding fear of the sovereign power is an aspect of personal revolution—one that is closely associated with the spirit of vigor, vitality, and hope. It is linked to dreaming the unknown, thinking the unthinkable. "Before the revolution, everyone would say, 'No, where are you going? You are a girl,' but now, boy or girl, we are all Egyptians," stated one of the many who volunteered to clean up the streets after Hosni Mubarak abdicated.[4] Here is a sense that changing society meant also changing oneself. Lifeworld, social beings' actual and immediate experience of life, was a domain where these desires for the transformation of self and society intersected. And the Tahrir moment embodied an early expression of such a lifeworld. It captured best the spirit of the event in these revolutions.

The episode of Tahrir inspired and informed the imagination of millions around the world who were fighting for social justice. It became a global emblem, a model inspiring the global Occupy movements that emerged in 80 countries and 500 cities around the world, including New York, Madrid, Athens, and Tel Aviv. Tahrir represented an extraordinary mix of a political space and novel political imagination.

Lying somewhere between the "political streets" of Beirut and Baghdad in 2019 and the "liberated zones" of the Zapatista Chiapas or the Kurdish Rajova, Tahrir appeared like a liberated street in the heart of a megacity, an improvisation to establish an alternative public order without and against the sovereign power.[5]

Here in this liberated square, activists organized mass rallies, prepared tracts, raised banners and stages, and before long set up makeshift tents in which to spend the night. Then came medical teams, cleaning crews, and security units. In the headquarters around the square, key organizers discussed strategies, assigned tasks, and allocated resources—food, resting locations, communication tools, and tract writing. In residential buildings surrounding the square, a number of apartments offered rest and respite, the places where revolutionaries would take breaks from the strain of the square, use lavatories, wash, rest, rejuvenate, and strategize next moves. Young men and women spent nights together in the comradely campsites. And Muslims and Christians assisted each other in their prayer services. Tech-savvy activists fed news into social media, while Al-Jazeera television continuously transmitted the events and images of Tahrir worldwide. As days passed, ordinary Cairenes—men, women, children, and elderly—would join the revolutionaries, turning the battlefield of Tahrir into playgrounds during the evenings, enjoying and boosting the trade of the street vendors whose mundane operations had merged into the monumental revolution. Travelers visited from provincial towns and villages, not missing the adventure of experiencing this moment in Tahrir. And young couples even held their marriage ceremonies or honeymooned in that extraordinary arena.

Tahrir, then, became a microcosm of an alternative social order to which the revolutionaries seem to aspire. Democratic governance, nonhierarchical organization, collective decision making, self-help, and altruism were all on full display. It was a liberated space wherein gender, religious, and class lines seemed to fade. Intrigued by this novel democratic politics, some observers portrayed Tahrir as a "theater" that staged an egalitarian, affective, and cooperative order that the Arab Spring appeared to herald.[6] Enthused by the appeal of agora in the eighteen days of Tahrir Square, philosophers Alain Badiou and Slavoj Žižek saw in these revolutionary moments the promise of a new social order that could serve as the foundation for a different future. For others, it was something like the ancient Greek polis, described by Hannah Arendt as a form of government that relied on self-rule and commonsense initiative with no particular single ruler.[7] The Tahrir moment then evolved and was imagined as a model of radical democracy, an alternative to a vanguard party, guerrilla tactics, or liberation war. It was this image, this new model of "future in the present," that lay behind its global appeal in a disenchanted world where the idea of old-fashioned revolution was dead, while the liberal democracy entangled in corporate interests and embattled by plutocracy had failed to address ordinary people's concerns for precarity, exclusion, and inequality.

While the *communitas* of Tahrir came to life in the exceptional days of the uprising, hundreds of new collectives emerged after to continue the spirit of popular sovereignty at a time when the state had lost full control and the people wished to "do something good" for their renewed societies. In both Tunisia and Egypt, thousands of youth groups came together to form Lijan al-Sha'biya, or Popular Committees, in the neighborhoods to protect people and property while the police had vanished from the public places. In the poor neighborhoods, some of these committees served to supply basic goods such as cooking gas and sugar and services such as garbage collection. Once the new regimes established authority, the committees turned into organs of local development, civic campaign, or dispute resolution. Notwithstanding their drawbacks—largely dominated by young male with women in the background—the Popular Committees embodied a democratic form of political participation that to some degree persisted despite the return of autocracy.[8] In Egypt, initiatives like Know Your Right and The

People Own along with hundreds of other committees worked to upgrade poor neighborhoods or provide essential goods and services such as subsidized bread, energy, waste collection, and the illumination of public places. In April 2011, Popular Committees held their first general conference at the national level. As the new governments moved to co-opt the committees, paying them lip service in order to garner revolutionary legitimacy, some committees remained oppositional (e.g., campaigning against gentrification in Cairo's Ramlet Boulaq), some worked with the state to use resources to empower their constituencies, and many others kept their distance and carried on with their grassroots ambitions.[9]

Thus, in Cairo's Basatin, the committee took care of safety and security, organized meetings with residents to beautify the neighborhood, clean up the streets, fix water fountains, and paint buildings. It set up symposia to offer political awareness, encouraging people to vote in the national and local elections. A committee member was chosen as a delegate in the Constituent Assembly in charge of drafting a new constitution. The Mit Oqba Popular Committee moved to upgrade the neighborhood, plant trees, pave roads, facilitate meaningful communication between residents and the local authorities, and oversee the local council's budget. With the help of the youth club and the local council (Mahaliyyat), it sustained the adjacent street vendors, while also making them orderly, clean, and respectful of pedestrians. In Dokki and Aghoza, the initiative was started by five youths in early 2012 to elevate public awareness on local issues, local councils, and problem solving. Their Facebook presence brought hundreds of supporters. The group conducted surveys to understand people's concerns, initiated training workshops on empowerment, and connected with other groups and popular committees to exchange ideas. Along this line, the Dokki and Aghoza council divided the area into ten districts to identify the neediest. In the meetings with the locals, pressing problems emerged: access to natural gas, subsidized bread, health care, and improved sanitation.

By the end of 2013, many of these problems had been tackled, but the efforts continued even after the coming to power of the new repressive government.[10]

One of the salient features of these neighborhoods was the proliferation of revolutionary aesthetics, in particular graffiti, that gave new life and color to the otherwise lifeless walls. In fact, an "artistic revolution" seemed to emerge from the eruption of artistic creation, graffiti, music, street arts, and calligraphy.[11] Tunisian women in particular pioneered a radically new artistic expression. They used documentary films, installations, cartoons, posters, and photographs to produce a new sociocritical discourse that promoted democracy and women's rights and discarded state feminism and religious extremism.[12] Graffiti art thrived from the very outset of the revolution both in Tunisia and Egypt and continued to expand years after the dictators were gone. The urban walls displayed an explosion of colors and inscriptions expressed in messages, slogans, signs, as well as spectacular portraits and iconic depictions. They spread news, expressed emotions, and blasted the rulers; they spoke of torture, injustice, rights, sexual harassment, police brutality, martyrdom, joy, and grief. In a way, the graffiti art served as the wallpapers of the revolutions, a vehicle for free speech, a barometer of public sentiments, a watchdog. If graffiti served as the wallpapers of the revolutions, the musical landscape acted as their soundtrack, voicing the demands, dreams, and indignant sentiments of the subaltern subjects, notably the incensed lower-class youth. In Egypt, when the authorities curtailed free expression after the 2013 coup, young artists resorted to quotidian drama to revive the utopian revolutionary sentiments. Through public performances, they carried on the dreams of the revolution even under the new repression.[13] Indeed, revolutionary habitus— expressed in genuine cooperation, comradery, and egalitarian spirit— seemed to continue even in the formidable times of despair, as in the Mubtadaa, an initiative of youth in their twenties that aimed to bring humanities knowledge to high school children.

Clearly, a new public sphere came to life in these societies. It had begun with the spontaneous gathering of people standing around in groups, each fifteen or twenty, on street corners in Kasbah, Bourguiba, or Tahrir debating diverse public issues ranging from the elections and democracy to corruption and social justice. These people were congregating in the new agonistic spaces of mixture and mélange that briefly subverted the dictates of the spatial ordering and elite attitude about where the poor could or could not go, sit, or loiter. Such free public debates, as I observed in postrevolution Tunis, Cairo, as well as 1979 Tehran, were part of a larger sphere that included not only art, graffiti, and countless associations but also print and digital media. Press, television, and radio programs, which previously were mostly the mouth-piece of the regimes, experienced a clear shift. Dozens of fresh newspapers of much higher quality were established both in Tunisia and Egypt, carrying informed news and debates. The state-run TV and radio stations became more open, and the private channels used innovative ideas and methods. The 25TV, a news start-up in Egypt integrating Facebook and Twitter into television content, wished to democratize news media even at the cost of conflicts with the authorities over its uncensored content.[14] Yet this new public sphere had to grapple with not only the hostility of the political elites but also the NGO-ization of civil society on a neoliberal schema that the Western governments were promoting through funding at these postrevolution moments.[15]

## COUNTERNORM CURRENTS

The revolutionary performance, the downfall of deep-rooted dictators, and the subsequent political opening prompted the Arab citizens to imagine their nations as if everything was now possible. Change in consciousness remained one of the most enduring, if invisible, legacies of the Arab uprisings, of which one expression was the sudden outburst of both highly conservative and liberal ideas in the Arab public sphere.

Thus, only days into the downfall of Mubarak and Ben Ali, the sudden appearance of ultraconservative bearded men, traditional garbs, and face-covered women gave a new aura to the public spaces. Bands of militant Salafis with long black beards and white galabia roamed around in the cities of Egypt and Tunisia to herald the coming of their divine social order. In Egypt, the newly founded association of Amr be Marouf wa Nahy an al-Monkar and its agents stopped women in the streets to impel them to observe "proper" moral behavior and dress codes. Even though the passersby, shopkeepers, and women themselves, for instance in the city of Suez, pushed back against these new moralizers, many felt apprehensive about these conservative shock waves.[16] In 2012, a Salafi sheikh in Egypt called for the death of the opposition leader, Muhamed El-Baradei. And the infamous Wagdi Ghoneim called for a jihad on those who were protesting against President Muhamed Morsi.[17]

The Tunisian religious radicals seemed even more intransigent. Shortly after the revolution, hardliners demanded female circumcision, marriage of underage girls, and polygamy.[18] In July 2012, in the capital's coastal suburb of La Marsa, Salafi groups attacked an art exhibition and destroyed artworks deemed to be "offensive." Earlier on, in the el-Kef region, others had ransacked a police station and bars selling alcohol.[19] Extremist groups further made a public uproar against the airing on TV of the Iranian film *Persepolis,* leveling a charge of blasphemy that a Tunisian court upheld. Other groups went so far as bringing down the national flag of Tunisia, replacing it with what came to symbolize ISIS, whose horrific brutality in Iraq and Syria took the world by surprise. Others raided the US Embassy in Tunis, and one of them assassinated the leftist activist Chokri Bel'aid in cold blood early in the morning. Even though these incidents remained sporadic, their shock waves reverberated across the Arab nations and fortified the idea that the Arab Spring was receding into an impending Islamist takeover. All this took place at a time when the religious parties were poised to assume governmental power.

But this was not the whole story. In parallel with these very conservative onslaughts emerged a series of contrapuntal, liberal sensibilities that shook conventional beliefs. Tunisia, already the most liberal Arab society, saw an upsurge in women's fury against the rise of aggressive Islamism and conservative Salafism. To protect their rights, they organized associations, staged street marches and sit-ins in prime minister offices, and campaigned on college campuses. The international Femen movement found its counterpart among some Tunisian women whose image of bare chests stirred much controversy at home and endorsement in the West, at a time when "saving Muslim women" had become part of the imperialist agenda of military intervention and regime change. The song "Hashrab Hashish" (I will smoke hash), by a young Egyptian woman who went by the name Luka Blue, caused much excitement among liberals and uproar among conservatives. At the regional level, no less dramatic was the pubic kissing of a dozen Moroccans in front of the parliament as a defiant protest against the arrest of three teenagers who had posted their affectionate photos on Facebook. "Our message is that [detained teenagers] are defending love, the freedom to love, and kiss freely," said one protester. Thousands supported the move.[20] And then came a campaign of "free hugs" in Saudi Arabia by groups who offer hugs to passersby in the streets to "brighten up their lives." The morality police would not tolerate such brazen public practice that had caused a moral panic over its possible implications. "Today it's one hug, tomorrow it's a free kiss, and the next day it'll be free sex," imagined a blogger.[21] Extralegal *urfi* marriage seemed a terrain where Salafi conservatism converged with liberal sensibilities. In Tunisia, *urfi* marriage grew among university students as the Salafis saw it as a space for young people to have (halal) sex before marriage, even though some 80 percent of male youth and 68 percent of female youth were already practicing sex before marriage.[22]

In Egypt, where religious sentiments and modesty in donning hijab, *khimar*, and niqab had dominated the public arenas since the 1980s, a new wave of deveiling came to life. The scale remained unknown, but it seemed to become a trend, as scores of veiled women ranging from TV presenters to those in the poor areas like Imbaba began to take off their headscarves.[23] "There is a wave of my friends doing it," a deveiled woman said.[24] Hala, for instance, was from a very religious family, with a grandfather who was a Sufi sheikh. Hala was recruited by a Muslim Brotherhood group, which looked "cool and upper middle class."[25] Finding them "such class snobs," she said, "I got traumatized and totally lost religion." But the turning point was just after the revolution when the Muslim Brothers came to power, when "they became a total failure." After grappling with the ideas of religion, freedom, and Muslim identity, she noted, eventually "I took off the veil." Of course, undergoing such dramatic change in identity, beyond personal trauma, became socially painful when family members, friends, or neighbors displayed disapproval. "Some people didn't talk to me anymore," Hala said. Yet the women continued in their new convictions "because [after the revolution] they felt so empowered." Whereas veiling was associated earlier with the "Islamic virtues of female modesty or piety," the end of the 2010s saw a dramatic shift.[26] "What is fascinating to me is that this language has almost completely shifted to one of doubt even among practicing Muslim women in Egypt today," concludes a scholar of religiosity in postrevolutionary Egypt. "Aside from the growing number of women taking the veil off, those who still have it on are bombarded with arguments against it, saying that there is little, if any, proof that it is a religious mandate. This has caused many women to question their decision to wear it."[27]

Only a revolution could cultivate such courage and confidence among Muslim women in a society where taking off hijab remained by far harder socially and religiously than putting it on. The revolution made these women believe that rules could be broken and norms could be altered, while the dispirited rule of the Muslim Brotherhood made them question the very wisdom behind that type of religiosity. Thus, women in particular exhibited a strong quest for autonomy and selfhood. "For me not wearing the veil," stated a deveiled woman, Meshraf, "I feel like myself for the first time in my life. . . . Only when men accepted this right for women could we say that we have a revolution," she said.[28]

The desire for selfhood and autonomy also found expression in many unmarried women, *mustaqillat*, deciding to live on their own, away from their families, as I discussed earlier in the book. If students brought the revolution to schools, farmers to farms, subaltern youth to communities, the *mustaqillat* brought the revolution to homes. In search of an autonomous life—from work to the home, from mobility to the control of their own bodies—the *mustaqillat* became "quite a phenomenon," according to Hala who knew many of them.[29] The conditions of checkpoints, curfews, and a general decline in the feeling of security after the revolution offered grounds for young women to justify their new counternormal lifestyle by arguing that commuting was unsafe and so they would be better off living on their own in the proximity of work or school. Others had already experienced life in a single-person household because their families had migrated to the Gulf states for work. But once the family returned, "the girls hated it," for they felt they had lost their independence.[30] It took some three decades after the revolution for a third of Iranian unmarried women (between twenty-five and thirty-five years of age) to live on their own (*zendegui-ye mojarradi*). It seemed to take only a few months for the Egyptian revolution to unleash such ideas of autonomy. "The revolution gave me one huge push," said a young *mustaqilla*. "As much as it failed on a national level, I believe I am leading my own miniature protest to the right path. I have created change, and maybe someday, it will happen for the country."[31] The highly publicized display of Alia el-Mahdi's nude image on her blog in protest of social control points as much to a profound frustration as to the courage and selfhood that many women felt. It certainly challenged long-standing gender norms, the disciplining of the body, and its commodification, as the scholar Laleh Khalili put it.[32]

But ordinary women's stealthy acts of defiance and subversion in everyday life proved to be more extensive and enduring than those spectacular undertakings.

Women were not alone in uttering such an overt counternormal disposition. Bolder expressions came from gays, whose lifestyle was deemed in the conventional moral codes as a Western disease, cultural threat, and a counterreligious force. Even though gays as collectives did endure before the revolution, frequenting certain bars, hangout places, or virtual space, they became extraordinarily vocal and visible just days after the revolution. So when an activist began an anti-homophobia campaign on Twitter, thousands joined within hours, with further support coming from other activists and celebrities. The move was to lay the foundation for a "distantiated" community.[33] Like others, gays had taken part in the revolution, fought street battles, and stayed in Tahrir Square for days and nights. The liminal space of Tahrir enabled them to venture "out," gain visibility, and set up headquarters to congregate and connect.[34] Not long after Mubarak's downfall, both male and female members in Cairo and Alexandria held gay nights in bars and private parties, or met in cafés, gyms, and beaches. Through the internet, they connected with wider communities beyond Egypt.

Being openly out, however, could not ensure tolerance. On the contrary, precisely because they became more visible and vocal, gays had to face increasing official witch-hunts of both Islamist and military-backed governments. In October 2013, the police raided a medical center arresting fifty-two gays, while in November a Valentine party in Alexandria Road came under police assault where the detainees were forcefully sent to "forensic examination."[35] In April 2014, police arrested four men at a gay party and, later, others detained for same-sex marriage on a boat in Cairo.[36] Gays had to grapple with the recurrent contradiction between going opaque and invisible to secure safety and being visible but unsafe. The controversy over flying rainbow flags during the Lebanese band Mashrou Leila's performance in Cairo brought this contradiction to the surface.[37] In the euphoria of exalting General Abdel Fattah al-Sisi to the "lion of Egypt" and the "real man" of the nation, the depiction of gays as "female-like" "half-men" could certainly serve the new national chauvinist narrative that the post-Morsi counterrevolutionaries championed. But neither this nor any other onslaught was able, of course, to stop gays from being gay. Rather, they would push the members from open activism to opacity and nonmovements—where they would go underground as noncollective actors to engage in passive networks waiting for the next chance to come out as collective agents in organized communities.

Things fared favorably in Tunisia, however. Gay rights groups gained an unprecedented space in the country where homosexuality was punishable by prison sentence. The first queer online magazine *GayDay* was launched in 2011, and the first ever LGBT association Shams came to surface shortly thereafter. Other organizations such as Damj, Chouf, and Mawjoudin openly supported queer rights. Mawjoudin organized film festivals to raise awareness on nonnormative gender identities.[38] Then came Shams Rad, the first LGBT-oriented radio station in the region, with the slogan "Dignity, Equality."[39] Expectedly, these efforts led to harassment, abuse, and even death threats. Even though Shams was suspended by the government in 2016 for not abiding by the nongovernmental organization (NGO) laws, it appealed the verdict and won its case, while the Ministry of Human Rights continued its legal support for the LGBT victims. In 2019, the Tunisian lawyer Mounir Baatour became the first openly gay candidate in the Arab world to officially run in a presidential election.[40] Bolstered by the new revolutionary mood, the trend had spread through the entire region. With only four associations advocating sexual rights in 2009, there developed by 2018 more than twenty social movements in the region where the nonnormative sexuality was seen as socially deviant, morally corrupt, and legally punishable. "I am a human like everyone else, and I have rights. I will defend those rights," said Ahmed, a gay man from Libya.[41]

Such public expression of personal liberties and lifestyle was unprecedented in scale and scope in the societies in which patriarchal sensibilities and conservative religiosity had gained extraordinary momentum since the 1970s. But the revolutions of 2011 shook many of the established ideas. "After taking down Mubarak," opined an activist, "I cannot think of anything that is not possible."[42] Even though such sentiments recognized later the difficulty of changing things under the postcoup repression, it is undeniable that the revolutions made the subaltern believe that rules could be broken, norms could be altered, and scared beliefs—even the very idea of God—could be questioned. And they were. In fact, a burgeoning "atheist movement," as it came to be known, emerged ironically at a time when the religious parties (in Morocco, Tunisia, and Egypt) had ascended to governmental power. Reportedly, some two million closet Arab atheists began to speak out in public—talking to journalists, organizing debates, and voicing their opinions on the web.[43] Multiple websites such as Egyptian Atheists, Atheists without Border, Atheist Brotherhood, Atheist against Religion, Atheist and Proud, and I Am an Atheist sprang up. In February 2013, a packed Cairo mosque hosted a debate between a group of atheists and a cleric. Others were aired on television.[44] A group of Egyptian atheists called on the prime minister about the new constitution to recognize "atheists'" rights." Emboldened by the revolutions, the movement went beyond Tunisia and Egypt to spread in the Arab world at large. In the Persian Gulf area, at least two television talk shows discussed atheism.[45] Protagonists, mostly young, expressed doubt about the credibility of a religion that "says we don't have free will, but we will still be accountable for what we do." A cleric testified how everyday parents would bring their disbelieving children to him for remedy.[46] In 2012, a poll by WIN-Gallup International found that almost a quarter of respondents in Saudi Arabia said they were nonreligious and 5–9 percent atheist.[47] Saudi atheists became so vocal and visible that the state issued a decree criminalizing any call for "atheist thought" and "questioning the fundamentals of Islam."[48] Some accounts spoke of over sixty Arabic-speaking atheist Facebook groups that emerged after the revolutions, ranging from Yemen with 25 followers to Sudan with 10,344 followers.[49]

Open disbelievers often faced insult, isolation, and even violence by family members and others. Basma Rabei was locked up for three weeks, receiving death threats from her brother, while Asmaa Omar endured a broken nose by her father for "insulting Islam," for becoming a "loose girl."[50] And police arrested youth for advocating atheism on Facebook.[51] Many continued to reject the idea of God, while others held their God but rejected religion, whether Islam or Christianity. The gender bias of actually existing religions seemed to drive more women than men to question the religious dogma.[52] The aggressive rise of Salafis in public spaces and of the religious parties in governments had placed religion at the center of social struggle precisely at a time when the revolutions had made the underdog fearless to express unorthodox views. As a Tunisian atheist claimed, "Before the revolution, people didn't see Islam as the problem, but after the revolution, they saw what political Islam was, and what Islam is."[53] This "atheist movement occurred, for the first time, in the history of Egypt, during the time that President Morsi and the Muslim Brotherhood were in power."[54] In 2014, the Egyptian Ministries of Youth and Endowments (Religious Affairs) convened to create a national plan to combat the rise in atheism by educational, religious, and psychological means.[55] By 2017, the parliament and al-Azhar were pushing to criminalize this "malicious call" and "poisonous thinking" amid a moral panic in the society.[56] Yet the trend seemed to continue even though less visibly in the virtual world and underground.

While atheists were defying God, the emergent anarchists defied organized power. The mysterious Black Bloc—with members wearing mask, hood, and black dress—surfaced on the streets in January 2013 to fight President Morsi and his "armed militias"—when nonviolent tactics were seen unable to halt the government's attacks against protesters, especially women.[57] The bloc operated in eight Egyptian cities, in the streets, and across several dozen Facebook pages. Suspicious of any type of systemic power, the bloc opposed all of the postrevolution governments, whether secular or religious. As a novel subculture of lower-class male youth, the bloc arose first to avenge the killing of a comrade known as Jika during the Muhammed Mahmoud battles with the military. But at its core, it expressed an indignant claim by the subaltern youths to public space controlled by the police and the privileged. Resonating with the Brazilian graffiti *pichadores*, it was a defiant proclamation: "I Matter," an expression of rejecting authority in all forms. The bloc reflected the rebellion of the subaltern but globalizing youngsters who had been operating under the heavy-handed command of fathers, elders, teachers, and rulers. Appearing in public and then vanishing mysteriously, just as the mythical image of Robin Hood, the Black Bloc transpired awe, admiration, and a mystical quality. But for the state intelligence, these do-gooder outlaws were a source of deep anxiety, prompting the secret police to infiltrate into their ranks to control them, sometimes going undercover as means to impair the Muslim Brotherhood and its rule. In Tunisia, anarchist practices were taken on more by the feminist group Feminism Attack whose members met in cafés, public places, and on Facebook to campaign and forge an identity. Sympathetic to Femen and close to Beck 7es, Disobedience, and Alberta but critical of the more established feminist organizations like the Tunisian Association of Women Democrats, the group aimed to raise awareness in favor of a culture of self-management and equality of men and women and to oppose "the system and the police generally" and the "extremist political parties which are all in the service of the same system."[58]

Clearly, the revolution redefined and brought to public scrutiny the relationship between religion and politics. The Moroccan scholar Montassir Hamadah observed an undeniable shift in religious discourse—oppositional and governmental Islam or Sufism and Salafism—in the

entire Arab world after 2011.[59] The short two years of religious rule by
the Muslim Brothers in Egypt and el-Nahda in Tunisia caused a remarkable change and misgiving in popular attitudes toward the merit
of religious state. In Tunisia, the Nahda Party responded by renouncing
the idea of a religious state, pursuing instead a post-Islamist line of promoting a secular state and pious society. But in Egypt, the intransigent
Islamism of the Muslim Brothers faced formidable dissent from both
Muslim citizens without, and from scores of prominent members, such
as Abdelmon'em Abulfotouh and Mokhtar Nouh, within the organization. Along with the youth of the Muslim Brothers, they formed a
half-dozen political parties such as Misr al-Qawiyya, Tayyar Masry,
and Hizb al-Adl that espoused a broadly post-Islamist orientation.
Indeed, the end of the 2010s saw a striking shift in the religiosity of
youth and women. Young men and women displayed a deep distrust
of religious authorities.[60] Even those lay "new preachers" (*du'ah al-judud*)
like Amr Khaled who once were household names lost their appeal in
a drastic fashion.[61] The young began to abandon organized religion
and political Islam in favor of either privatized faith, Sufism, or total
disbelief.[62]

The public display of such counternormal ideas—whether deveiling,
alternative sexuality, atheism, or anarchism—exemplified a broader phenomenon typical of most postrevolution moments, a phenomenon
whose enduring manifestations can only be traced in the long run. I
am referring to the revolutionary rupture that gives rise to all sorts of
new acts, ideas, and trends in society, when new perceptions and practices unsettle established hierarchies, when citizens challenge the rulers,
youth the elders, women men, workers bosses, pupils teachers, and
laymen the clergy. These new subjectivities, if sustained, would serve
as a precursor for changes to power relations, social roles, values, and
expectations that altogether coalesce to a social transformation. A quiet
revolution transpires in those layers of society that often remain invisible and undetected.

## THE SOCIAL QUESTION

One salient but suppressed feature of this historic juncture was the rise of the "social question" driven by the poor but dismissed by the political class. Surely, the most visible players on the revolutionary stage— youth and women—caught the most attention and for good reasons. Youth had moved from the "immature and emotional" subjects into the "courageous and responsible" children of the nation. They had taken charge of street politics and stunned the elders, gaining their respect by their dedication, discipline, and wisdom. Self-confident and empowered, the young now began to demand institutional respect and accountability. In the meantime, the uprisings had brought millions of women onto the streets for days and nights during which they marched with men, chanted slogans, formed groups, battled with the police, and helped the injured. Many of them spent nighttimes away from home and family in the streets along with male comrades, often in defiance of their anxious fathers, brothers, and elders. Indeed, women's unprecedented voice and visibility had caused grave anxiety among conservative men and those in power, sparking an alarming wave of sexual harassment aimed at driving women off the public squares. But in response, women forged their most genuine movements from below to campaign for equal rights and criminalization of sexual harassment.[63]

Yet beyond the main squares and at the backstage of the revolution, as I described earlier, the poor were emerging from their neighborhoods, factories, and farms to challenge their bosses, patrons, and politicians in pursuit of dignity and enhanced life chances. The revolution and the collapse of police control had cultivated an extraordinary sense of self-confidence and entitlement in the poor, who took the opportunity to claim inclusion, redistribution, and local self-rule. Hundreds of thousands of low-income people defied the authorities to set up street subsistence work, trade goods, and offer services in strategic spots in the city centers, where economic and administrative disruptions had left millions without work. At the fury of the elites and authorities who described them as an "incurable disease," street vendors moved for the first time to organize themselves in unions and to bring about change in laws regarding urban space.

Land grabbing, informal home construction, and extralegal extension went unheeded. In Egypt, within the first two years after the revolution, hundreds of thousands of hectares of agricultural land turned illegally into plots to construct homes. Thousands of poor families seized half-built apartments, campaigned to acquire state housing, and fought rent increases and gentrification. Scores of small farmers seized farmlands or took legal action to reclaim what they considered their lands but had been taken away by large landowners. Many joined campaigns to demand agrarian reform, land to the tillers, and a supply of irrigation water and fertilizer. In the midst of this, Nubian youth in Egypt rose to claim return to their historic homeland from which their families had been displaced in the 1960s, owing to the construction of the Aswan Dam. Their powerful mobilization compelled the postrevolution constitution in 2014 to guarantee their "right to return," even though the actual practice remained contested.[64] Meanwhile, in Tunisia thousands of landless and small farmers appropriated land to till, while others demanded the return of large plots and state lands that they maintained belonged to their ancestors. Indeed, small farmers questioned the wisdom behind state ownership, asking instead for land reform and redistribution. Farmers in Testour and Medjez el-Bab went ahead "stealing" water and refusing to pay electricity bills to energy companies until the government intervened to waive half of their energy debt. Some farmers insisted on abolishing price liberalization and debt payment, while others staged sit-ins calling for an official increase in the price of their products. In a dramatic move, residents of the dategrowing oasis of Jemna collectively appropriated hundreds of hectares of farmland belonging to Ben Ali's crony investors. The farmers settled in and began to operate, managing their activities through establishing an association. They increased the output substantially and spent the surplus on improving life in the community—better jobs, schools, a marketplace, and health care.

The poor pushed for their claims often through direct actions to acquire what they wanted or otherwise forced the government to address their demands. But when their gains were threatened and demands ignored, they organized a spate of extraordinary street protests, strikes, and acts of civil disobedience. By 2013, Tunisia experienced the highest rate of protests in the world, while Egypt's social protests reached their height in 2012 when basic services such as electricity, running water, or sewage system came in short supply. Indeed, the campaigns such as Ramlet Boulaq in Cairo symbolized poor people's resolve to resist the state's plans to gentrify, demolish informal settlements, and relocate lives, a strategy that assumed greater momentum after the coup in 2013 when President Sisi sought to refigure Cairo in the image of the city-states of the Persian Gulf.

Most of these protests enjoyed a good degree of organization. In fact, building organizations became a common feature of poor people's politics after years of restriction. In Tunisia, small farmers pushed for the democratization of the existing unions or otherwise created new ones. In Egypt, farmers' efforts to organize resulted in four new unions and federations with some 700,000 members. In the cities, plant workers moved to revitalize their unions or establish new independent syndicates. Beyond the workplaces, neighborhoods were also being organized. Most Popular Committees that sprang up during the uprisings turned into neighborhood associations when some normality returned. Informal settlements in Cairo formed their first association of *ashwaiyyat* to work toward securing and upgrading slum communities. They called for the removal of corrupt local officials and the establishment of genuine representation. Residents in popular quarters joined forces to pave roads, create maps, paint buildings, set up libraries, publish local newspapers, or construct crossings and access ramps to connect their secluded neighborhoods to the main highways. These poor residents were vying to practice self-governance but insisted on integrating their communities into the larger urban world.

Such instances of local self-rule and democracy in the rural settings, as reported by the anthropologist Lila Abu-Lughod, was expressed best in an Upper Egypt village where youths took over the responsibility of their local situation immediately after Mubarak's ouster. They formed a Popular Committee, protected their village from "thugs," formed a Facebook page, tackled the distribution crisis (of bread, cooking gas), high price of meat, and garbage collection; and went on organizing literacy programs. The village youths set up a weekly market, helped the displaced people in the community, and fought the corrupt village council. The villagers, especially women and girls, developed a sense that they could now freely talk about and discuss matters of their community as well as engage in local and national politics. They enthusiastically participated in all elections. For the villagers, this represented a new subjectivity, a product and producer of revolutionary movement. "They did not speak of democracy; but in tackling problems directly and personally, they were living democracy."[65]

These radical acts and expectations clearly showed how very different the concerns of the poor were from those of the political class who took the economic status quo of neoliberal market, precarity, and disparity for granted. Even by 2015, Tunisia's president Beji Caid Essebsi would not hesitate to propose an "economic reconciliation" bill that would practically exonerate corrupt officials and businessmen guilty of crimes. But the bill faced a formidable resistance from one of the country's most inspiring grassroots social movements, Maneesh Msameh (I Will Not Forgive). The movement sparked an intense public debate about the meaning of "truth and reconciliation" and the enduring questions of corruption and structural inequality.[66]

Thus, to the dismay of the new elites and authorities, these poor people inadvertently brought the "social question"—poverty, exclusion, and inequality—onto center stage of the revolution. They did so through their acts and claims to challenge property norms, redistribute wealth, and practice local self-rule. Indeed, what the poor in Tunisia and Egypt were proclaiming was akin to what Hannah Arendt might see as the spoiler of "revolution," a fundamentally *political* act of opening space for freedom. In Arendt's view, the desperate poor do not have the luxury of caring for freedom; all they want is freedom from everyday necessities. Furthermore, the zeal, passion, and violence involved in doing good for the poor and in fighting against miserable social conditions would entail coercion, terror, and tyranny, as happened in France, Russia, or Cuba because of their revolutions. Only, the American Revolution was immune from tyranny because it ignored the "social question"—that is, it overlooked the misery of the slaves. Arendt hoped that the question of misery and poverty would be tackled through solidarity and rational democratic deliberation. For her, poverty was not a matter of class exploitation and exclusion but a natural phenomenon that had always existed.[67]

An Arendtian might contend that the revolutions in Tunisia and Egypt entailed pluralism rather than tyranny because the revolutionaries ignored the social question. Even though, as I suggested at the outset, this pluralism had more to do with the refolutionary character of the Arab revolutions, neither American democracy nor those in Tunisia and Egypt properly addressed their enduring social questions.[68] In the United States, the civil rights movement took up racial discrimination and structural inequality, while in Tunisia and Egypt, the poor people themselves moved to claim dignity, redistribution, and local self-rule. Even though Arendt speaks specifically of the "wretched" and "miserable," those who can only think of survival or freedom from basic needs, her overall outlook, nonetheless, does not give due credit to poor people's capacity to engage in politics.[69] Her rigid separation of the social and the political reduces the social, as well as everyday life, merely to apolitical struggles for survival and freedom from material necessities. Whereas everyday life, for Arendt, is the domain where people labor to strive and work to build things, politics lies in action, where humans engage in speech, communication, discussion, and consensus building. Politics is expressed in such activities as townhall meetings, organized civic activism, or mass demonstrations where conscious deliberation for freedom occurs.[70]

But I think that politics can be and at times is woven into the realm of labor, the everyday, and struggle for survival. For instance, the factory councils in the Soviet Republic and the Hungarian Revolution (which Arendt praised for their political novelty), or those in the Iranian revolution of 1979, or plant occupation by the Argentinian workers during the 2001 financial crisis, emerged primarily as a result of the necessity of workers operating the workplaces to keep jobs and earn a living when the bosses had abandoned their enterprises. But such endeavors by workers involved intense deliberation and imagination, affect and action, and new ways of conducting working and communal life. Even if the poor are mostly preoccupied with issues of survival and bettering their lot, their endeavors are often informed by the ethics of dignity, norms of cooperation, and acts of deliberation. What the poor in Tunisia and Egypt were practicing was not all about survival. Rather, they were involved in aspects of what Marina Sitrin, drawing on the experience of Argentina in 2001, calls *horizontalidad,* a form of grassroots initiatives that does not seek state power but building alternative power to the state through new ways of organizing social and economic life at the base of the society.[71] By resorting to self-governance, mutual assistance, solidarity, and local trust—what the sociologist Mohammed Bamyeh calls anarchism—the poor deployed the spontaneity of their daily life to engage in the revolution.[72]

ALTHOUGH THE REVOLUTIONS FAILED to alter significantly the power structure at the top of the society, much happened at the bottom, in the social realm. For some fleeting time, ordinary citizens lived a revolutionary life. Against all odds, they enacted and imagined a new order of things in their immediate environs—in their neighborhoods, in schools and art spaces, on farms, or among their families. At times, their struggles found selective synergy with middle-class activism and organizations. It was here in the social domain that claims for social justice and self-realization assumed tangible meaning, and the revolutionary ethics of solidarity and civic responsibility went hand in hand with insurgent ideas about challenging hierarchies and altering established norms. What transpired was not trivial. It expressed the radical impulse of the social, according to which change assumes a self-perpetuating dynamic. One change may lead to another, setting the structural conditions for others to surface. In this sense and against all odds, revolutions tend often to resist their own end. They propel a new structure of expectations and outlooks that in turn produces the unexpected.

*Chapter 8*

# Whatever Happened to
# the Revolution?

WHAT DO THE NARRATIVES IN THIS BOOK tell us about how
to understand revolution? And how do we account for the place of everyday life and ordinary people in times of extraordinary political upheaval? As discussed earlier, the standard thinking on revolution takes
a political, macrostructural and state-centric approach focusing on the
state, elites, ideologies, and power bloc at the top to determine the success, failure, or the direction of the revolutions. This perspective, as I
have emphasized, is indispensable for any understanding of revolution.
But it is not adequate. We need to know what revolution means at the
base of society, how it plays out in the social realm, in everyday life,
and among the grassroots. This social side of revolution, however, is
overwhelmingly absent from the analytical schema of the prevailing
scholarship on revolutions. Indeed, little effort has been made to bring
the perspectives on everyday life and popular politics into a conversation with contentious politics or revolution in a meaningful analytical
frame. The scholarship on revolution barely speaks of the everyday and
popular politics, and works on the everyday and popular politics seldom
address revolution. I hope that through delving into the everyday of
the Arab Spring, this book is a first step in bridging this analytical
disconnect.

The book has highlighted the place of the popular in the story of the remarkable revolutions that swept across the Arab world in the 2010s. It has described and documented the diverse ways in which the ordinary people, the poor, marginalized youth, women, and social minorities helped bring the revolutions in Tunisia and Egypt to fruition. It has equally tried to show how and to what extent these revolutions changed the lives of the subaltern. Surely, it was youth activists who primarily initiated and pushed forward the uprisings. But as I have emphasized, youth on their own can never generate a revolutionary breakthrough; the breakthrough comes only when the ordinary people get engaged in the extraordinary acts of collective contention, when the elderly, housewives, parents, children, farmers, and working people cease the routine of their lives to come out in the streets and backstreets of contention. By their vast participation in these uprisings, ordinary people pushed the young protagonists' marginal, though spectacular, campaign into the social mainstream. Here, the involvement of women in particular proved instrumental in "feminizing," "civilizing," and thus immunizing the body politic of the uprisings from excessive acts of uncivility and violence.

The very experience of the uprisings by the subaltern—the experience of solidarity, unity, and equality—planted in them the seeds of a new consciousness that grew before long to inform a revolutionary "rupture" or "event." These subaltern subjects then came to imagine a new order of things in their immediate social world, taking practical steps to realize their novel claims. They had shed their fear. Many of them thought and did things that they had never imagined thinking or doing before. Many women, for instance, refused to abide by gender norms; students rejected the archaic education system; and youth moved to "build," to "do something" for their nation. Social minorities claimed recognition, as peasants did land, water, security of tenure, and local natural resources. Workers demanded security of employment and representative organization, and the poor emphasized respect, redistribution, and self-rule. Indeed, the radical claims of the poor for respect, redistribution, and self-rule brought to the fore the overlooked social question of the revolution, the claim for social justice. But to what extent did these struggles result in new policies, practices, and perceptions? How much of the changes and gains made by the subaltern groups persisted over time? And to what degree did the very dynamics of the revolution shape social policies of the postrevolutionary regimes notwithstanding their repressive rule? Even though it may be too early to judge, indications point to a complex outcome.

## ON BALANCE

It is undeniable that the subaltern groups were making their claims within and against a multifaceted web of rigid power structures, entrenched interests, and dominant norms. The nonradical and refolutionary character of these uprisings meant that many of the dominant socioeconomic and political ideas, institutions, and interests associated with the old order persisted. Altogether, they formed a bulwark that selectively ignored or actively defied quests for fundamental reform, policy change, or state support in favor of the subaltern groups. The popular term *deep state* (*al-dawla al-amiqa*) pointed precisely to the persistence of the structures of status quo and counterrevolutionary interests within the postrevolutionary regimes. Without allies in the government or among the political class, the subaltern people had a formidable task at hand. They were confronting powerful forces that ranged from political authorities, economic elites, patriarchal agents, and the security apparatus, to counterrevolutionary operators, foreign states, and even the World Bank and International Monetary Fund.

The Tunisian revolution did succeed in establishing and / or reaffirming electoral democracy, political liberty, freedom of expression and organization, and women's legal rights. These were fundamental achievements on their own that radically distinguished Tunisia from Egypt's path to a police state. Indeed, Tunisian procedural democracy that owed much to the organized labor and unemployed movements seemed to factor in relatively better development indicators. Yet it dangerously fell short of addressing the subaltern claims for inclusion, social justice, and equality. If anything, the contempt of the elites and their media vis-à-vis the subalterns was hardened. Police and media attacks on youths of the poor neighborhoods for disregarding COVID-19 restrictions were only the latest pretext for depicting the subaltern youth as agents of deviance and disorder.[1] A deep disenchantment with the revolution resulted, even a nostalgia for Ben Ali's era. Yet there was also a determination to fight on. In a January 2019 conversation in Tunis, a college graduate taxi driver told me, "There is no revolution. The situation is worse than before [the revolution]." "But we have now freedom to speak out," he went on.

Obstacles against the subaltern radical claims were daunting, particularly in Egypt, where the military coup occasioned the restoration of the counterrevolution. Even capitalist economies conditioned many of their educated middle-class poor into a cruel hope, not the kind of hope that energizes the desperate to move forward but one that consumes their energy by driving them into the endless labyrinths of start-ups, self-help, call centers, training, and retraining in hopes that one day they will make it.[2] The new elites and their allies in both countries fought hard to retrieve what the subaltern struggles had won in the revolution—sense of citizenship, land, housing, opportunities, independent organizations, and a culture of social movement. Nevertheless, a good number of gains made by the subaltern struggles continued to hold both in Egypt and especially Tunisia, where democratic polity allowed more room for popular resistance. While by the end of the 2010s, Egyptian activists fell victim to the severe repression of the regime, in Tunisia a youth-led citizen movement like Hasebhom (Hold Them to Account) backed by rights organizations could still thwart a government draft law that would give leeway to security officers in the use of lethal force.[3]

Popular campaigns and direct actions largely failed to bring fundamental policy changes because the subaltern groups mostly lacked support among the new postrevolutionary authorities. But a significant number of them did, because even the autocratic counter-revolutionary regimes could not escape from the effects and expectations that the revolutions had unleashed. For instance, new policies came to life with respect to illegal appropriation by the poor of land, housing, and urban services. New legislations were introduced in favor of women's personal status and against sexual violence. Others pertained to the "usage of public space in cities" pushed by the union of street vendors in Egypt, or democratic governance in universities and solidarity economy in Tunisia.[4] The Tunisian government was pushed to enhance development initiatives in favor of low-income women in provinces such as Safaqs, Tourz, and Tunis in the fields of employment and traditional enterprises.[5] By 2015, two dozen centers for women's development had been set up to promote the policy. Such efforts culminated in 2020 with a parliamentary bill to establish a solidarity economy. In Egypt, a 2017 law aimed, though with no clear guidelines, to legalize adverse possessions on state lands. Up until March 2020, some 11,000 out of 300,000 applications had been approved. Meanwhile, many informal buildings gained access to proper electricity, even though the coded meters without names meant to deny them of legal recognition.[6] Another law in 2019 moved to recognize informal housing both on state and private lands.[7] While many squatters of the state housing were evicted, others (e.g., in Madinat al-Nahda and Qattamiyya) were recognized or received alternative housing.[8]

Even in cases where no supportive legislations resulted, the actual gains from the popular direct actions, nevertheless, remained. These included most of the land encroachments, unlawful home constructions, and housing allocations, not to mention the upgraded neighborhoods. Many of the Popular Committees in Egypt continued their work variably even after the 2013 coup when severe restrictions on independent civil associations mounted. A number of small farmers retained the lands they had occupied, but others succumbed to lawsuits by the owners, despite that many owners also failed "to return to the lands because they had lost their power in the villages."[9] In Tunisia, the self-managed Jemna oasis, despite numerous legal contests, continued to operate. After years of contestation, the government eventually agreed to the self-management of the palm plantation by the local people but retained ownership of the land.

The Jemna experiment had already set a precursor for other communities to continue a few years later to reclaim land, carry out occupation, and demand control of local natural resources such as water, minerals, and oil.[10] Thus, in March 2017, the El-Kamour community in south Tatouine would launch a series of remarkable protests to demand shares of local resources, oil, jobs, and infrastructure. Their radical repertoires, occupying the oil pumping station, forced the reluctant government to agree on several reforms including creating jobs and an allocated budget for regional development. Enraged by the authorities' inaction, the locals rose up again in May through November 2020 to undertake general strikes, blocking roads and impairing the production and transfer of oil. This time, they compelled the government to commit to both the earlier demands and new ones including job creation, earmarked development budget, investment, and credit for over 1,000 projects to be delivered before the end of 2020.[11] This followed the parliament to adopt in June 2020 a bill to set up a solidarity economy. El-Kamour signaled the radical spirit of the subalterns in keeping the revolution alive. Their unparalleled social protests—amounting to 10,452 in 2017 (up from 4,416 in 2015)—were to ensure that the social questions of poverty and inequality, indeed a new social contract, remained on the revolutionary agenda.[12]

Then there were some enduring changes in social norms and values. These included the revolutionary practices of solidarity and civic responsibility on the one hand and defiance of some entrenched hierarchies on the other hand. Thus, six years after the revolution in Tunisia, ordinary citizens would still take the initiative to clean the streets after violent demonstrations (in Kasserine), bringing order to the sidewalks and direction to the chaotic traffic. Such collective acts of citizenship by the ordinary people were likely to be the legacy of the earlier revolutionary impetus—those liminal moments of intense civility and self-rule.[13] At the same time, many citizens, youth and women in particular, continued to challenge conservative gender norms, cultural standards, religious orthodoxy, and hierarchical power. The immersion of religious and moral authorities, whether sheikhs, Salafis, Muslim Brothers, or al-Nahda, into the dirty businesses of realpolitik had by 2019 driven many youths away from ritualistic religion and political Islam toward either adopting privatized faith and Sufism or abandoning religion altogether.[14] Given the gender prejudice of orthodox religion, more women than men experienced such a shift in religious sensibilities. Broadly speaking, there was a sense that women spoke out about what they thought or felt. In Egypt, more and more of them would now curse, smoke shisha, ride bikes, appear in secular clothing, or speak out about male sexual harassment in public. The trends of Muslim women taking off the hijab, or unmarried women leaving home to live on their own, did not appear to diminish.[15] If anything, the desire for self-assertion and autonomy, albeit with associated tensions, seemed to amplify. Women-initiated divorces, or *khul‘*, for instance, jumped from 66 percent in 2010 to 88.4 percent in 2019.[16] And in a significant shift, the hijab began to be disassociated from Islamic virtues of female modesty and piety and linked instead to extremism and lower-class culture. In the end, the astonishing participation of women in the second wave of the Arab uprisings in Sudan, Algeria, Iraq, and Lebanon in 2019 indicated that the legacy of public presence by the Arab women persisted in earnest.

Perhaps the most lasting legacy of the revolutions was the change in popular subjectivities stemming from the very experience of revolt, the brief moments of unity, equality, and altruism, the loss of fear, and the feeling of freedom. The memory of these episodes and the social ethics they occasioned (commitment, cooperation, self-rule) can serve as an ideational basis for a different organization of social life when the opportunity arises and new possibilities open up, as we witnessed in the experiences of the French or Iranian revolutions.[17] By the end of the decade, over 58 percent of Arabs would express positive views on the uprisings despite some of the horrific consequences seen in Syria, Libya, Yemen, or Egypt. The post-Islamist spirit of the revolutions continued to hold. According to Arab Barometer polls in 2018–2019, fewer than 20 percent of people in Tunisia and Egypt (as well as Algeria, Jordan, Iraq, and Libya) trusted Islamist parties. Over 76 percent would favor democracy and civil state.[18] On the tenth anniversary of the Egyptian revolution, an activist would insist that the "revolution will remain the most beautiful thing that happened to me." "I am the son of the revolution and was raised by it," he went on. "Every event of it, no matter how small, has left a mark and impact on me."[19]

The chronicle of the Arab Spring, then, is not simply doom, gloom, and failure, but also the rise of a new imaginary and expectations as well as some social and personal transformation, which the new rulers could not simply overlook. Even the political reforms pushed by King Mohammad VI in Morocco or Mohammed bin Salman's overhaul of the cultural, artistic, and religious fields in Saudi Arabia cannot be disentangled from the political course that the Arab revolutions set, let alone President Sisi's modernization of education, energy, and infrastructure despite his authoritarian rule.[20] Some observers distinguish these top-down and authoritarian reforms as the real Arab revolution that stands against the "miserable failure" of the "bottom-up" Arab spring.[21] But in truth these top-down modernization drives are some of the consequences of those very bottom-up revolutions. These top-down initiatives represent a kind of Gramscian passive revolutions where the elites, wounded and worried about popular revolts, spearhead reforms primarily to regain or retain hegemony. They project revolutionary pretensions while wishing to break away from revolution. Their initiatives are shaped by the force and fury of the very bottom-up revolutions which they strive to tarnish and transcend.

## CHALLENGES AHEAD

After years of absence following the cold war, "revolution" seems to be back on the political stage, not only in the Arab region but throughout the world. The past decade has seen an unparalleled number of mass protests escalating annually by an average of 11.5 percent from 2009 to 2019.[22] One can hardly keep up with the news of the nationwide protests stretching from Latin America (Haiti, Chile, Mexico, Brazil, Colombia) to Africa (Gambia, Ethiopia, Kenya, South Africa, and Nigeria); from the Arab world and Iran to Belarus, Ukraine, and Spain; and from Hong Kong and India to the global movements inspired by Black Lives Matter in 2020.

Some have characterized these examples of political unrest in terms of the intra-elite war for wealth and status. Simply, there is an overproduction of educated elites who fight for few positions, the argument goes. The Occupy Wall Street or the right-wing nationalist movement galvanized by Donald Trump represent such intra-elite conflicts that can possibly lead to social breakdown.[23] Those on the left, for instance the Marxist journal *Endnotes*, while enthusiastic about these global revolts, express doubts about their revolutionary potential. If anything, they argue, these protests voice "revolutionaries without revolution." Behaving like nonmovements, these global protests embody fragmented claims and collectives with a mix of basic and liberal demands, little strategy, and no ideology. All they can do, the argument goes, is to render their societies ungovernable.[24]

Taking a global perspective, I contend, these movements seem to result not simply from a war between elites but are related to three underlying roots: first, political exclusion and electoral fraud; second, the neoliberal economies of exclusion resulting in heightened precarity and disparity; and third, the new digital technologies that facilitate mobilization on unprecedented scale. An important actor in these movements is the segment of educated middle classes who under the current economy of exclusion are losing their old privileges and becoming the precariat. But placing all of these movements—from the Arab uprisings to Occupy Wall Street, the *gilets jaunes*, and FeesMustFall— under the same rubric obscures the significant differences between these movements' dynamics and outcomes. The protests that emerged under democracies, such as those in France, Chile, South Africa, or the United States, took the repertoire of the Occupy movement in that they brought together fragmented claims and collectives into a loose network of dissenting constituencies. But those that occurred under and against the autocratic Arab regimes assumed the repertoire of uprising, calling for regime change. I characterized these repertoires in the Arab Spring as refolutions. They were marked by a disjunction between the radical claims of the subaltern and the nonradical visions of the political class. These refolutions, as we saw earlier, could address neither the *political question* of these episodes—the question of the state and its transformation—nor, for that matter, their *social question* of poverty, exclusion, and inequality. It was left to the subaltern groups to push for radical change in both domains.

Once again, the ordinary people—the poor, peasants, workers, middle-class poor, as well as the racial minorities and politically marginalized—have forged remarkable global upheavals. They have created a revolutionary mood and brought hope for the subalterns to imagine different futures. But the challenges they face remain formidable. It is certainly true that the increasingly educated classes are experiencing precarity and proletarianization, turning into the middle-class poor, the indignant potential revolutionary that played a crucial role in the Arab revolutions. Moreover, today's masses are different from *les misérables* of Victor Hugo that Arendt might have had in mind. Not simply aloof, illiterate, isolated, and wretched, they are equipped with extended networks, social awareness, college-educated children, and a sense of citizenship. But the chief question in this new revolutionary era is how these subaltern subjects and their radical claims can break through the structures of entrenched interests, power, and privilege. Here, I am not just referring to the old and new elites, big business, large landholders, military chiefs, intelligence captains, cultural patriarchs, media tycoons, or religious-moral authorities and their foot soldiers. The international and regional power blocs also exert a debilitating counterrevolutionary force. The Arab revolutions were particularly subject to the dictates of geopolitics in the Middle East. Interventions by Iran, Israel, Turkey, Saudi Arabia, the United States, Qatar, the United Arab Emirates (UAE), Egypt, and ISIS turned the revolutions in Syria, Yemen, and Libya into theaters of war to settle geopolitical scores.[25] Deeply apprehensive of revolutions both domestically and in their backyards, Saudi Arabia and the UAE in particular strived to subvert any democratic openings in the neighborhood through a strategy of destabilization and economic leverage. Riyadh supported Salafi extremists, provoked sectarian discord, backed an early version of ISIS, and used financial blackmail to dissuade Egypt's postcoup government from any reconciliation with the opposition.[26] Thus, as much as examining how the revolutionary movements operate, we need to understand how the counterrevolution works. I am not speaking simply of the authoritarian regimes and their institutional power but more their counterrevolutionary strategies and fragilities—their modes of surveillance, ideological operations, domestic bases, and international grids.

There is currently a clear asymmetry of knowledge / power between the movements and countermovements, revolutionaries and counterrevolutionaries, citizens and the states. While movements have become increasingly open and transparent, the states have grown more enigmatic and watchful. In the current surveillance society, states and their economic allies know far more about how the movements operate than movements know about how the states, corporations, and their power bloc think.[27] This might be expected as a natural order of modern politics, but it is important to bear in mind that in the past, revolutionaries often operated underground with elaborate systems of concealed communication and networking to protect information about how their agents think. In the Algerian anti-colonial revolution, for example, the French colonists had to use horrific torture to extract information from the revolutionaries about their ideas and strategies. But today, all such information is brandished on the movements' websites or social media communications. Opacity lies at the heart of the power of the subaltern (non)movements. This asymmetry of knowledge remains a critical disadvantage for the revolutionary movements of today.

Of course, open movements have the advantage of overcoming the perils of closed vanguardism and succeed in drawing a staggering number of participants from all walks of life. Popular uprisings of immense constituencies are potentially able to generate a revolutionary rupture, an event, by sheer people's power, despite and next to the web of power and privilege and forces of coercion. The new radical ideas and practices produced in the event, in favor of dignity, equality, inclusion, and recognition, can produce a glitch in the operating machine of the powerful and privileged. More significantly, they may form a new subjectivity and serve, moreover, as a moral resource for a deeper change yet to come. Nevertheless, they still leave the *political question*—that is, a meaningful overhaul of the state institutions, ideology, and power block—unresolved. This crucial problem in current revolutionary movements remains to be tackled.

It is then fair to wonder why people continue to embrace revolutions despite their associated uncertainty, disruption, and even terror. Why is it that a poor driver, a father of four children living in a Cairo's *ashwaiyyat*, would tell me at the height of state repression in 2015 that "now there is no revolution anymore; but a second revolution will come soon, the revolution of the hungry [*al-thawra al-jiya*]."[28] Why is it that despite the destructive repertoire of the Syrian revolution, which the rational choice argument would deem as the basis for avoiding uprisings elsewhere, mass revolts erupted not just in Algeria and Sudan but also in Lebanon, Iraq, and Iran almost simultaneously? Because, as I have suggested, people rarely decide to make revolutions willingly and voluntarily; rather, they are conditioned and compelled by circumstance to do so.[29] If there is a truism in this painful dialectic, then it is only plausible to embrace and extend revolutions when they actually transpire. This book has described what can emerge even in those "failed" revolutions, marked most immediately by the mystical moments of people actually experiencing freedom, unity, equality, when they become sovereign subjects, when they reclaim and realize their humanity. People embrace revolutions not only because there is much more to these historical events than simply turmoil and terror but also because, as the great historian E. P. Thompson put it, "stability, no less than revolution, may have its own kind of terror."[30]

# Notes

## 1. EVERYDAY LIFE AND REVOLUTION

1. Max de Haldevang, "Coronavirus Has Crippled Global Protest Movements," *Quartz*, April 1, 2020, https://qz.com/1828468/coronavirus-has-crippled-global-protest-movements/.

2. For a fine discussion of such conventional wisdom among social scientists, see Gregory Gause, "Why Middle East Studies Missed the Arab Spring: The Myth of Authoritarian Stability," *Foreign Affairs*, July–August 2011.

3. Yazid Sayigh, "Missed Opportunity: The Politics of Police Reform in Egypt and Tunisia," Beirut, Carnegie Middle East Center, March 2015.

4. Tunisian sociologist Abdelwahab Ben Hadiedh, Tunis, June 2017.

5. Ayad Ben Ashour, *Tunis: Thawra fi Bilad al-Islam* (Tunis: Ma'had Tunis Lil-Tarjama, 2018). Ben Ashour, who presided over the Supreme Commission for the Realization of the Objectives of the Revolution, suggests that the Tunisia revolution was "historically unprecedented," the like of which never happened before, and "from this comes its challenges and problems" (11).

6. Hannah Arendt, "The Lecture: Thoughts on Poverty, Misery and the Great Revolutions of History," *New England Review*, June 2017, 12, https://lithub.com/never-before-published-hannah-arendt-on-what-freedom-and-revolution-really-mean/.

7. Here, I focus primarily on Tunisia, Egypt, and Yemen. I do not speak of Syria and Libya where the extraordinary intervention of foreign forces radically altered the nonviolent trajectories of these revolutions into devastating armed

conflicts. See Assad Achi, "How the Syrian Civil Society Lost Its Independence in a War of Conflicting Agendas," in *Contentious Politics in the Syrian Conflict*, ed. Maha Yahya (Beirut: Carnegie Middle East Center, May 15, 2020).

8. In a different and important take, Hamid Dabashi welcomes the exhaustion of these three ideologies (anti-colonial nationalism, Marxism-Leninism [or third world socialism], and Islamism) as "the end of post-colonialism." For not only did they serve as ideological cushions for the postcolonial repressive regimes but also because their exhaustion made possible for the Arab Spring to pursue a postideological posture; Hamid Dabashi, *The Arab Spring: The End of Post-Colonialism* (London: Zed Books, 2012).

9. In an interesting international perspective, Daniel Ritter goes as far as attributing the outbreak of the Arab revolutions to the international regimes of human rights after the 1975 Helsinki accords. "Commitment" to human rights placed the Western-aligned autocratic regimes in an "iron cage of liberalism" while empowering the opposition to mobilize for democracy through "unarmed" revolutions; Daniel Ritter, *The Iron Cage of Liberalism: International Politics and Unarmed Revolutions in the Middle East and North Africa* (Oxford: Oxford University Press, 2015).

10. Fawwaz Traboulsi, *Thawrat Bila Thuwwar* [Revolutions without revolutionaries] (Beirut: Riyad El-Rayyes Books, 2014).

11. Yassin al-Hajj Saleh, "An al-Siyasah wal-Hubb wal-Thawra" [On politics, love, and revolution], https://www.ahewar.org/debat/show.art.asp?aid=664766. Given that revolutions are essentially relational (i.e., what happens in one revolution may change things in the next one), this model of "refolution" is subject to change. Algerian revolutionaries already declared in 2019 that "Algeria is not from the family of the Arab spring," indicating how they wish to avoid the shortcomings of the Arab Spring (Panel discussion on the Algerian Revolution, MESA, November 15, 2019, New Orleans). In the same fashion, the Sudanese revolutionaries in the late 2010s attempted to adopt more organized and systematic mobilization, a process in which both the Sudanese Professional Association and the Communist Party played a significant part.

12. Alain Badiou, *The Rebirth of History: Times of Riots and Uprisings* (London: Verso, 2012).

13. For the concept of "lifeworld" see Jurgen Habermas, *The Theory of Communicative Action* (2 vols.; Boston: Beacon Press, 1987) where he counterposes "lifeworld" against the standardizing political or economic "systems."

14. George Lawson, *Anatomies of Revolution* (Cambridge: Cambridge University Press, 2019).

15. Lawson, *Anatomies of Revolution*.

16. Maria Stephans and Erica Chenoweth, *Why Civil Resistance Works* (New York: Columbia University Press, 2011).

17. Sharon Nepstad, *Non-Violent Revolutions: Civil Resistance in the Late 20th Century* (Oxford: Oxford University Press, 2011).

18. Karl Marx and Friedrich Engels, *The Communist Manifesto* (New York: International Publishers Co., 2014); Eric Hobsbawm, *How to Change the World: Reflections on Marx and Marxism* (New Haven, CT: Yale University Press, 2011).

19. Rosa Luxemburg, *Reform or Revolution* (Atlanta, GA: Pathfinder, 1973); V. I. Lenin, *What Is to Be Done?*, trans. Joe Fineberg and George Hanna (London: Penguin, 1990).

20. Lise Vogel, *Marxism and the Oppression of Women* (New Brunswick, NJ: Rutgers University Press, 1983); Alexandra Kollontai, "Communism and the Family," in *Selected Writings of Alexandra Kollontai* (London: Allison & Busby, 1977), https://www.marxists.org/archive/kollonta/1920/communism-family.htm.

21. Ernesto Che Guevara, *Guerrilla Warfare* (New York: Skyhouse Publishing, 2013); Ernesto Che Guevara, "Socialism and Man," in *Che Guevara Reader: Writings on Politics and Revolution*, ed. David Deutschmann and Maria del Carmen Ariet (Melbourne: Ocean Press, 2013).

22. Antonio Gramsci, *The Antonio Gramsci Reader: Selected Writings 1916–1935* (New York: New York University Press, 2000), 210.

23. See Asef Bayat, "Reminiscing Gramsci," *Jadaliyya*, June 18, 2017.

24. For a very useful critical overview of this genre, see Anna Johansson and Stellan Vinthagen, *Conceptualizing Everyday Resistance: A Transdisciplinary Approach* (Abingdon, UK: Routledge, 2020). The *Journal of Resistance Studies* carries current research and debate.

25. Michel de Certeau, *The Practice of Everyday Life* (Berkeley: University of California Press, 2011).

26. Asef Bayat, "Reclaiming Youthfulness," in *Being Young and Muslim: New Cultural Politics in the Global South and North*, ed. Linda Herrera and Asef Bayat (New York: Oxford University Press, 2010).

27. James Scott, *Weapons of the Weak: Everyday Forms of Peasant Resistance* (New Haven, CT: Yale University Press, 1985).

28. Matthew Gutmann, "The Ritual of Resistance: A Critique of the Theory of Everyday Forms of Resistance," *Latin American Perspectives* 20, no. 2 (Spring 1993).

29. Asef Bayat, "From 'Dangerous Classes' to Quiet Rebels: Politics of the Urban Subaltern in the Global South," *International Sociology*, September 1, 2000.

30. James Scott, "Everyday Forms of Resistance," *Copenhagen Journal of Asian Studies* 4, no. 1 (2008): 57–58; see also Johansson and Vinthagen, *Conceptualizing Everyday Resistance.*

31. See an interesting conceptual survey of "resistance" in Mona Lilja and Stellan Vinthagen, "Dispersed Resistance: Unpacking the Spectrum and Properties of Glaring and Everyday Resistance," *Journal of Political Power* 11, no. 2 (2018), 14: "The relationship between resistance and social change is fundamentally unclear."

32. We perhaps need an anthropology of revolution, which we really do not have (as testified by Biorn Thomassen, "Notes towards an Anthropology of Political Revolutions," *Comparative Studies in Society and History* 54, no. 3 [July 2012]: 679–706) except perhaps for dispersed ethnographies on different aspects of revolutions. Even useful, it does not offer a comprehensive perspective. Social history of revolutions may perhaps be a more productive field for such studies. We have valuable studies on French or Russian revolutions such as those by Jean Hunt on culture in France or Sheila Fitzpatrick on Russia. I believe that a historical sociology approach may yield the best results in conjoining history and theory.

33. Jeff Goodwin, "Why We Were Surprised (Again) by the Arab Spring," *Swiss Political Science Review* 17, no. 4 (2011): 452–456.

34. Timur Kuran, "The East European Revolution of 1989: Is It Surprising That We Were Surprised?" *American Economic Review* 81, no. 2 (1991): 121–125.

35. Charles Kurzman, *The Unthinkable Revolution in Iran* (Cambridge, MA: Harvard University Press, 2004).

36. Carlton Coon, *Caravan: The Story of the Middle East* (New York: Holt, 1958). See also how an observer describes the Arab revolutions as more about "neo-traditionalist politics" than about "democracy and civil rights per se"; in other words, they were about reviving old cultures, religious values, sectarian or tribal loyalties; see Asher Susser, "The Contemporary Middle East: The Resistance of Traditional Society," *Tel Aviv Notes* 8, no. 7 (2014).

37. "When we use such complex words as revolution, they have different resonance in Islamic society against the background of Islamic history and tradition from which they have in the West," argued Bernard Lewis during the well-known MESA debate with Edward Said. "In the Western world the association of revolution are the major revolutions of the modern history—American, French or Russian. In the Islamic world, there is a quite different revolutionary tradition nurtured on different scriptures and classics alluding to different history. What

matters, the evocative symbol is not storming the Bastille but the battle of Karbala." Bernard Lewis, "The MESA Debate: 'The Scholars, the Media, and the Middle East,'" November 22, 1986, Boston. Needless to say, probably none of those millions who battled in the streets of the Arab revolutions did invoke the Battle of Karbala nor, for that matter, any religious symbols or slogans. They were thinking of different concerns as this book will show.

38. Reductionist Marxist approach was represented most pervasively by the variety of Marxist-Leninist groups, often pro-Soviet or Trotskyists, that operated in the Middle Eastern countries before the collapse of the USSR.

39. Hisham Sharabi, *Neopatriarchy: A Theory of Distorted Change in Arab Society* (Oxford: Oxford University Press, 1992).

40. Tribal links and solidarities in Tunisia are highlighted by Nick Hopkins, who argues that the state basically ignored them; see Nicholas Hopkins, "Water-User Associations in Rural Central Tunisia," in *Anthropology and Development in North Africa and the Middle East*, ed. Muneera Salem-Murdock and Michael M. Horowitz (Boulder, CO: Westview, 1990), 74–94.

41. Hua Hsu, "What Jacques Derrida Understood about Friendship," *New Yorker*, December 3, 2019.

42. Jodi Dean, public lecture on "Comrade," University of Illinois, Urbana-Champaign, October 9, 2017. See also her book *Comrade: An Essay on Political Belonging* (London: Verso, 2019).

43. Jacques Derrida, *The Politics of Friendship* (London: Verso, 2006).

44. For details of how friendship and close circles contributed to youth political activism in prerevolution Egypt, see Henri Onodera, "Friendship and Youth Activism in Pre-revolutionary Egypt," in *What Politics? Youth and Political Engagement in Africa*, ed. E. Oinas, H. Onodera, and L. Suurpää (Leiden: Brill, 2018), 42–57.

45. Robert Springborg, "Professional Syndicates in Egyptian Politics, 1952–1970," *International Journal of Middle East Studies* 9, no. 3 (1978).

46. Friedrich-Ebert-Stiftung, *Arab Youth Survey 2016*, conducted among 9,000 young people (between sixteen and thirty) in Bahrain, Egypt, Jordan, Lebanon, Morocco, Palestine, Tunisia, Yemen, and Syrian refugees.

47. See, for instance, Lisa Wedeen, "The Politics of Deliberation: Qat Chews as Public Spheres in Yemen," *Public Culture*, December 2007.

48. See Taghi Azad Armaki, *Patouq and the Iranian Modernity* (Tehran: Avay-e Nour, 2011)). Robert Putnam, "Bowling Alone: America's Declining Social Capital," *Journal of Democracy* 6, no. 1 (1995).

49. Amelie Le Renard, *Society of Young Women: Opportunities of Power, Place, and Reform in Saudi Arabia* (Palo Alto, CA: Stanford University Press, 2014).

50. Conversation with Abdelrahman, Cairo, June 2013.

51. Pascale Menoret, "Leaving Islamic Activism Behind: Ambiguous Disengagement in Saudi Arabia," in *Social Movements, Mobilization, and Contestation in the Middle East*, ed. Joel Beinin and Frédéric Vairel (Palo Alto, CA: Stanford University Press, 2013), 82.

52. The concept of counterpublics comes from Nancy Fraser, "Rethinking the Public Sphere: A Contribution to the Critique of Actually Existing Democracy," *Social Text*, nos. 25–26 (1990): 67.

53. For details on the concept and practices of nonmovements, see Asef Bayat, *Life as Politics: How Ordinary People Change the Middle East* (Palo Alto, CA: Stanford University Press, 2013).

54. See Linda Herrera and Asef Bayat, eds., *Being Young and Muslim: Cultural Politics in the Global South and North* (New York: Oxford University Press, 2013) for a documentation of some of these practices.

55. Scott, "Everyday Forms of Resistance," 54–55.

56. I am grateful to David Dyzenhaus, professor of philosophy at the University of Toronto, for bringing these remarks to my attention following my lecture on "Nonmovements" at Wissenschaftskolleg in Berlin; February 27, 2017.

57. Katrin Klingan, curator of Berlin House of World Culture; email correspondence about her articulation of my notion of nonmovements, September 30, 2012.

58. Václav Havel, *The Power of the Powerless: Citizens against the State in Central Eastern Europe* (Abingdon, UK: Routledge, 1985).

59. Alexei Yurchak, *Everything Was Forever, until It Was No More* (Princeton, NJ: Princeton University Press, 2006).

60. See Beinin and Vairel, *Social Movements*; Rabab El-Mahdi, ed., *Egypt: The Moment of Change* (London: Zed Books, 2009); Bayat, *Revolution without Revolutionaries*.

61. Antonio Gramsci, *Selections from the Prison Notebooks of Antonio Gramsci*, ed. and trans. Quintin Hoare and Geoffrey Nowell Smith (London: Lawrence and Wishart, 1971), 326–327, 333.

62. This might explain the quandaries such as that of the renown Iranian novelist Gholam-Hussein Saedi, who wondered how the Iranians who in their millions voted for the shah's single Rastakhiz Party would not long after rise

against him in the revolution of 1979; see Habib Lajevardi, *Interview with Gholam-Gussein Saedi,* Oral History Project, Harvard University, 1984.

63. See for details, Asef Bayat, "Radical Religion and the Habitus of the Dispossessed: Does Islamic Militancy Have an Urban Ecology?" *International Journal of Urban and Regional Research* 31, no. 3 (2007).

64. https://mideastsoccer.blogspot.com/2018/06/morocco-may-have-lost -world-cup-but.html.

65. Stephen Clarke, "The Panopticon of the Public Protest: Technology and Surveillance," *Res Cogitans* 4, no. 1 (2013): 173–180; Robert Pelzer, "Policing of Terrorism Using Data from Social Media," *European Journal for Security Research* 3, no. 2 (2018): 163–179. The organization of the protests in January 25, 2011 in Egypt was successful largely because some eight groups reportedly met in secret to coordinate and discuss how to proceed with the protests. In doing so, the activists denied the state of accessing their mobilization tactics. At the same time, activists also managed to acquire information about the police countertactics that a retired police officer had offered to the opposition, advising them where and when to demonstrate, where to avoid, and such like. This knowledge proved to be instrumental in the success of the protests.

66. For instance, Beinin and Vairel, *Social Movements;* Habib Ayeb, "Social and Political Geography of Tunisian Revolution," *Review of African Political Economy* 38, no. 129 (2011); Maha Abdelrahman, *Egypt's Long Revolution: Protest Movements and Uprisings* (Abingdon, UK: Routledge, 2014); Bahgat Korany and Rabab El-Mahdi, eds., *Arab Spring in Egypt: Revolution and Beyond* (Cairo: American University in Cairo Press, 2014).

67. Gustav Le Bon, *The Crowd: A Study of the Popular Mind* (New York: Cosimo, 2006).

68. Alain Badiou, *The Rebirth of History: Times of Riots and Uprisings* (London: Verso, 2012), 108–109.

69. Ayman El-Desouky, "The Amāra on the Square: Connective Agency and the Aesthetics of the Egyptian Revolution," *Contention* 5, no. 1 (2017): 51–83.

70. Manuel Castells, *The Network Society,* 2nd ed. (Oxford: Blackwell, 2009).

71. W. Lance Bennett and Alexandra Segerberg, "The Logic of Connective Action," *Information, Communication and Society* 15, no. 5 (2012): 739–768.

72. Zeynep Tufekci, *Twitter and Teargas: The Power and Fragility of Networked Protest* (New Haven, CT: Yale University Press, 2017).

73. Ekaterina Stepanova, "The Role of Information Communication Technologies in the 'Arab Spring,'" PONARS Eurasia Policy Memo no. 159, May 2011, http://pircenter.org/kosdata/page_doc/p2594_2.pdf; see also Carrington Malin, "Middle East and North Africa Facebook Demographics," Spot on Public Relations, May 2010, https://www.spotonpr.com/wp-content/uploads/2017/10/FacebookMENA_24May10.pdf.

74. For a perceptive critique of those who exaggerate the digital at the expense of the physical in Egypt, see Hossam El-Hamalawy, "Al-Internet wa al-Thawra," *Al-Eshtiraki*, January 24, 2021, https://revsoc.me/politics/43522/?fbclid=IwAR2CEL9Mf5DQG—IRURiaeTQCl4vIxS6P8i4gi7eFaqnA5VnOdkU1f-GjX6U.

75. John Thompson, "The New Visibility," *Theory, Culture and Society* 22, no. 6 (2005).

76. Asef Bayat, "The Fire That Fueled the Iran Protests," *The Atlantic*, January 27, 2018, https://www.theatlantic.com/international/archive/2018/01/iran-protest-mashaad-green-class-labor-economy/551690/.

77. Hannah Arendt, "The Social Question," in *On Revolution* (London: Penguin, 1963).

78. See the insightful essay by Mohammed Bamyeh, "Anarchist Method, Liberal Intention, Authoritarian Lesson: The Arab Spring between Three Enlightenments," *Constellations* 20, no. 2 (2013): 188.

79. Lawson, *Anatomies of Revolution*, 16.

## 2. THE SUBALTERN UNDER AUTOCRACIES

1. https://freedomhouse.org/regions/middle-east-and-north-africa

2. United Nations Development Programme, *Arab Human Development Report 2002* (New York: UNDP, 2002).

3. Adam Hanieh, *Lineages of Revolt: Issues of Contemporary Capitalism in the Middle East* (Chicago: Haymarket Books, 2013), 145–149.

4. Habitat, *The State of the Arab Countries* (Nairobi: Habitat, 2012).

5. Conversation with Hamza Meddeb, June 2017, Tunis.

6. Conversation with Hamza Meddeb, June 2017, Tunis.

7. Beatrice Hibou, *The Force of Obedience: Political Economy of Repression in Tunisia* (London: Polity, 2011).

8. Hazem Qandil, *Soldiers, Spies, Statemen: Egypt's Road to Revolt* (London: Verso, 2012).

9. According to Wealth X report.

10. Eberhard Kienle, *A Grand Delusion: Democracy and Economic Reform in Egypt* (London: I. B. Tauris, 2001).

11. Eric Denis, "Demographic Surprises Foreshadow Change in Neoliberal Egypt," *Middle East Report*, no. 246.

12. Egypt remains well below "water poverty line" of 1,000 cubic meter per person per year. See Karen Piper, "Egypt's Arab Spring: A Revolution of the Thirsty," *designobserver.com*, accessed August 24, 2012.

13. According to Egyptian National Research Center, reported in Mohamed el-Dahshan, "Developing World's Megacities Struggle to Consume Water," *al-Masry al-Youm*, September 12, 2010.

14. See also Shahira Amin, "Egypt's Farmers Desperate for Clean Water," CNN, November 10, 2010.

15. *Al-Dastour*, December 28, 2009, 14.

16. According to the Institute for International Urban Development, Harvard University, http://i2ud.org/2012/12/4210/.

17. Habib Ayeb, "Rural Revolution in Tunisia," unpublished paper, 2014.

18. Kora Andrieu, Wahid Ferchichi, Simon Robins, Ahmed Aloui, and Hajer Ben Hamza, *The Victim Zone and Collective Reparation in Tunisia: Ain Drahem and Sidi Makhlouf* (New York: Transitional Justice Barometer, May 2016), 9.

19. In 2010, Tunisia had a "high" Human Development Index (0.714), according to the UNDP data, compared to Egypt's "medium" rate of 0.671.

20. Karim Trabelssi, *Current State of the Informal Economy in Tunisia as Seen through Its Stakeholders: Facts and Alternatives* (Tunis: UGTT, 2014).

21. Cited in Larry Michalak, "Merchants at the Margins: The Politics of Petty-Commerce in Tunisia," unpublished paper, August 2014, p. 2.

22. Michalak, "Merchants at the Margins," 3.

23. Denis, "Demographic Surprises."

24. See Asef Bayat, "Cairo Poor: Dilemmas of Survival and Solidarity," *Middle East Report*, December 1, 1997.

25. See report by Dirk Wanrooij, "The Egyptian Uprising: Imbaba" (master's thesis, University of Amsterdam, 2011), 88.

26. See excellent study by Salwa Ismail, "The Egyptian Revolution against the Police," *Social Research* 79, no. 2 (2012); see also Salwa Ismail, *Political Life in Cairo's New Urban Quarters* (Minneapolis: University of Minnesota Press, 2006).

27. Ismail, "Egyptian Revolution against Police," 451.

28. Reported in *Al-Shorouq*, December 22, 2009.

29. Reported in Amin Allal, "Becoming Revolutionary in Tunisia, 2007–2011," in *Social Movements, Mobilization, and Contestation in the Middle East and North Africa*, 2nd ed., ed. Joel Beinin and Frederic Vairel (Palo Alto, CA: Stanford University Press, 2013), 194.

30. Asef Bayat, *Life as Politics: How Ordinary People Change the Middle East* (Palo Alto, CA: Stanford University Press, 2013); see also Chapter 5 of this volume.

31. Habib Ayeb, "Social and Political Geography of the Tunisian Revolution: The Alfa Grass Revolution," *Review of African Political Economy* 38, no. 129 (2011); Habib Ayeb, "Rural Revolution in Tunisia," unpublished paper, 2014.

32. For Tunisia, see Mouldi Lahmar, *This Other Hidden Face of the Tunisian Revolution: Its Rurality* (Oslo: Norwegian Peacebuilding Resource Center, June 2015). For Egypt, see a critical view on the social transformation of Egyptian village, Ahmed Zayed, "Al-Tahadur al-Ashwaii fi al-Rif wal-Hadar: Al-Wajh al-Akhar Li-Thaqafah al-Tabaqat al-Wustaa," *Al-Dimuqratiya*, no. 74 (April 2019). Earlier and informed ethnographic studies in Upper Egypt can be found in Nicholas Hopkins, ed., *Upper Egypt: Identity and Change*, Cairo (Cairo: American University in Cairo Press, 2004).

33. The narrative draws on Habib Ayeb, documentary film, 2014.

34. See Ayeb, documentary film, 2014.

35. This is based on my own observation in Iran. Also Eric Hooglund, "Change in Rural Patterns—Shiraz, Iran," paper presented at the workshop "Twentieth Century Iran: History from Below," Amsterdam, May 24–26, 2001; see also Lila Abu-Lughod, "Taking Back the Village: Rural Youth in a Moral Revolution," *Middle East Report*, no. 272 (Fall 2015).

36. Friedrich Ebert Stiftung, *Arab Youth Survey 2016*, Berlin, 2016.

37. *Tunis Times*, June 30, 2013.

38. Asef Bayat, "The Fire That Fueled the Iran Protests," *The Atlantic*, January 27, 2018, https://www.theatlantic.com/international/archive/2018/01/iran-protest-mashaad-green-class-labor-economy/551690/.

39. Habib Ayeb's post in Facebook, January 15, 2018.

40. See Heba Khalil, "The Lawyers of Egypt: Class, Precarity, Politics" (PhD diss., University of Illinois, Urbana-Champaign, 2021).

41. For theoretical elaborations on "youth," "youthfulness," and "youth politics," see Asef Bayat, "Reclaiming Youthfulness," in *Life as Politics*; and Asef Bayat, "Is There a Youth Politics?" *Middle East Topics and Arguments* 9 (2017).

42. My conversation, March 2003, American University in Cairo.

43. Interview conducted by Rime Naghib, 2002, Cairo.

44. My conversation, March 2013, Cairo.

45. Baher Ibrahim, "The Eid al-Adha Bribe," in *Arab Spring Dreams*, ed. Nasser Weddady and Sohrab Ahmari (London: Palgrave, 2012), 68, 70–71.

46. Ibrahim, "The Eid al-Adha Bribe," 70.

47. For Tunisia, see Jonas Röllin, "On the Concepts of 'Youth' and 'Generation' in the Contemporary Tunisian Context," Working paper (2016), 2–3.

48. Drawn on the conclusion of a debate in Majlis el-Shura, reported in *Al-Ahram*, July 14, 2000, 7.

49. This information is based on my interview with the minister of Youths and Sports, Dr. Ali Eddin Hilal, November 3, 2001, Cairo.

50. The Ministry of Local Development was to extend some of these loans. See *Al-Ahram*, July 14, 2000, 7.

51. On Tunisia, see Röllin, "On the Concepts of 'Youth,'" 3.

52. Sylvie Floris, *Studies on Youth Policies in the Mediterranean Partner Countries: Tunisia* (MarlyleRoi, France: EuroMed, 2009), 8.

53. Conversation with cyberactivist Tarek, July 2011, Tunis. Single names are all fictitious.

54. Ahmed Tohami Abdel-Hayy, "al-Tawajjhat al-Syasiyya al-Ajyal al-Jadid" [The political orientations of the new generations], *Al-Demoqratiyya*, no. 6 (Spring 2002): 120, 122.

55. Abdel-Hayy, "al-Tawajjhat al-Syasiyya al-Ajyal al-Jadid," 120.

56. My conversation, 2002, Cairo.

57. Interview with Maya Jribi, leader of the Progressive Democratic Party of Unisia, "Our Youth Have neither Hope nor Future," *Nawaat*, February 5, 2009, https://nawaat.org/portail/2009/02/05/interview-with-maya-jribi-leader-of -the-progressive-democratic-party-of-tunisia-our-youth-have-neither-hope -nor-future/.

58. Sherine el-Taraboulsi, "Spaces of Citizenship: Youth Civic Engagement and Pathways to the January 25th Revolution," in *Youth Activism and Social Space in Egypt* (Cairo: John Gerhart Center, American University in Cairo, 2011).

59. Life Makers had branches in Egypt, Morocco, and the United Kingdom. The initiative was perhaps similar to the programs of the Turkish religious leaders Fatullah Gulen's "market Islam" or the Indonesian Abdullah Gymnastiar known as Aa Gym, who held a program of "managing hearts" influenced by the American self-improvement paradigm. Amr Khaled came to be recognized by *Time* magazine as one of the 100 most influential people in the world in 2007.

60. See Dirk Wanrooij, "The Egyptian Uprising: Imbaba" (master thesis, University of Amsterdam, 2011).

61. Based on interviews by Rime Naghib, 2002, Cairo; Ghada Abdel-Shafiq's survey, "Youths in Egypt," term paper, American University in Cairo, Fall 2001.

62. Conversation with Abdelrahman, June 2013, Cairo. Single names are all fictitious.

63. Narrated in Alia Mossallam, "On the Love of Life and Alaa's Detention," *Mada Masr,* January 4, 2014.

64. Conversation with Hossam, July 2011, Alexandria, Egypt.

65. Conversation with Abdelrahman, August 2015, Champaign, IL.

66. Conversation with a teacher / mentor activist, May 2012, Tunis.

67. Allal, "Becoming Revolutionary in Tunisia," 185–204.

68. Conversation with Elyssa, a Tunisian youth, May 2017, Berlin.

69. Conversation with Elyssa, a Tunisian youth, May 2017, Berlin.

70. For more details, see Asef Bayat, "Claiming Youthfulness," in *Life as Politics.*

71. Cited in Riham Adel, "Married, or Maybe Not," *Al-Ahram Weekly,* December 10–16, 2009, 8.

72. As stated by a law student in Cairo; cited in Rime Naguib, "Egyptian Youth: A Tentative Study," unpublished paper, Spring 2002.

73. My conversations, March 2002, American University in Cairo.

74. Bayat, "Reclaiming Youthfulness."

75. Conversations with Ghassan and Tariq, July 2012, Tunis.

76. Linda Herrera, *Revolution in the Age of Social Media: Egyptian Popular Insurrection and the Internet* (London: Verso, 2014), 12–16.

77. Hania Sholkamy, "The Jaded Gender and Development Paradigm," *IDS Bulletin* 43, no. 1 (January 2012): 94.

78. Jack Shenker, *The Egyptians: A Radical Story* (London: Allen Labe, 2016), 138–139.

79. Cited in Ursula Lindsey, "Some Gains, Many Sacrifices: Women's Rights in Tunisia," *Al-Fanar Media,* July 10, 2017.

80. Jihen Laghmari and Caroline Alexander, "Woman Running for President Shows Tunisia's Arab Spring Progress," Bloomberg News, November 13, 2014.

81. For a fine analysis of this kind of developmentalist paradigm with respect to the poor, see Julia Elyachar, *The Markets of Dispossession: NGOs, Economic Development, and the State in Cairo* (Durham, NC: Duke University Press, 2005).

82. Islah Jad, "The NGO-ization of the Arab Women's Movements," *IDS Bulletin* 35, no. 4 (2004).

83. Mervat Hatem, "Economic and Political Liberation in Egypt and the Demise of State Feminism," *International Journal of Middle East Studies* 24, no. 2 (1992).

84. CARE International, *Arab Spring or Arab Autumn: Women's Political Participation in the Uprisings and Beyond* (London: CARE, 2012). See also http://english .ahram.org.eg/NewsContent/3/12/101284/Business/Economy/Almost-a-fifth -of-Egyptian-households-are-headed-b.aspx.

85. Ahmed El Amraoui and Rabii Kalboussi, "The Gender Faultline in Tunisia, *Aljazeera*, 24 October 2015.

86. Nadje Al-Ali, *Secularism, Gender and the State in the Middle East: The Egyptian Women's* Movement (Cambridge: Cambridge University Press, 2000).

87. Helen Rizzo, Anne M. Price, and Katherine Meyer, "Anti-Sexual Harassment Campaign in Egypt," *Mobilization: An International Journal* 17, no. 4 (2012): 457–475.

88. Nadje al-Ali, *Women's Movement in the Middle East: Case Studies of Egypt and Turkey* (Geneva: UNRISD, 2003), 18.

89. Conversation with Alaa, July 2016, Cairo.

90. Andrieu et al., *The Victim Zone*, 39.

91. Andrieu et al., *The Victim Zone*, 40.

92. Samar al-Mazghani, "The Cart at the Border Crossing," in *Arab Spring Dreamers: The Next Generation Speaks Out for Freedom and Justice from North Africa to Iran,* ed. Nasser Weddady, Sohran Ahmari and Gloria Steinem (New York: St. Martin's Press, 2012), 106.

93. Story based on her own testimony in Dalia Ziada, "My Sacred NO," in *Arab Spring Dreamers*, 132.

94. Nadje Al-Ali, "Gendering the Arab Spring," *Middle East Journal of Cultural Communication* 5, no. 1 (2012).

95. Conversation with Ghosoun, July 2016, Cairo.

96. Sara Lei Sparre, *Muslim Youth Organizations in Egypt: Actors of Reform and Development* (Copenhagen: Danish Institute for International Studies, January 2008).

97. For details on Egypt's women *halaqat*, see Asef Bayat, *Making Islam Democratic: Social Movements and the Post-Islamist Turn* (Palo Alto: Stanford University Press, 2007), 155–161.

98. Fatma El-Zanaty and Ann Way, *Egypt Demographic and Health Survey 2008* (Cairo: Ministry of Health, El-Zanaty and Associates, and Marco International, 2009).

99. Homa Hoodfar, *Between Marriage and the Market: Intimate Politics and Survival in Cairo* (Berkeley: University of California Press, 1997).

100. Neveen Beshier, "Knowing the Ropes: Autonomy in the Everyday Life of Egyptian Married Women" (master thesis, American University in Cairo, 2010).

101. In a survey conducted by the New Women Research Centre and El-Nadim Centre, 93 percent of women considered forced intercourse by their husbands as rape; see Nemat Guenena and Nadia Wassef, *Unfulfilled Promises: Women's Rights in Egypt* (Cairo: Population Council, 1999), 37.

102. Diane Singerman, "Rewriting Divorce in Egypt: Reclaiming Islam, Legal Activism, and Coalition Politics," in *Remaking Muslim Politics: Pluralism, Contestation, Democratization,* ed. Robert W. Hefner (Princeton, NJ: Princeton University Press, 2005).

103. Conversation with Asmaa, thirty-two-year-old college graduate of languages, August 2016, Cairo.

104. Amal Ghandour, "The Art of Presence," October 18, 2012, https://aeon.co/essays/inch-by-inch-what-next-for-the-women-of-the-arab-spring.

105. Human Rights Watch, *In a Time of Torture: The Assault on Justice in Egypt's Crackdown on Homosexual Conduct: APPENDIX: Laws Affecting Male Homosexual Conduct in Egypt* (New York: Human Rights Watch, 2004), http://hrw.org/reports/2004/egypt0304/9.htm#_Toc63760431.

106. Ghassan Moussawi, "(Un-)Critically Queer Organizing: Towards a More Complex Analysis of LGBTQ Organizing in Lebanon," *Sexualities* 18, nos. 5–6 (2015).

107. See, for instance, https://www.gaytravel.com/gay-blog/spotlight-on-egypt-a-gay-bloggers-pov/.

108. An anonymous gay man, July 2018, Berlin.

109. https://www.gaytravel.com/gay-blog/spotlight-on-egypt-a-gay-bloggers-pov/.

110. *Cairo Scene,* https://www.cairoscene.com/LifeStyle/Egypt's-Gay-Guide; https://www.gaytravel.com/gay-blog/spotlight-on-egypt-a-gay-bloggers-pov/.

111. https://www.cairoscene.com/LifeStyle/Egyptian-Cops-Using-Grindr-To-Hunt-Gays.

112. The book *Bareed Mista3jil* [Express mail] by Meem (Beirut: Ciel Paperback, 2009) provides some insights into the underground lives of queer women in Lebanon.

113. "Sidi-Bouzid: Darurah al-Takfir fi Hall Laa-iqaf al-Nazif" [The necessity of thinking for a solution to stop the bloodshed], *al-Masdar al-Tunisiyah,* December 28, 2010.

114. The rebellion of Gafsa in 2009 was, according to the opposition figure Maya Jribi, "the first movement of youth" in their twenties. See Jribi, "Our Youth Have neither Hope nor Future."

115. Lina Ben Mhenni, "My Arab Spring: Tunisia's Revolution Was a Dream," *Aljazeera,* December 2015. Also interview with Mabrouk Jebahi, July 2012, Tunis.

116. Röllin, "On the Concepts of 'Youth,'" 8.

117. Habib Ayeb, "Social Geography of the Tunisian Revolution," *Review of African Political Economy* 38, no. 129 (2011), 473–485; Nizar Shaqroun, *Rawaya al-Thawra al-Tunisiya* (Tunis and Bahrain: Al-Dosari, 2011).

118. According to human rights organizations.

119. *Al-Masdar al-Tunsiyya,* December 1 and 9, 2010.

120. Some of the known victims included Nawal Ali Mohamed (journalist), Rabaa Fahmy (lawyer), Nashwa Talaat, Alshaymaa Abu Elkheir (journalist), Sara Eldeeb (correspondent with the Associated Press), Eman Taha (journalist), Abeer Elaskary (journalist), Magda Adly (doctor and member of the Nadeem Center), Aida Seif Eldawla (doctor and member of the Nadeem Center), Ranwa Yehia (correspondent with the German News Agency), Rabab Ahmed Elmahdy (professor at the American University in Cairo), Safaa Zaki Murad (lawyer), and Laila Sueif (professor at Cairo University).

121. Between 1998 and 2010, Egypt had seen more than 3,300 worker strikes, sit-ins, and other forms of protest. See Joel Beinin, *Political Economy and Social Movement Theory Perspectives on Tunisian and Egyptian Popular Uprisings of 2011* (London: LSE Middle East Center, January 2016).

122. Steven Viney, "Zabaleen Sidelined by Morsy's 'Clean Homeland' Campaign," *al-Masry al-Youm,* August 14, 2012.

123. Heba Abdel Hamid, "Evicted Duweiqa Residents Demand New Homes," *Egypt Independent,* January 16, 2010.

124. *Al-Sharq,* December 16, 2009.

125. In the city of Port Said, when sixty-six families from Zerzara were offered insufficient help from the government for their burned-down homes, they blocked a main urban road following a series of protests in the city center. *Al-Masry al-Youm,* July 16, 2010.

126. Mohsen Semeika, "Opposition Stages Protests in Matarya over Power Cuts, Bread Prices," *Masry al-Youm,* August 26, 2010.

127. *Al-Masri al-Youm,* January 5, 2010, 2.

128. *Al-Masy al-Youm,* June 3, 2012.

129. *Al-Dastour,* January 5, 2010, 2.

130. *Al-Shorouq,* January 2, 2010, 2. A year earlier, women of Minyat Sandoub village in al-Duqliyya had gathered in front of the State Council (majlis al-dawla) asking for help against the Housing Cooperative Council, which they claimed, had encroached on their lands. The women displayed a large sign outlining their demands. *Al-Shorouq,* December 22, 2009.

131. Cited in Habib Ayeb and Ray Bush, "Small Farmers Uprisings and Rural Neglect in Egypt and Tunisia," *Middle East Report* 44, no. 272 (Fall 2014).

132. Karima Khalil, "Politically Active Youth Groups in Egypt, Post-January 25," unpublished report, January 2012.

133. Mariam Bazeed, "Anonymous No More," in *Arab Spring Dreams: The Next Generation Speaks Out for Freedom and Injustice from North Africa to Iran,* ed. Nasser Weddady and Sohrab Ahmari (New York: St. Martin's Press, 2012), 204.

134. Conversation with Abdelrahman, 2014, Champaign, IL.

135. Conversation with Abdelrahman, June 2012, Cairo.

136. Henri Onodera has documented how friendship and close circles contributed to youth political activism in prerevolution Egypt. See Henri Onodera, "Friendship and Youth Activism in Pre-Revolutionary Egypt," in *What Politics? Youth and Political Engagement in Africa,* ed. Elina Oinas, Henri Onodera, and Leena Suurpää (Leiden: Brill, 2018), 42–57.

### 3. THE SUBALTERN IN THE UPRISINGS

1. Mark R. Beissinger, Amaney Jamal, and Kevin Mazur, "Who Participated in the Arab Spring? A Comparison of Egyptian and Tunisian Revolutions," https://www.researchgate.net/publication/256026784_Who_Participated_in _the_Arab_Spring_A_Comparison_of_Egyptian_and_Tunisian_Revolutions.

2. Elena Lanchovichina, *Eruptions of Popular Anger: The Economics of the Arab Spring and Its Aftermath* (Washington, DC: World Bank, 2018), 117.

3. There is a useful debate about whether towns like Sidi Bouzid are "urban" or "rural." See, for instance, Mouldi Lahmar, *The Other Hidden Face of the Tunisian Revolution: It's Rurality* (Oslo: NOREF Norwegian Peacebuilding Resource Centre, June 2015). It seems to me that places like Sidi Bouzid are hybrid social formations marked by the mix of both "rural" and "urban" features, as the Lahmar report suggests.

4. See Malek Saghiri's fascinating essay "Greetings to the Dawn: Living through the Bittersweet Revolution (Tunisia)," in *Diaries of an Unfinished Revolution: Voices from Tunis to Damascus,* ed. Layla al-Zubaidi and Matthew Cassel (London: Penguin, 2013), 9–47.

5. Jonas Röllin, "On the Concepts of 'Youth' and 'Generation' in the Contemporary Tunisian context," Working paper, Marburg, 2016, pp. 9–10.

6. Conversation with Elyssa from Tunis, June 1, 2017, Berlin.

7. Cited in Choukri Hmed, "Abeyance, Networks, Contingency and Structures: History and Origins of the Tunisian Revolution," *Revue française de science politique* 62, nos. 5–6 (2012): 48.

8. Hmed, "Abeyance, Networks, Contingency and Structures," 48.

9. Reported in Muhammad Yaghi, "In the Tunisian and Egyptian Revolutions: How the Powerless Activists Overcame the Resource Problem" (paper, International Studies Association, Toronto, March 26–29, 2014).

10. Saghiri, "Greetings to the Dawn," 33–34.

11. Lanchovichina, *Eruptions of Popular Anger,* 117.

12. Yaghi, "In the Tunisian and Egyptian Revolutions," 12–13.

13. Yaghi, "In the Tunisian and Egyptian Revolutions," 13.

14. Saghiri, "Greetings to the Dawn," 33–34.

15. Yaghi, "In the Tunisian and Egyptian Revolutions," 16.

16. Yaghi, "In the Tunisian and Egyptian Revolutions," 16.

17. See Hela Yousfi, *Trade Unions and Arab Revolutions: The Tunisian Case of UGTT* (New York: Routledge, 2018).

18. Hmed, "Abeyance, Networks, Contingency and Structures," 39–40.

19. Conversation with Rasha, July 26, 2011, Tunis.

20. Conversation with Elyssa, June 2017, Berlin.

21. Conversation with Fadwa, twenty-four years old, July 27, 2011, Tunis.

22. Conversation with Nuwress, June 14, 2017, Tunis.

23. Conversation with Nuwress, June 14, 2017, Tunis.

24. Conversation with Qamar, June 2017, Tunis.

25. Conversation with Abdelrahman Mansour, a co-administrator of We Are All Khaled Said Facebook page, July 2013, Cairo.

26. Conversation with Abdelrahman J., March 27, 2011, Cairo.

27. Conversation with Abdelrahman J., March 27, 2011, Cairo.

28. Ahdaf Soueif, *Cairo: Memoire of a City Transformed* (New York: Pantheon, 2014), 38–39.

29. Aia Mossallam, "Permanent Temporariness," Heinrich Böll Stiftung website, January 20, 2021; https://www.boell.de/en/2021/01/20/permanent -temporariness.

30. Some of these *shillas* and nonmovements were connected to open groups such as the Popular Committee to Defend Imbaba Airport Land, the leftist Tajammu' Selma Said, a middle-class activist who established a network in the Tajammu branch in Imbaba. They had set up the Center for the Families of Imbaba, which aimed to help the residents on local issues. They organized workshops and discussions concerning children and family matters. See Dirk Wanrooij, "The Egyptian Uprising: Imbaba" (MA thesis, University of Amsterdam, 2011), 66.

31. Heba Afify, "Youth Coalition Calls on Protestors to Leave Tahrir Square," *AlMasry Alyoum,* February 12, 2011.

32. Lanchovichina, "Eruptions of Popular Anger," 117.

33. Nadia Idle and Alex Nunns, *Tweets from Tahrir* (New York: OR Books, 2011), 223.

34. Soueif, *Cairo,* 19.

35. Cited in Paul Mason, *Why It's Kicking Off Everywhere* (London: Verso, 2012), 15.

36. Khalil Abu-Shadi, "layali Atfaal al-Shawari' fi Maidan Tahrir" [Nights of the children of streets in Tahrir Square], *Al-Youm al-Sabi'a,* December 28, 2011. See also Wanrooij, "The Egyptian Uprising."

37. Egyptian cyberactivists had taken the idea of Day of Anger from the Jordanian youth who, inspired by the events in Tunisia, were planning for such a day in Amman.

38. Scenes from video clip "Uprising in Imbaba" by Mathew Cassel, www .youtube.com/watch?v=ABfVEq7JIMW.

39. Video clip "A Visit to Imbaba," directed by Neveen Shalaby, Amnesty International.

40. See a very interesting eyewitness account by an American photojournalist, Mathew Cassel, *Aljazeera.net,* February 10, 2011. See also Wanrooij, "The Egyptian Uprising."

41. See Asef Bayat, "Does Radical Islam Have an Urban Ecology?" in *Life as Politics: How Ordinary People Change the Middle East,* 2nd ed. (Palo Alto, CA: Stanford University Press, 2013).

42. Anthony Shadid, "Few Focus on Religion in One Cairo Neighborhood," *New York Times,* February 15, 2011.

43. Gamal Eid, a report on January 28, Day of Anger, his Facebook page.

44. Abu-Shadi, "layali Atfaal al-Shawari' fi Maidan Tahrir."

45. Neil Ketchley, *Egypt in a Time of Revolution: Contentious Politics and the Arab Spring* (Cambridge: Cambridge University Press, 2017).

46. See Erica Chenoweth and Maria Stephan, *Why Civil Resistance Works: The Strategic Logic of Nonviolent Conflict* (New York: Columbia University Press, 2011).

47. Cited in Yaghi, "In the Tunisian and Egyptian Revolutions," 27.

48. Two paragraphs in this section heavily draw on my article "Plebeians of the Arab Spring," *Current Anthropology* 56, no. S11 (2015).

49. Beissinger et al., "Who Participated in the Arab Spring?" 13.

50. Joel Beinin, "The Middle East's Working-Class Revolutions?" *The Nation*, August 24, 2011, 5.

51. According to the reports of the human rights organizations.

52. Amnesty International, *We Are Not Dirt: Forced Evictions in Egypt's Informal Settlements* (London: Amnesty International, 2011), 3.

53. Conversation with the revolutionary activist Alaa Abdel-Fattah, June 2013, Cairo.

54. Sara Carr, "Informal Settlement Dwellers Evicted despite Housing Promises," *Al-Masry al-Youm*, July 31, 2011.

55. Soueif, *Cairo*, 13.

56. Lanchovichina, "Eruptions of Popular Anger."

57. Hania Sholkamy, "The Jaded Gender and Development Paradigm," *IDS Bulletin* 43, no. 1 (2012), 95.

58. Nehad Abou El-Komsan, *The Freedom of the Square: Reflections on the Course of the Egyptian Revolution and the Participation of Women* (New York: UN Entity for Gender Equality, 2013), 8.

59. There were also Heba Abdel Sayed, Nadia al-Halabi, Amira Badr, and Maheetab al-Geelani, among many others. For biographies and activism of these women, see Abou El-Komsan, *The Freedom of the Square*, 111–133.

60. Abou El-Komsan, *The Freedom of the Square*.

61. Conversation with Asmaa, August 2016, Cairo.

62. Conversation with Alaa, August 2016, Cairo.

63. Conversation with Hoda, fifties, from Haram, August 2016, Cairo.

64. Conversation with Ghouson, August 2016, Cairo.

65. Conversation with Mona, fifty-five-year-old medical doctor, July 2016, Cairo.

66. Conversation with Hoda, August 2016, Cairo.

67. Abou El-Komsan, *The Freedom of the Square*, 42.

68. Conversation with Radwa, twenty-four years old, July 2016, Cairo.

69. Nadje Al-Ali, "Gendering the Arab Spring," *Middle East Journal of Culture and Communication* 5 (2012): 26–31; Dalia Said Mostafa, "Introduction: Egyptian Women, Revolution and Protest Culture," *Journal of Cultural Research* 19, no. 2 (2015): 123.

70. Conversation with Ghouson, August 2016, Cairo.

71. Abou El-Komsan, *The Freedom of the Square*, 127.

72. Narrated by Soueif, *Cairo*, 21

73. For Tunisia, see Andrea Khalil, "Tunisia's Women: Partners in Revolution," *Journal of North African Studies* 19, no. 2 (2014): 186–199; for Egypt, see Nermin Allam, *Women and the Egyptian Revolution: Engagement and Activism during the 2011 Arab Uprisings* (Cambridge: Cambridge University Press, 2017)

74. "Spotlight on Egypt: A Gay's Blogger's POV," February 8, 2011, https://www.gaytravel.com/gay-blog/spotlight-on-egypt-a-gay-bloggers-pov/.

75. Conversation with a gay man from Egypt, July 2018, Berlin.

76. Statistical data about those killed during the Egyptian uprising, Wiki Thawra, https://wikithawra.wordpress.com/2013/10/23/25jan18dayscasualities/.

77. For detailed discussion, see Asef Bayat, "Is There Youth Politics?" *Middle East Topics and Argument*, no. 9 (2017).

78. Literature on youth and the Arab revolutions abounds. See, for instance, Haggai Erlich, *Youth and Revolution in the Changing Middle East, 1908–1914* (London: Lynn Rienner, 2015); Edward Sayer and Tarik Yousef, eds., *Young Generation Awakening: Economics, Society, and Policy on the Eve of the Arab Spring* (Oxford: Oxford University Press, 2016); Raj Desai, Anders Olofsgard, and Tarik Yousef, "Days of Rage and Silence: Explaining Political Action by Arab Youth," in *Young Generation Awakening: Economics, Society, and Policy on the Eve of the Arab Spring*, ed. Edward Sayer and Tarik Yousef (Oxford: Oxford University Press, 2016); Nadine Abdalla, "Youth Movements in the Egyptian Transformation: Strategies and Repertoires of Political Participation," *Mediterranean Politics* 21, no. 1 (2016); Dina Shehata, "Youth Movements and the 25th January Revolution," in *Arab Spring in Egypt: Revolution and Beyond*, ed. Bahgat Korany and Rabab El-Mahdi (Cairo: American University in Cairo Press, 2012), 105–124; Magdalena Delgado, "Contentious Copts: The Emergence, Success, and Decline of the Maspero Youth Movement in Egypt," in *Contentious Politics in the Middle East*, ed. Fawaz Gerges (London: Palgrave, 2015). The existing literature mostly treats youth as incidental

or tangential to events, with little analyses about the specificities of youth claims and presence. The studies that do focus on youths as a central subject are still concerned not about "youth politics" as such but "youth *in* politics." For an elaboration on this "youth politics," see Bayat, "Is There Youth Politics?"

79. See Anastasia Tsioulcas, "Emel Mathlouthi Is the 21st Century's Catalyst for Change," NPR, November 8, 2018, https://www.npr.org/2018/11/08/665200790/emel-mathlouthi-is-the-21st-centurys-catalyst-for-change.

80. Xan Rice et al., "Women Have Emerged as Key Players in the Arab Spring," *The Guardian*, April 22, 2011.

81. Deniz Kandiyoti, ed., *Women, Islam and the State* (London: Macmillan, 1991).

82. Rice et al., "Women Have Emerged as Key Players."

83. Muhamed Turkey al-Rabi'ou, "Jahadiyya Badawiyyat wa Malakat Gamal Kurdiyyat," *al-Quds al Arabi*, November 23, 2108. See also https://time.com/2921491/hope-solo-women-violence/.

84. Khalil, "Tunisia's Women," 186. See also Shirin Abul-Nagah, "How to Read Gender Now," *al-Arabi al-Jadid*, December 5, 2018, https://www.alaraby.co.uk/diffah/opinions/2018/11/25/%D9%83%D9%8A%D9%81-%D9%86%D9%82%D8%B1%D8%A3-%D8%A7%D9%84%D8%AC%D9%86%D8%AF%D8%B1-%D8%A7%D9%84%D8%A2%D9%86.

85. Conversation with Norhan, twenty-four years old at the time of the uprising, July 2016, Cairo.

86. Khalil, "Tunisia's Women," 188.

87. Allam, *Women and the Egyptian Revolution*.

88. Khalil, "Tunisia's Women," 186.

89. Mozn Hassan, director of the Nazra Feminist Studies Centre in Cairo; cited in Nadine Sikka and Yasmine Khodary, "One Step Forward, Two Steps Back? Egyptian Women within the Confines of Authoritarianism," *Journal of International Women's Studies* 13, no. 5 (2012): 97. See also Lucia Sorbera, "Challenges of Thinking Feminism and Revolution in Egypt between 2011 and 2014," *Postcolonial Studies* 17, no. 1 (2014): 68. Kathambi Kinoti, "The Role of Women in Egypt's Popular Uprising," June 30, 2011, https://www.awid.org/news-and-analysis/role-women-egypts-popular-uprising.

90. Nehad Aboul Komsan, "The Status of Egyptian Women in 2011," December 29, 2011, https://ecwronline.org/?p=1116.

91. See Asef Bayat, "Islamism and Social Movement Theory," *Third World Quarterly* 26, no. 6 (2005): 901.

92. Heidi Hartmann, "The Unhappy Marriage of Marxism and Feminism: Towards a More Progressive Union," *Capital and Class* 3, no. 2 (1979): 2.

93. See, for instance, Islah Jad, *Palestinian Women's Activism: Nationalism, Secularism, Islamism* (Syracuse, NY: Syracuse University Press, 2018).

94. This is reflected, for instance, in the position of Khaled Ali, a labor lawyer and director of the Egyptian Center for Economic and Social Rights, who suggested that workers' protests during the uprising gave "the revolution an economic and social slant besides the political demands." See Beinin, "The Middle East's Working-Class Revolutions?" 5.

95. See Asef Bayat, *Street Politics: Poor People's Movements in Iran* (New York: Columbia University Press, 1997).

96. For ideological pragmaticism of the poor, see Asef Bayat, "Radical Religion and the Habitus of the Dispossessed: Does Islamic Militancy Have an Urban Ecology?" *International Journal of Urban and Regional Research* 31, no. 3 (2007).

97. The next few passages draw heavily on Bayat, "Plebeians of the Arab Spring."

98. The historian Khaled Ziadeh suggests that the very poor did not participate in the uprising or in the protests because they "colluded" with the autocratic regimes, for they saw their interests, quiet encroachment, served under the prerevolution governments; see interview with Khaled Ziadeh, "Poor People's Encroachment Is Not Innocent," *Al-Modon*, December 8, 2018 (in Arabic).

99. Hernando de Soto, "The Free Market Secret of the Arab Revolutions," *Financial Times*, November 8, 2011.

100. Hernando de Soto, "Poor People Also Have the Right to Buy and Sell," public lecture in Royal Society for Encouragement of Arts, Manufacturing and Commerce, March 21, 2013.

101. I have to admit that my analysis of Egypt, unlike Tunisia, focuses more on the capital, Cairo. But there is no doubt that the revolutionary uprising spread also to such delta areas as Alexandria, Suez, Port Said, Mansoura, as well as the southern regions of Minya, Asyut, and Aswan.

102. For Iran protests of the late December 2017, see Asef Bayat, "The Fire That Fueled the Iran Protests," *The Atlantic*, January 27, 2018.

103. This is similar to what Badiou calls historical riot, but Badiou's formulation is exceedingly Egypt-centric; in fact, it is Tahrir-centric when he emphasizes the spatial unity or gathering of rioters in one place, like Tahrir Square; see Alain Badiou, *The Rebirth of History: Times of Riots and Uprisings* (London: Verso, 2012), 35.

104. Hanan Sabea, "A 'Time out of Time': Tahrir, the Political and the Imaginary in the Context of the January 25th Revolution in Egypt," Field Sights—Hot Spots, *Cultural Anthropology Online*, May 9, 2013, http://www.culanth.org/fieldsights/211-a-time-out-of-time-tahrir-the-political-and-the-imaginary-in-the-context-of-the-january-25th-revolution-in-egypt.

4. THE POOR AND PLEBEIAN

1. Hazem Kandil, "Revolt in Egypt: An Interview," *New Left Review*, no, 68 (March–April 2011).

2. For a perceptive critique of such views, see Nasser Abourahmeh, "'The Street' and 'the Sum': Political Form and Urban Life in Egypt's Revolt," *City* 6 (2013): 716–728.

3. Hernando de Soto, "The Free Market Secret of the Arab Revolutions," *Financial Times*, November 8, 2011.

4. Eberhard Kienle, *Changed Regimes, Changed Priorities? Economic and Social Policies after the 2011 Revolutions in Tunisia and Egypt* (Cairo: Economic Research Forum, July 2015), 25.

5. "Close to 700,000 Unemployed by the Coming July," [in Arabic] *al-Masdar al-Tunisiya*, April 5, 2011.

6. "Hundreds of Tunisian Journalists Face the Threat of Unemployment," [in Arabic] *al-Masdar al-Tunisiya*, March 14, 2011.

7. Mona Ghanmi, "University Grads Accept Menial Jobs," *Maghrebia*, February 15, 2011.

8. D. W. Duechewille, www.dw.de, June 12, 2013 [in Arabic].

9. See news item at www.tunisia-live.net/category/news/August2016.

10. *Al-Arabi al-Jadid*, October 13, 2014.

11. "Terrorism, Unemployment and High Prices, of Most Important Problems," [in Arabic] *al-Masdar al-Tunisiya*, April 28, 2015.

12. Kora Andrieu, Wahid Ferchichi, Simon Robins, Ahmed Aloui, and Hajer Ben Hamza, *The Victim Zone and Collective Reparation: Ain Draham and Sidi Makhlouf* (Tunis: Transitional Justice Barometer, May 2016), http://www.simonrobins.com/TJ%20Barometer%20-%20The%20victim%20zone%20ENG.pdf.

13. "A Young Man Sets Himself on Fire in Nasrullah in Front of Police Station," [in Arabic] *al-Masdar al-Tunisiya*, February 19, 2011.

14. "Stopping 180 Youths before Setting Fire to the Capital," [in Arabic] *al-Masdar al-Tunisiya*, March 1, 2011.

15. "Jajib al-Uyoun Youth Setting Themselves in Fire to Commit Collective Suicide," [in Arabic] *al-Masdar al-Tunisiya*, May 2, 2011.

16. Johannes Frische, "Getting By at the Urban Periphery: Everyday Struggles of Informal Merchants in Tunisia," *Middle East Topics and Arguments*, 5 (2015): 67.

17. Ramzi Zaeri, "Souq Sidi-Mendil," *Bawaba Afrikiya al-Akhbariya*, May 14, 2014.

18. Frische, "Getting By," 71.

19. "Tunis, Republic of Chaos Has Taken Over Our Capital," [in Arabic] *Al-Masdar al-Tunisiya*, March 15, 2011; Zaeri, "Souq Sidi-Mendil."

20. Larry Michalak, "Merchants at the Margins: The Politics of Petty-Commerce in Tunisia," unpublished paper, August 2014, p. 8.

21. "Is Causing Chaos a Legitimate Right?" [in Arabic] *Al-Masdar al-Tunisiya*, February 12, 2011.

22. Michalak, "Merchants at the Margins," 16.

23. Michalak, "Merchants at the Margins," 8.

24. Alia Gana, "The Rural and Agricultural Roots of the Tunisian Revolution: When Food Security Matters," *International Journal of Sociology of Agriculture and Food* 19, no. 2 (2013): 205.

25. Gana, "The Rural and Agricultural Roots," 208.

26. Habib Ayeb, "Rural Revolution in Tunisia," unpublished paper, 2014.

27. Based on report by Ghassan Ben-Khalifa, "Henshir STIL fi Jemna: Al-Maslaha al-Amma Qabl al-Ribh al-Khas" [Public interests come before private gain], *Nawwat*, July 11, 2015.

28. Gana, "The Rural and Agricultural Roots of the Tunisian Revolution."

29. Alia Gana, *Agriculteurs et paysans, nouveaux acteurs de la société civile et de la transition démocratique en Tunisie* (Tunis: Observatoire Tunisien de la Transition Démocratique, éditions Diwan, 2011).

30. Hela Yousfi, *Trade Unions and Arab Revolutions: The Tunisian Case of UGTT* (New York: Routledge, 2018).

31. "Cultural Demonstration of UGTT in Celebration of Labor Festival," [in Arabic] *Al-Mastar al-Tunisiya*, May 2, 2011.

32. Hala Yousefi, "Mafariq Toroq Imam al-Hayat al-Niqabiyya fi Tunis," *Al-Safir al-Arabi*, March 5, 2015, http://arabi.assafir.com/Article/25/2020; see a fine study, Joel Beinin, *Workers and Thieves: Labor Movements and Popular Uprisings in Tunisia and Egypt* (Palo Alto, CA: Stanford University Press, 2014).

33. Mahdi al-Zaghlami, "Negotiations around Pay Rise Begins in Late February," [in Arabic] *Al-Masdar al-Tunisiya,* February 14, 2011. Later on, when the Federation of Tunisian Industry rejected the UGTT's demand for a 6 percent pay rise in the private sector, the rank and file opted for a mass industrial action. And when its negotiations with the Tunis Transportation Company failed in November 2014, a general strike brought transportation and many social and economic activities to a halt. www.leconomistemaghrebin.fr, December 26, 2014; *Al-Sharq al-Awsat,* November 13, 2014.

34. The Union of the Unemployed Degree Holders, established in 2006 under Ben Ali, functioned illegally; it emerged into the open, gained legal status in February 2011, and attracted 10,000 members in twenty-four branches in different parts of Tunisia. Its members called for the right to work and regional development.

35. "Plan to Employ Immediately 50,000 Youths," [in Arabic] *Al-Masdar al-Tunisiya,* February 23, 2011.

36. "Chaos at Offices of Employment to Claim Unemployment Benefits," [in Arabic] *Al-Masdar al Tunisiya,* March 3, 2011.

37. "Délice Danone Offers 300 Jobs in Sidi-Bouzid," [in Arabic] *Al-Masdar al-Tunisiya,* April 8, 2011.

38. "Chaos and Protests at Headquarters of Tunis Governorate," [in Arabic] *al-Masdar al-Tunisiya,* February 8, 2011.

39. "Traffic Chaos Following News of Strike in Gas Stations," [in Arabic] *al-Masdar al-Tunisiya,* February 8, 2011.

40. "Protests of Taxi Drivers," [in Arabic] *al-Masdar al-Tunisiya,* February 24, 2011.

41. "Surprise Strike of Metro Workers Disrupts Transfer of Commuters," [in Arabic] *al-Masdar al-Tunisiya,* February 3, 2011; "Report of New Strikes by Metro Employees," [in Arabic] *al-Masdar al-Tunisiya,* February 9, 2011.

42. "Customs Workers Demonstrate Demanding to Work," [in Arabic] *al-Masdar al-Tunisiya,* March 3, 2011.

43. "Strike in National Transport Co. Transtu," [in Arabic] *al-Masdar al-Tunisiya,* March 10, 2011; also *al-Masdar al-Tunisiya,* March 12, 2011.

44. "Over 150 Security Guards Organize Protests," [in Arabic] *al-Masdar al-Tunisiya,* February 8, 2011.

45. "Strike in All Handling Companies on Next Wednesday," [in Arabic] *al-Masdar al-Tunisiya,* May 2, 2011; "Strike Plan of Finance Employees on May 4–5,

2011," [in Arabic] *al-Masdar al-Tunisiya*, May 5, 2011; also "Tunisian Airline Workers Resort to Strike," [in Arabic] *al-Masdar al-Tunisiya*, May 12, 2011.

46. "Tunis-Closure of All Municipalities and Disruption of Citizen Work," [in Arabic] *al-Masdar al-Tunisiya*, May 9, 2011.

47. "Tunis: Over 90,000 Teachers Enter a General Strike for Two Days," [in Arabic] *al-Masdar al-Tunisiya*, January 20, 2015.

48. "After Secondary Education, 63,000 Teachers Begin Strikes," [in Arabic] *al-Masdar al-Tunisiya*, April 13, 2015.

49. "Hot Indicators in Social and Media Situations," [in Arabic] *al-Masdar al-Tunisiya*, February 5, 2011.

50. "Protests of Journalists and Reporters in Sfax Governorate," [in Arabic] *al-Masdar al-Tunisiya*, April 27, 2011.

51. "Employees of Gafsa Enter into an Open-Ended Strike," [in Arabic] *al-Masdar al-Tunisiya*, April 22, 2011.

52. Heba Saleh, "Strikes and Political Divisions Plague Tunisian Phosphate Industry," *Financial Times*, February 19, 2014.

53. Saleh, "Strikes and Political Divisions."

54. "Absence of Ramadan Charity and Aid Cause Road Suspensions," [in Arabic] *al-Masdar al-Tunisiya*, August 4, 2011.

55. The poll (1,395) was conducted by the Egyptian Center for Public Opinion Research, Baseera, in September 2013; reported in "Egyptians' Living Conditions and Their Expectations of the Future: Poll," *Daily News-Egypt*, September 8, 2013.

56. For the figures, see Nafeez Mosaddeq Ahmed, "How Resource Shortages Sparked Egypt's Months Long Crisis," *The Atlantic*, August 19, 2013.

57. Amr Abdel Abotawila, "Understanding Egyptian Social Housing Squatting Phenomenon Post January 2011" (MA thesis, Ain Shams University, Cairo, 2017), 19–20, 41.

58. Cited in Abotawila, "Understanding Egyptian Social Housing Squatting," 64.

59. *Al-Maal*, June 11, 2013.

60. *Al-Ahram Online*, June 10, 2014. In a 2011 report, the Central Administration for Protecting Arable Lands identified 108,316 cases of encroachments on arable lands across the Nile and delta, between January 25 and March 31, 2011; see Raghda Mohamed, "To Curtail Encroachments Egypt Seeks to Build New Cornish," *Al-Masry al-Youm*, May 7, 2012.

61. According to the Housing Directorate of Alexandria reported in David Sims, "Understanding Cairo's Informal Development," in *Learning from Cairo*,

Cairo, ed. Beth Stryker, Omar Nejati and Magda Mostafa (Cairo: American University in Cairo Press, 2012), 38.

62. Mohamed, "To Curtail Encroachments."

63. *Al-Ahram Online*, June 10, 2014.

64. *Al-Masry al-Youm*, June 20, 2013.

65. *Ahram Online*, http://english.ahram.org?NewsContentPrint/, November 18, 2012.

66. Jamie Farniss, "Post-Revolutionary Land Encroachment in Cairo," *Singapore Journal of Tropical Geography* 37, no. 3 (September 2016).

67. These sections and others in this chapter contain passages from my essay "The Plebeians of the Arab Spring," *Current Anthropology* 56, no. 11S (2015).

68. *Al-youm Essabe'a*, March 17, 2013.

69. *Al-Badil*, May 23, 2013.

70. *Veto*, May 16, 2013; *Al-youm Essabe'a*, March 1, 2013.

71. *Al-Ahram*, October 5, 2013.

72. In December 2012, tens of youths eligible to obtain apartments in the Ab'adiya Project in Damanhour staged a protest in front of the governorate building asking for a reduction in their down payment from EGP 20,000 to EGP5,000. Others disrupted traffic in anger. "I was working in tourism in Sharm al-Shaikh, but have been sitting at home without work for two years. How can I pay this huge amount for an apartment I have been waiting for seven years?" one protester lamented. *Al-Sabah*, December 4, 2012.

73. Abdelkarim al-Jaberi, "Shagarat Maryam Residents Threatened with Eviction," *Al-Masry al-Youm*, September 8, 2012.

74. *Al-Masry al-Youm*, March 14, 2013.

75. Nada Tarbush, "Cairo2050: Urban Dream or Modernist Delusion?" *Journal of International Affairs* 65, no. 2 (2012): 176.

76. Tome Dale, "Cairo's Central Slum under Threat," *al-Masry al-Youm*, July 5, 2012.

77. Video interview made by the architect and anthropologist Omnia Khalil, 2013, Cairo.

78. Abdel-Karim al-Jaberi, "Update: Gunfire, Tear Gas Continue in Bulaq," *al-Masry al-Youm*, July 2, 2012.

79. Abdel Karim al-Jaberi, "Wave of Arrests, Threat of Eviction Plague Ramlet Bulaq," *al-Masry al-Youm*, August 7, 2012.

80. Omnia Khalil, "The People of the City Space: Laboring and Power in the Quest of Unraveling the HOW in Ramlet Bulaq" (MA thesis, American

University in Cairo, April 2014); see also Omina Khalil, "Th Everyday in Ramlet Bulaq," *Middle East Report*, no. 274 (Spring 2015).

81. Tom Dale, "Land Rights, Labor and Violence in a Cairo Slum," *Egypt Independent*, July 15, 2012.

82. *Daily News*, August 28, 2013.

83. For instance, since 2011, Egyptians have been using over three million air conditioners in their homes; Omar Halawa, "Searching for Water: Residents of Giza Protest Unstable Supply," *al-Masry al-Youm*, July 23, 2012.

84. *Al-Youm Assabe'a*, May 22, 2013; *Al-Badil*, May 22, 2013.

85. The government subsidized 22.5 piasters of 35 piaster cost per kilowatt-hour; Omar Halwa, "Out in the Dark," *al-Masry al-Youm*, August 5, 2012.

86. *Al-Masry al-Youm*, June 7, 2013; *al-Shorouk*, May 29, 2013; *Al-Masry al-Youm*, June 20, 2013; *Al-Youm Assabe'a*, February 9, 2013; *Al-Watan*, June 6, 2013; *Al-Shorouk*, May 23, 2013 [all in Arabic].

87. See the report at https://www.telesurenglish.net/opinion/US-Regime -Change-Blueprint-Proposed-Venezuelan-Electricity-Blackouts-as-Watershed -Event-for-Galvanizing-Public-Unrest-20190315-0017.html?fbclid=IwAR0N8rChb _VCic85ktBCs_6SKW8OMdG5lz-t6YvGVr6dycU1XjAHB_G7ZIU.

88. Narmin Najdi, "Esna Residents Protest Over the Authorities' Neglect," *Al-Dostour*, March 17, 2013; *Al-Badil*, March 10, 2013; *Al-Ahram*, March 8, 2013; *Al-Balad*, May 29, 2013; Ahmed al-Gamal, "Dismissal of Head of Hayy al-Dawahi in Port Said," [in Arabic] *Al-Dostour*, June 10, 2013.

89. *Al-Ahram Online*, January 9, 2013.

90. Al-Masry al-Youm, "Daqahlia Village Residents Launch Sit-In over Lack of Facilities," *al-Masry al-Youm*, English ed., September 10, 2012.

91. *Masr al-Jadid*, April 23, 2012.

92. *Al-Masry al-Youm*, May 19, 2013.

93. *Al-Shorouk*, June 11, 2013.

94. Report by the Egyptian Center for Social and Economic Rights, 2013. Egyptian Ministry of Manpower reported that during 2011, workers organized 335 strikes (including 135 sit-ins in the public sector and 123 in private sector) and 4,460 complaints to the ministry; *al-Masry al-Youm*, January 17, 2012.

95. Office of the President Morsi, published in a poster and distributed officially, June 2013.

96. See a critical view on the social transformation of Egyptian village, Ahmed Zayed, "Al-Tahadur al-Ashwaii fi al-Rif wal-Hadar: Al-Wajh al-Akhar Li-Thaqafah al-Tabaqat al-Wustaa," *Al-Dimuqratiya*, no. 74 (April 2019).

Earlier and informed ethnographic studies in Upper Egypt can be found in Nicholas Hopkins, ed., *Upper Egypt: Identity and Change* (Cairo: American University in Cairo Press, 2004). For Tunisia, see Mouldi Lahmar, *This Other Hidden Face of the Tunisian Revolution: Its Rurality* (Oslo: Norwegian Peacebuilding Resource Center, June 2015).

97. Asef Bayat and Eric Denis, "Who Is Afraid of the *Ashwaiyyat?* Urban Change and Politics in Egypt," *Environment and Urbanization* 12, no. 2 (October 2000).

98. Yasmine Laveille, "Contention in Marginalized Spaces: Egypt after the 2011 Revolution" (PhD diss., London School of Economics, 2016), 99.

99. Yasmine Laveille, "Villagers Demand a Football Field," *Mada Masr*, December 20, 2015.

100. Saker El-Nour, "Small Farmers and the Revolution in Egypt: The Forgotten Actors," *Contemporary Arab Affairs* 8, no. 2 (2015): 199.

101. El-Nour, "Small Farmers," 202.

102. Egyptian Center for Economic and Social Rights (ECESR), *Yearly Protest Report 2013* (Cairo: ECESR, 2014).

103. Yasmine Moataz Ahmed, "The Union Effect and the State Effect," paper presented at "Tunisia and Egypt: A Comparative Reading of a Revolutionary Process," Tunis, November 9–10, 2012.

104. Personal communication, March 2019, Cairo.

105. These included Egyptian Federation of Small Farmers, General Union of Small Farmers (with 500,000 members), Independent Union of Small Farmers (organizing those with less than five feddans), and the Syndicate of Small Farmers affiliated to Muslim Brothers. El-Nour, "Small Farmers," 204.

106. Moataz Ahmed, "The Union Effect and the State Effect."

107. Ragui Assad, "Labor Supply, Employment and Unemployment in the Egyptian Economy, 1988–2006," in *The Egyptian Labor Market Revisited*, ed. Ragui Assad (Cairo: American University in Cairo Press, 2009).

108. *Al-Masry al-Youm*, March 14, 2012, www.egyptindependent.com.

109. Interview with Hossam, an eyewitness, July 2011, Alexandria.

110. Mohamed, "To Curtail Encroachments."

111. Jano Charbel, "Street Vendors Forming Union to Combat State Crackdown," *al-Masry al-Youm*, December 9, 2012.

112. EIPR Report on "Economic and Social Justice," [in Arabic] December 9, 2012.

113. Kamal Murad, "The Return of the Street Vendors to Downtown on Thursday after Security Forces Withdraw," [in Arabic] *Al-Masry al-Youm,* September 25, 2014; *Al-Masry al-Youm,* September 15, 2014; *Al-Masry al-Youm,* September 17, 2014; *Al-Masry al-Youm,* September 20, 2014.

114. *Al-Masry al-Youm,* September 9, 2012.

115. At a time when unemployment jumped from the prerevolution 9 percent to 31 percent, or 5.3 million, of whom 72 percent had lost jobs, and one out of three had college degrees. According to Abu-Bakr al-Gindi, the head of CAPMAS, cited in *al-Shorouk,* March 15, 2013.

116. Amr Adly, "Challenging Spatial and Economic Order: The Rise of Street Vendors Movement," in Arab Reform Initiative, *Effervescent Egypt: Venues of Mobilization and the Interrupted Legacy of 2011* (Beirut: Arab Reform Initiative, 2018), 31.

117. Charbel, "Street Vendors Forming Union."

118. *Al-Dostour,* March 24, 2011.

119. Steve Viney, "Zabaleen Sidelined by Morsi's 'Clean Homeland' Campaign," *al-Masry al-Youm,* August 14, 2012.

120. Studies in Fayyoum, Minya, and Asyut in 2010 showed a great number of children, notably girls age sixteen, worked between five to ten hours per day for an EGP100–300 monthly pay. Wael Gamal, "Ahlan bi Aamilaat al-Manazil fi Aalam al-Amal al-Aam," *Al-Shorouk,* September 10, 2012.

121. For elaboration, see the excellent study by Heba Khalil, "The Lawyers of Egypt: Class, Precarity, Politics" (PhD diss., University of Illinois, Urbana-Champaign, 2021), chapter 4.

122. Esra' Mohammed Ali, "Ehya' Bel-Esm Faqat," *Al-Masry al-Youm,* April 1, 2013.

123. Wael Gamal, "Blackouts in Egypt Are Also Politics," *Al-Ahram Weekly,* July 31, 2012.

124. Omar Nagati and Beth Stryker, *Archiving the City in Flux: Cairo's Shifting Urban Landscape since the January 25th Revolution* (Cairo: American University in Cairo Press, 2013), 54.

125. *Al-Watan,* May 16, 2015.

126. Omar Nagati, video lecture, American University of Beirut, The City Debate, 2013.

127. Tadamun, http://www.tadamun.info/?post_type=city&p=2741&lang=en&lang=en#.WCdkBbU-764.

128. Tadamun, http://www.tadamun.info/?post_type=city&p=2741&lang=en&lang=en#.WCdkBbU-764.

129. "Mubadera al-Maktabat al-Karama," http://www.tadamun.info/?post_type=initiative&p=5226#.WCeCrbU-7AK.

130. See http://elkarama.anhri.net/?p=366.

131. Safa Harafi, "Living in Slums," *al-Masry al-Youm*, September 9, 2012.

132. Wael Eskandar, "Wa Mazaalat Estrategiyya 'Modon al-Ashbah' Mostamerrah," http://eipr.org, May 15, 2013.

133. Ahmed Hamed, *al-Ahram Daily*, December 21, 2013.

134. Yahya Shawkat, "On a Minister of New Communities and Ministry of Housing the Egyptians Deserve," [in Arabic] *Mada Masr*, March 5, 2014; Yahya Shawkat, "Government Failure to Upgrade Informal Settlements in Egypt," *Open Democracy*, November 23, 2015. See also Lama Tawakkol, "Reclaiming the City's Core: Urban Accumulation, Surplus (Re)production and Discipline in Cairo," *Geoforum*, https://doi.org/10.1016/j.geoforum.2019.12.014.

135. Frische, "Getting By," 67.

136. Cited in Habib Ayeb, "The Social, Economic and Spatial Marginality in Two Neighborhoods in Tunisia," [in Arabic], unpublished paper, 2015, p. 23.

137. Ayeb, "The Social, Economic, and Spatial Marginality," 23–24.

138. Muhamed Abdel-Baqy, "Living on the Edge," *al-Ahram Weekly*, December 17, 2013. In May 2015, the justice minister Mahfouz Saber disparagingly stated that a "son of garbage collector [*ibn zabaleen*] cannot become a judge." There developed a national uproar in the streets and social media forcing him to resign. The campaign People Want to Appoint a Garbage Collector Son as Judge went viral; *Al-Watan*, May 12 and 13, 2015.

139. For an interesting discussion of the exclusionary attitudes of the Egyptian middle-class activists toward the poor, see Jessica Winegar, "A Civilized Revolution: Aesthetics and Political Action in Egypt," *American Ethnologist* 43, no. 4 (2016): 609–622.

140. Cited in Hoda Mansour, "Ghazhab al-Ashwaiyat," *Rowz al-Yousuf*, August 25, 2012.

141. Cited in Mathew Cassel, "Egypt: Impatient in Imbaba," *Electronic Intifada*, July 12, 2013.

142. Cited in Anthony Shadid, "Few Focus on Religion in One Cairo Neighborhood," *New York Times*, February 15, 2011.

143. Transcript of the complaints of a female food vendor in Cairo's Sayyid Nafisah captured on video, رصد حركة البيع في سوق السيدة نفيسة في العاصمة المصرية posted in Aljazeera, 2018.

144. Hannah Arendt, "The Lecture: Thoughts on Poverty, Misery and the Great Revolutions of History," *New England Review,* June 2017, 12, https://lithub.com/never-before-published-hannah-arendt-on-what-freedom-and-revolution-really-mean/.

145. Asef Bayat, *Workers and Revolution in Iran* (London: Zed books, 1987); Asef Bayat, *Street Politics: Poor People's Movements in Iran* (New York: Columbia University Press, 1997).

146. See Asef Bayat, *Revolution without Revolutionaries: Making Sense of the Arab Spring* (Palo Alto: Stanford University Press, 2017), chapter 3.

147. Joel Beinin, "Political Economy and Social Movement Theory Perspectives on the Tunisian and Egyptian Popular Uprisings of 2011," LSE Middle East Center Paper Series, no. 14 (2016), https://www.academia.edu/22618960/_Political_Economy_and_Social_Movement_Theory_Perspectives_on_the_Tunisian_and_Egyptian_Popular_Uprisings_of_2011_LSE_Middle_East_Centre_Paper_Series_no_11_January_2016_?email_work_card=title.

148. This is based on a comparison of the (United Nations Development Programme) Human Development Indexes adjusted against inequality between Tunisia and Egypt during 2010 and 2018, combined with "indicators of democracy" found in Polity Index covering the same period; http://www.systemicpeace.org/.

149. Conversation with worker activist Fatma Ramadan, Egyptian Initiative for Personal Rights, June 9, 2013.

150. Even though the ex-president Marzouki supported the Jemna experiment, the Nahda / Essebsi governments deemed the practice "illegitimate" and caused much bureaucratic bottleneck. For instance, the Association of the Protection of Jemna Oasis that represented the project could not secure social security for its workers because it lacked legal status, never mind how much good it had done to local people and their community.

151. Ahmed Khalil Tawfik, *Tweetat Al-'osoor al-Wusta* (Cairo: Al-mu'assasah al-'arabiyyah al-hadithah, 2014); cited in Khalil, "The Lawyers of Egypt," 14.

## 5. MOTHERS, DAUGHTERS, AND THE GENDER PARADOX

1. Xan Rice, Katherine Marsh, Tom Finn, Harriet Sherwood, Angelique Chrisafis, and Robert Booth, "Women Have Emerged as Key Players in the Arab Spring," *The Guardian,* April 22, 2011; BBC News website, June 15, 2019, https://www.bbc.com/news/world-africa-48634150.

2. For a detailed discussion, see Chapter 3 in this book.

3. Nicola Pratt, "Gender, Neoliberalism, Social Justice, and Egyptian Revolution," paper presented at "Rethinking the 'Woman Question' in the New Middle East," Amman, Jordan, May 3–4, 2014.

4. Valentine M. Moghadam, "Modernizing Women and Democratization after the Arab Spring," *Journal of North African Studies* 19, no. 2 (2014): 137–142

5. Valentine Moghadam has in particular spearheaded such endeavors with reference to the Middle East and beyond; see, for instance, Valentine M. Moghadam, "Feminism and the Future of Revolutions," *Socialism and Democracy* 32, no.1 (2018): 31–53.

6. Cited in Lucia Sobrera, "Challenges of Thinking Feminism and Revolution in Egypt between 2011 and 2014," *Postcolonial Studies* 17, no. 1 (2014): 69.

7. Pratt, "Gender, Neoliberalism, Social Justice, and Egyptian Revolution."

8. Rice et al., "Women Have Emerged as Key Players"; BBC News website, June 15, 2019, https://www.bbc.com/news/world-africa-48634150.

9. Sheila Rowbotham, *Women, Resistance, and Revolution: A History of Women and Revolution in the Modern World* (London: Verso, 2014), 1.

10. See Chapter 3 for more elaboration on Tunisia and Egypt. Similar pattern seems to be at work in Bahrain and Libya. Thus, for the Bahraini Noor Jilal, "women are not calling for their own rights but those of everyone"; according to a Benghazi, Libyan, female protestor, "We want to be able to speak our minds, to be ourselves"; and according to Faiza Suliman in Yemen, "Our demands are somehow similar to men, starting with freedom, equal citizenship, and giving women greater role in society"; see Rice et al., "Women Have Emerged as Key Players."

11. https://www.aljazeera.com/indepth/opinion/2012/03/201231613312920 1850.html.

12. See the video of the incident at https://www.youtube.com/watch?v =gtPFHw65aIs.

13. No wonder victims would often remain perplexed as to "who should I blame for this? I don't know who to blame," as one wondered after being assaulted.[1] "But I am really angry at many religious leaders . . . our political leaders. . . . I am angry at all the mothers who teach their sons that they are superior just because they are men . . . and tell their daughters that they are inferior just because they are women. . . . I am angry, but I am not broken"; see El-Nadeem Center for Rehabilitation of Victims of Violence and Torture, Nazra

for Feminist Studies, and New Woman Foundation, *Sexual Assault and Rape in Tahrir: A Compendium of Sources 2011–2013* (Cairo: El-Nadeem Center for Rehabilitation of Victims of Violence and Torture, Nazra for Feminist Studies, and New Woman Foundation, 2013), 6.

14. Hanan Hammad, "Sexual Harassment in Egypt: An Old Plague in a New Revolutionary Order," *Gender*, no. 1 (2017): 44–63.

15. Egyptian Center for Women's Rights, Cairo, 2008.

16. See El-Nadeem Center for Rehabilitation of Victims of Violence and Torture et al., *Sexual Assault and Rape in Tahrir Square*, 8.

17. Yasmine El-Rifae, "What the Egyptian Revolution Can Offer #MeToo," *Nation*, January 22, 2018. Between November 2012 and January 2014, more than 250 cases of sexual violations including rapes were documented to have taken place. Only on June 8, 2014, in Tahrir Square to celebrate the inauguration of the new president, nine cases of heinous mob sexual assaults were documented.

18. Catherine Byaruhanga, "Rape and Revolution: They Were Crying and Screaming," BBC News website, June 15, 2019; see also BBC, "Letter from Africa: How Cheating Husbands Are Linked to Sudan Protests," BBC News website, February 20, 2019.

19. In Syria, the regime encouraged the perpetrators to make video clips of rapes so that they could be circulated. Aljazeera, "Silent War: How Rape Became a Weapon in Syria," https://www.aljazeera.com/programmes/witness/2018/06/silent-war-rape-weapon-syria-180611071447939.html?fbclid=IwAR19tIaWwDpFvY_8o3NuNizH1AIHyRAVSyV31wE2YbDxUo_8UpF__PlF3po.

20. El-Nadeem Center for Rehabilitation of Victims of Violence and Torture et al., *Sexual Assault and Rape in Tahrir Square*, 4.

21. Hammad, "Sexual Harassment in Egypt." Sherine Hafez also plausibly suggests "these acts of public violence against women aim at regaining a sense of lost power by males making women as the weaker sex, sexual objects to be pillaged, touched, and humiliated" (*Women of the Midan* [Bloomington: Indiana University Press, 2019], 51). But we also need to ask what is the role of the "revolution" in this episode of violence, and why the eighteen days were mostly free from such acts.

22. Interview with Deniz Kandiyoti, *Borderlines*, March 13, 2020, https://www.borderlines-cssaame.org/posts/2020/3/13/gender-governance-and-islam-book-launch-an-interview-with-deniz-kandiyoti.

23. Aliya Jessa, "Staring Down Street Harassment: Women's Perspectives of Street Harassment in Tunisia," SIT Graduate Institute / SIT Study Abroad SIT Digital Collections, Fall 2017. See also https://www.youtube.com/watch?v=XDmInIYJBNM.

24. According to the report on gender-based violence made by the Center of Research, Study, Documentation and Information on Women; http://www.stopstreetharassment.org/tag/tunisia/.

25. See Moghadam, "Modernizing Women and Democratization after the Arab Spring." Nadje Al-Ali and Nicola Pratt also point to this dilemma in "Gender, Protest and Political Transition in the Middle East and North Africa," in *Handbook on Gender in World Politics,* ed. Jill Steans and Daniella Tepe-Belfrage (Chichester, UK: Edward Edgar, 2016).

26. Cited in Andrea Khalil, "Tunisia's Women: Partners in Revolution," *Journal of North African Studies* 19, no. 2 (2014): 196.

27. The association of women with nation, and men with the state is discussed in Suad Joseph, "Gendering Citizenship in the Middle East," in *Gender and Citizenship in the Middle East,* ed. Suad Joseph (Syracuse, NY: Syracuse University Press, 2000), 3–30. According to Beth Baron, nationalists in Egypt deployed female honor to mobilize men against foreign domination; they gendered the country as a woman obligating men to protect the nation in the same way as they would protect their women's honor. Beth Baron, *Egypt as a Woman: Nationalism, Gender, and Politics* (Berkeley: University of California Press, 2005), 40–42.

28. See an interesting discussion in Lucia Sobrera, "Challenges of Thinking Feminism and Revolution in Egypt between 2011 and 2014," *Postcolonial Studies* 17, no. 1 (2014).

29. She expressed it to Catherine Ashton, the European Union foreign policy supremo during a recent visit to Tahrir Square in March 2011; Rice et al., "Women Have Emerged as Key Players"; BBC News website, June 15, 2019, https://www.bbc.com/news/world-africa-48634150.

30. Conversation with Radwa, July 2016, Cairo.

31. Conversation with Ghouson, August 2016, Cairo.

32. Cited in Shaza Abdel-Lateef, "Emancipatory Future: Women and Agitational Politics in Revolutionary Egypt" (MA thesis, American University in Cairo, 2013), 42.

33. Cited in Abdel-Lateef, "Emancipatory Future," 28.

34. Conversation with Asma, August 2016, Cairo.

35. Conversation with Rasha, female activist, July 26, 2011, Tunis.

36. Conversation with Qamar, June 16, 2017, Tunis.

37. Samia Mehrez, ed., *Translating Egypt's Revolution: The Language of Tahrir* (Cairo: American University in Cairo Press, 2012), 14.

38. Cited in http://english.alarabiya.net/en/life-style/2012/12/21/Egypt-activist-who-protested-nude-says-she-wants-to-make-change-differently.html.

39. Marwan M. Kraidy, "The Revolutionary Body Politic: Preliminary Thoughts on a Neglected Medium in the Arab Uprisings," *Middle East Journal of Culture and Communication* 5, no. 1 (2012); Marwan M. Kraidy, "New Texts Out Now: Marwan M. Kraidy, The Naked Blogger of Cairo: Creative Insurgency in the Arab World," *Jadaliyya,* March 1, 2017, https://www.jadaliyya.com/Details/34062.

40. Sherine Hafez, *Women of Midan* (Bloomington: Indiana University Press, 2019), 142.

41. Carlotta Gall, "Tunisians Are Shaken as Young Women Turn to Extremism," *New York Times,* November 20, 2014.

42. http://iknowpolitics.org/ar/news/world-news/%D8%AA%D9%88%D9%86%D8%B3-%D9%86%D8%B3%D8%A7%D8%A1-%D8%A7%D9%84%D8%AC%D9%86%D9%88%D8%A8%D8%AF%D9%8A%D9%85%D9%82%D8%B1%D8%A7%D8%B7%D9%8A%D8%A7%D8%AA-%D9%8A%D8%A4%D9%8A%D8%AF%D9%86-%D8%A7%D9%84%D9%85%D9%86%D8%A7%D8%B5%D9%81%D8%A9.

43. Doris H. Gray and Terry Coonan, "Notes from the Field: Silence Kills! Women and the Transitional Justice Process in Post-Revolutionary Tunisia," *International Journal of Transitional Justice* 7 (2013): 350–351.

44. https://foreignpolicy.com/2014/02/07/will-tunisian-women-finally-inherit-what-they-deserve/ 350.

45. https://www.reuters.com/article/tunisia-women-idAFLDE73G0CP 20110427.

46. Jihen Laghmari and Caroline Alexander, "Woman Running for President Shows Tunisia's Arab Spring Progress," Bloomberg, November 13, 2014.

47. See Moghadam, "Modernizing Women and Democratization after the Arab Spring," 140.

48. Ursula Lindsey, "Some Gains, Many Sacrifices: Women's Rights in Tunisia," Al-Fanar Media, July 10, 2017.

49. Khalil, "Tunisia's Women," 197.

50. Gabriella Borovsky and Asma Ben Yahia, "Women's Political Participation in Tunisia after the Revolution: Findings from Focus Groups in Tunisia," conducted February 17–28, 2012, Washington, DC.

51. Conversation with Nermin, women's rights activist, June 20, 2019, Tunis.

52. "Tunisian Women Portraits: Rafika, a Powerful Woman, Hiding Another," *Huffington Post* Tunisia, April 17, 2015, http://www.huffpostmaghreb.com/2015/03/17/femmes-tunisiennes_n_6879608.html?utm_hp_ref=societe-tunisie.

53. Rehab Sakr, "Occupying New Public Spaces: Facebook, Underground Economy, and the Response of Egyptian Women to the Economic Crises after 2011 Revolution," unpublished paper, Cairo, 2015.

54. Stated by a thirty-year-old housewife from Sfax cited in Borovsky and Ben Yahia, "Women's Political Participation in Tunisia," 19.

55. https://foreignpolicy.com/2014/02/07/will-tunisian-women-finally-inherit-what-they-deserve/.

56. Sandro Lutyens, "Manich Manich to Provide Women with Necessary Means to Defend Their Rights," *Huffpost* Tunisia, April 1, 2015, http://www.huffpostmaghreb.com/2015/04/01/tunisie-manich-manich-femmes_n_6967888.html.

57. https://thehill.com/blogs/congress-blog/foreign-policy/201830-women-activism-and-resistance-in-rural-upper-and-lower.

58. https://thehill.com/blogs/congress-blog/foreign-policy/201830-women-activism-and-resistance-in-rural-upper-and-lower.

59. https://thehill.com/blogs/congress-blog/foreign-policy/201830-women-activism-and-resistance-in-rural-upper-and-lower.

60. Conversation with Radwa, August 2016, Cairo.

61. Conversation with Hoda, August 2016, Cairo.

62. Conversation with Hoda, August 2016, Cairo.

63. Conversation with Alaa, August 2016, Cairo.

64. Sami Zlitni and Zeineb Touati, "Social Networks and Women's Mobilization in Tunisia," *Journal of International Women's Studies* 13, no. 5, (2012): 53–54.

65. Giulia Daniele, "Tunisian Women's Activism after the January 14 Revolution: Looking within and towards the Other Side of the Mediterranean," *Journal of International Women's Studies* 15, no. 2 (2014): 25.

66. "For me, feminism is liberating women and liberating women is offering the opportunities and allowing them to choose," according to Ben Said; Katie Nadworny and Danielle Villasana, "Grassroots Efforts in Tunisia to Advance Women's Right," November 6, 2017, https://www.pri.org/stories/2017-11-06/grassroots-efforts-tunisia-advance-women-s-rights.

67. For a detailed discussion, see Mounira M. Charrad and Amina Zarrugh, "Equal or Complementary? Women in the New Tunisian Constitution after the Arab Spring," *Journal of North African Studies* 19, no. 2 (2014): 230–243.

68. Lilia Balise, "New Generation of Feminists Strike Out in Tunisia," *Middle East Eye*, July 28, 2016, https://www.middleeasteye.net/features/new-generation-feminists-strike-out-tunisia; see also https://www.nswp.org/es/node/2652.

69. https://www.alaraby.co.uk/english/indepth/2017/11/16/choufthounna-the-feminist-art-festival-in-tunisia.

70. Magdalena Mach, "Tunisian Women Take Over Male-Dominated Street with Art," Words in the Bucket, July 23, 2018, https://www.wordsinthebucket.com/tunisian-women-paint-the-city-walls-with-their-feminine-power.

71. Lilia Labidi, "Political, Aesthetic, and Ethical Positions of Tunisian Women Artists, 2011–13," *Journal of North African Studies* 19, no. 2 (2014): 157–171.

72. El-Rifae, "What the Egyptian Revolution Can Offer #MeToo."

73. In a statement, the feminist group Nazra confirmed, "We stress the need to confront all attempts to use this discussion as a means to 'protect' women that may lead to their exclusion or infringe on their right to demonstrate or take part in various political activities." The statement can be found in El-Nadeem Center for Rehabilitation of Victims of Violence and Torture et al., *Sexual Assault and Rape in Tahrir Square*, 56.

74. Abdel-Lateef, "Emancipatory Future," 72.

75. See the very interesting report of the Women's March at https://www.youtube.com/watch?v=EKRe-MONpNo.

76. The organizations included El-Nadeem Center for Rehabilitation of Victims of Violence and Torture, New Woman Foundation, Women and Memory Forum, Baheya Ya Masr, Center for Egyptian Women's Legal Assistance, Sahm al-Theka Foundation, the Alliance for Arab Women, the Voice of Egyptian Women, and Egyptian Women for Change, among many others. See El-Nadeem Center for Rehabilitation of Victims of Violence and Torture et al., *Sexual Assault and Rape in Tahrir Square*.

77. Cited in Ghadeer Ahmed Eldamaty, "Mustaqillat: Navigating Women's Mobilities in Post-2011 Egypt" (MA thesis, American University in Cairo, 2019).

78. For some details, see Nadine Sika and Yasmine El-Khodary, "One Step Forward, Two Steps Back? Egyptian Women within the Confines of Authoritarianism," *Journal of International Women's Studies* 13, no. 5 (2012).

79. Abdel-Lateef, "Emancipatory Future," 49, 98–99.

80. See comments by women activist Lina Ben-Mehli on Tunisian TV at https://www.youtube.com/watch?v=7PdsbssePBo.

81. Sarah Yerkes and Maro Youssef, "Coronavirus Reveals Tunisia's Revolutionary Gains Exist Only on Paper," The New Arab, June 22, 2020, https://english .alaraby.co.uk/english/comment/2020/6/22/coronavirus-reveals-tunisias -revolutionary-gains-only-exist-on-paper.

82. https://www.bbc.com/news/world-africa-35743663.

83. Messaoud Romdhani, "Gender Equality in Tunisia: Still a Long Way to Go," *Alternatives International*, September 1, 2019.

84. Gender Concerns International, "The Situation of Women in Tunisia," http://www.genderconcerns.org/country-in-focus/tunisia/the-situation-of -women-in-tunisia/.

85. Aida al-Ahwal and Sonya Zeinoubi, women activists; see https://www .youtube.com/watch?v=hhBkW_Pqn7I.

86. https://www.npr.org/templates/story/story.php?storyId=201851115.

87. https://imagesmena.org/wp-content/uploads/sites/5/2017/05/IMAGES -MENA-Multi-Country-Report-EN-16May2017-web.pdf.

88. See Nadia Sonneveld and Monika Lindbekk, "A Revolution in Muslim Family Law? Egypt's Pre- and Post-Revolutionary Period (2011–2013) Compared," *New Middle Eastern Studies*, no. 5 (2015).

89. https://www.loc.gov/law/foreign-news/article/tunisia-cabinet-approves -bill-requiring-equal-inheritance-shares-for-men-and-women/.

90. https://www.opendemocracy.net/en/north-africa-west-asia/living -double-life-behind-lies-of-womens-daily-lives-in-egyp/.

91. Conversation with Mona, July 2016, Cairo.

92. Conversation with Qamar, June 16, 2017, Tunis.

93. Ali Gamal, "The Lure for Girls of Living Alone," BBC, July 21, 2015, https://www.bbc.com/news/world-middle-east-33347904.

94. See Eldamaty, "Mustaqillat."

95. Cited in Eldamaty, "Mustaqillat," 31.

96. Gamal, "The Lure for Girls of Living Alone."

97. Conversation with Hala in her twenties, April 2015, Cairo.

98. Eldamaty, "Mustaqillat."

99. I discuss the phenomenon of veiling in Asef Bayat, *Making Islam Democratic: Social Movements and the Post-Islamist Turn* (Palo Alto: Stanford University Press, 2007).

100. Cited in Valentina Primo, "Are Egyptian Women Taking Off Their Veils?" *Cairo Scene*, August 9, 2014; Gamal, "The Lure for Girls of Living Alone."

101. Noha Darwish, "Unveiling the Trend: Egyptian Women Rethink the Veil," What Women Want, December 2, 2012, http://whatwomenwant-mag .com/2012/12/02/unveiling-the-trend-egyptian-women-re-think-the-veil.

102. Cited in Primo, "Are Egyptian Women Taking Off Their Veils?"

103. https://scoopempire.com/veiled-egypt-becoming-extremely-difficult/

104. Justin Lynch, "Women Fueled Sudan's Revolution, but Then They Were Pushed Aside," *Independent*, August 5, 2019, https://www.independent.co.uk /news/world/africa/sudan-revolution-women-uprising-democratic-transition -army-bashir-a9038786.html. Similarly, women were involved in both Algerian and Moroccan independence revolutions including street protests. But after the independence, they were told to go back home "where they belonged"; Fatima Saddiqi, "Contestations of Women's and Gender Rights in Morocco: A Reading from the 'Center,'" Zoom lecture, December 8, 2020.

## 6. CHILDREN OF REVOLUTION

1. Alexis de Tocqueville, *The Ancien Régime and the Revolution* (London: Penguin, 2008), 10.

2. For details, see Chapter 3.

3. See in particular Linda Herrera, *Revolution in the Age of Social Media* (London: Verso, 2014); Linda Herrera, ed., *Wired Citizenship: Youth Learning and Activism in the Middle East* (London: Routledge, 2014).

4. Haggai Erlich, *Youth and Revolution in the Changing Middle East, 1908–1914* (London: Lynne Rienner, 2015); Edward Sayer and Tarik Yousef, eds., *Young Generation Awakening: Economics, Society, and Policy on the Eve of the Arab Spring* (Oxford: Oxford University Press, 2016); Raj Desai, Anders Olofsgard, and Tarik Yousef, "Days of Rage and Silence: Explaining Political Action by Arab Youth," in *Young Generation Awakening: Economics, Society, and Policy on the Eve of the Arab Spring*, ed. Edward Sayer and Tarik Yousef (Oxford: Oxford University Press, 2016); Nadine Abdalla, "Youth Movements in the Egyptian Transformation: Strategies and Repertoires of Political Participation," *Mediterranean Politics* 21, no. 1 (2016); Dina Shehata, "Youth Movements and the 25th January Revolution," in *Arab Spring in Egypt: Revolution and Beyond*, ed. Bahgat Korany and Rabab El-Mahdi (Cairo: American University in Cairo Press, 2012), 105–124; Magdalena Delgado, "Contentious Copts: The Emergence, Success, and Decline of the Maspero Youth Movement in Egypt," in *Contentious Politics in the Middle East*, ed. Fawaz Gerges (London: Palgrave, 2015).

5. See, for instance, Nur Laiq, *Talking to Arab Youth: Revolution and Counterrevolution in Egypt and Tunisia* (New York: International Peace Institute, 2013). The book contains very useful interviews with youth engaged in the political or civic institutions.

6. See, for instance, Jon Abbink and Ineke van Kessel, eds., *Vanguard or Vandals: Youth, Politics and Conflict in Africa* (Leiden: Brill, 2005).

7. This paragraph draws heavily on Asef Bayat, "Is There a Youth Politics?" *Middle East Topics & Arguments* 9 (December 2017).

8. More details may found in Asef Bayat, "Muslim Youth and the Claims of Youthfulness," in *Being Young and Muslim: Cultural Politics in the Global South and North*, ed. Linda Herrera and Asef Bayat (Oxford: Oxford University Press, 2013).

9. https://twitter.com/Khaqani_M/status/1190408839771967490

10. I have discussed the notions of youth, youthfulness, and youthful politics in Asef Bayat, "Reclaiming Youthfulness," in *Being Young and Muslim*, ed. Linda Herrera and Asef Bayat (London: Oxford University Press, 2010); and Bayat, "Is There a Youth Politics?"

11. A very positive projection of youth in the Middle East may be found in Jared Cohen, *Children of Jihad* (New York: Gotham Books, 2007), where youth are seen as the agents of democracy and tolerance.

12. See Pierre Bourdieu, "Youth Is Just a Word," in *Sociology in Question* (London: Sage, 1993); Mayssoun Sukarieh and Stuart Tannock, *Youth Rising?* (London: Routledge, 2015); and Bayat, "Is There a Youth Politics?"

13. https://www.bbc.com/news/world-africa-12200493.

14. http://nawaat.org/portail/2015/12/30/revolution-my-love/.

15. Conversation with Rasha, July 26, 2011, Tunis.

16. Nicholas Collins, *Voices of a Revolution: Conversations with Tunisia's Youth* (Tunis: National Democratic Institute, 2011).

17. Conversation with Hossam, June 2012, Alexandria.

18. https://www.youtube.com/watch?v=Fgw_zfLLvh8.

19. https://www.anthropology.northwestern.edu/documents/people/TakingOuttheTrash_Winegar.pdf.

20. Cited in Alcinda Honwana, "Youth and the Tunisian Revolution," paper presented at the "Conflict Prevention and Peace Forum," 2011, p. 15.

21. I observed this in a conference that the Youth of Ekhwan had organized in Cairo, March 2011, against the will of their leaders.

22. Much violence occurred in the Tahrir protests in March and April, episode of virginity tests, Imbaba clashes in May, protests of the Ministry of

Interior in July, Israeli Embassy in September, Maspero massacre in October, and Muhammad Mahmoud Street battles in November that resulted in fifty deaths. Things were also bad in the protests in People's Assembly in December, over Kamal Ganzouri's cabinet, and the suspicious bombing of the Qadesseen (Two Saints) church to cause sectarian discord.

23. Karima Khalil has documented dozens of the newly emerged youth organizations in detail. Karima Khalil, "Politically Active Youth Groups in Egypt," unpublished research report, Cairo, January 2012, Paper 1.

24. These included the April 6th, young Muslim Brothers, the Mohamed ElBaradei Support Campaign, Al Karama, Justice and Freedom (Leftists), and Tagammu.

25. These groups included Hashd; Popular Democratic Movement for Change; Youth for Justice and Freedom (Shabab Min Agl al Adala wel Horreya); Revolution Protection Council (Majliss Hemayet el Thawra); Support Baradei for President Campaign; Revolutionary Committees for the Defense of the Revolution (al Ligan el Thawriyya lil Difa'a an al Thawra); the Revolutionary Youth Union; Democratic Forces Coalition (Tahalof al Qowa al Demoqratiya); Kollena Khaled Said (We Are All Khaled Said); just to name a few.

26. Conversation with Abdelrahman, June 2013, Cairo.

27. For an excellent portrayal and analysis, see Mona Abaza, "Walls, Segregating Downtown Cairo and the Mohammed Mahmud Street Graffiti," *Theory, Culture and Society* 30, no. 1 (2013); Mona Abaza, "Intimation and Resistance: Imagining Gender in Cairene Graffiti," *Jadaliyya*, June 30, 2013.

28. Daniel Farrell, "The Role of Artistic Protest Movements in the Egyptian Revolution," in *Youth, Revolt, Recognition: The Young Generation during and after the Arab Spring*, ed. Isabel Schäfer (Berlin: Mediterranean Institute Berlin (MIB) / Humboldt University Berlin, 2015).

29. Abdalla F. Hassan, "Rap Group at the Leading Edge of Egyptian Rebellion," *New York Times*, May 17, 2012, https://www.nytimes.com/2012/05/17/world/middleeast/17iht-m17-egypt-alexandria.html.

30. Mustapha Farouq, "Revolution Records," Al-Bawabah News, January 23, 2016, https://www.albawabhnews.com/1733558.

31. Conversation with Hossam, July 2011, Alexandria.

32. See Tadamun, http://www.tadamun.info/?post_type=initiative&p=7461#.WCiyCbU-7AI.

33. Conversation with Omran, July 2016, Cairo.

34. Conversation with Omran, July 2016, Cairo.

35. Linda Herrera, "Youth and Citizenship in the Digital Age: A View from Egypt," *Harvard Educational Review* 82, no. 3 (2012).

36. "Student Groups Demand Dismissal of Higher Education, Interior Ministers," Ahram Online, November 30, 2013.

37. Farah Ramzi, "Student Activism in Post-2011 Egypt: Understanding a Contentious Arena in a Fluctuating Context," Arab Reform Initiative, April 2016, p. 9, https://www.arab-reform.net/publication/student-activism-in-post-2011 -egypt-understanding-a-contentious-arena-in-a-fluctuating-context/.

38. Florian Kohstall, "From Reform to Resistance: Universities and Student Mobilisation in Egypt and Morocco before and after the Arab Uprisings," *British Journal of Middle Eastern Studies* 42, no. 1 (2015): 64, https://www.tandfonline .com/doi/abs/10.1080/13530194.2015.973183.

39. Conversation, Fall 2013, Illinois, United States.

40. These sentiments were expressed by the interviews conducted by Ramzy, "Student Activism in Post-2011 Egypt."

41. Interview with Rabab al-Mahdi, "Ultras Soccer Fans Ignite Revolutionary Fever," news@auc, August 30, 2012.

42. Heba Afifi, "Children of Revolution: Youth Wage Street Battles," *Al-Masry AlYoum*, March 14, 2013.

43. Afifi, "Children of Revolution."

44. Conversation with a young couple, Ahmed and Narmeen, July 2012, Montazah Park, Alexandria.

45. David Kirkpatrick and Mayy El-Sheick, "In Egypt a Chasm Grows between Young and Old," *New York Times*, February 16, 2014.

46. Kirkpatrick and El-Sheick, "In Egypt a Chasm Grows."

47. Ramzy, "Student Activism in Post-2011 Egypt," 12.

48. In 2010, some 35 percent of the Egyptian population were youth between fifteen and thirty-five years of age. Muslim Brothers have an estimated 600,000–700,000 members. This means that over 200,000 young people were affiliated with the Muslim Brotherhood; Charlotte Biegler-König, "The Attractiveness of Political Islam for Youth in North Africa," in *Youth, Revolt, Recognition: The Young Generation during and after the Arab Spring*, ed. Isabel Schäfer (Berlin: Mediterranean Institute Berlin (MIB) / Humboldt University Berlin, 2015), 39.

49. https://www.seechangemagazine.com/?p=2225; https://www.huffpost .com/entry/the-rise-of-the-social-en_b_6787054.

50. https://www.egyptindependent.com/call-center-industry-obstacles -and-potential/. See also https://www.aljazeera.com/indepth/features/2013 /08/20138113261070378s.html.

51. Harry Pettit, "The Cruelty of Hope: Emotional Cultures of Precarity in Neoliberal Cairo," *Environment and Planning D: Society and Space* 37, no. 4 (2019).

52. Harry Pettit, "Learning to Hope: 'Solving' a Youth Unemployment Crisis in Egypt," Tadwin Publishing, March 31, 2016.

53. Cited in Kirkpatrick and El-Sheick, "In Egypt a Chasm Grows between Young and Old."

54. Conversation with Hossam, June 2012, Alexandria.

55. On the experience of trauma in Egypt, see Vivienne Matthies-Boon, "Trauma as a Counterrevolutionary Strategy," *Middle East Report* 292, no. 3 (2019).

56. EuroMed, *Youth Work in Tunisia after the Revolution* (Brussels: European Union, 2013), 10. See also Tunisia-Live.net, Op-Ed, March 24, 2014.

57. Cited in Honwana, "Youth and the Tunisian Revolution," 16.

58. https://www.euronews.com/2016/03/18/taking-the-tunisian-revolution -into-the-schools-forging-a-21st-century-system.

59. Conversation with sociologists Hayet Mousa and Rida Ben Amer, January 2013, Tunisia. See also interviews in Fredrich Ebert Stiftung Youth Survey, Berlin, 2017.

60. Conversation with sociologists Hayet Mousa and Rida Ben Amer, January 2013, Tunisia.

61. Interviews conducted by Fredrich Ebert Stiftung, Tunisia, 2017, Interview no. 2.

62. Conversation with Ghassan, July 2011, Tunis.

63. Bjørn Thomassen, "Notes towards an Anthropology of Political Revolution," *Comparative Studies in Society and History* 54, no. 3 (2012), 684.

64. Interview Ghassan, July 2011, Tunis.

65. Charis Boutieri, "Jihadists and Activists: Tunisian Youth Five Years Later," *Open Democracy*, July 29, 2015, https://www.opendemocracy.net/en /author/charis-boutieri/.

66. Conversation with Elyssa, a college student in Tunis during and after the revolution, January 2020, Berlin.

67. Sarah Lynch, "In Tunisia, Academic 'Families' Protect University Campuses," *Al-Fanar Media*, February 23, 2014, https://www.al-fanarmedia.org/2014 /02/in-tunisia-academic-families-protect-university-campuses/.

68. Nadine El-Sayed, "In Tunisia, a Once Banned Student Union Rises Again," *Al-Fanar Media*, March 19, 2019, https://www.al-fanarmedia.org/2014/03/tunisia-banned-student-union-rises/.

69. Mohamed Abdel Salam, "Student Unions and Politics in Post-Revolution Tunisia," Atlantic Council, January 20, 2015, https://www.atlanticcouncil.org/blogs/menasource/student-unions-and-politics-in-post-revolution-tunisia/.

70. Carolina Silveira, "Youth as Political Actors after the 'Arab Spring': The Case of Tunisia," in *Youth, Revolt, Recognition: The Young Generation during and after the Arab Spring*, ed. Isabel Schäfer (Berlin: Mediterranean Institute Berlin (MIB) / Humboldt University Berlin, 2015), 21–22.

71. Kiran Alevi, "Will Tunisia's Youth Head to the Ballots?" Al-Jazeera, September 26, 2014.

72. "Tunisian Youth: Between Political Exclusion and Civic Engagement," *Tunisia Live*, June 14, 2013, http://www.tunisia-live.net/2013/06/14/tunisian-youth-between-political-exclusion-and-civic-engagement/#sthash.8tWkIcpI.dpuf.

73. Michael Robbins, "Tunisia Five Years after the Revolution: Findings from the Arab Barometer," in *Arab Barometer Country Wave IV Reports*, May 15, 2016, p. 8, http://www.arabbarometer.org/country/tunisia.

74. Fredrich Ebert Stiftung Youth Survey, Berlin, 2017, Tunisia, Interview no. 2.

75. Interviews with young people, Fredrich Ebert Stiftung Youth Survey, Berlin, 2017, Tunisia, Interview no. 2.

76. Interview with the activist Hamza Abidi in "Refusing to Forgive: Tunisia's Maneesh M'sameh Campaign," *Middle East Report*, no. 281 (2016): 31.

77. "Experiences and Perceptions of Young People in Tunisia: The Case of Douar Hicher and Ettadhamen Quantitative Survey: Preliminary Findings," International Alert, February 2015, pp. 4–5.

78. "Experiences and Perceptions of Young People in Tunisia."

79. Close to 90 percent said work was the most important, while 10 percent said politics. "Experiences and Perceptions of Young People in Tunisia."

80. World Bank Group, *Tunisia, Breaking the Barriers to Youth Inclusion* (Washington, DC: World Bank, 2014), 19, https://www.worldbank.org/en/country/tunisia/publication/tunisia-breaking-the-barriers-to-youth-inclusion.

81. Qualitative interviews, Tunisia, Fredrich Ebert Stiftung Youth Survey, Berlin 2017.

82. Conversation with Ayat and Ridaa, sociologists, January 2013, Tunis.

83. Inken Bartels, "Reconfiguration of Tunisian Migration Politics after the 'Arab Spring': The Role of Young Civil Society Movements," in *Youth, Revolt, Recognition*, ed. Isabel Schäfer (Berlin: Mediterranean Institute Berlin (MIB) / Humboldt University Berlin, 2015).

84. Kevin Sullivan, "Tunisia, after Igniting Arab Spring, Sends the Most Fighters to Islamic State in Syria," *Washington Post*, October 28, 2014, https://www.washingtonpost.com/world/national-security/tunisia-after-igniting-arab-spring-sends-the-most-fighters-to-islamic-state-in-syria/2014/10/28/b5db4faa-5971-11e4-8264-deed989ae9a2_story.html; also Monica Marks, "Youth Politics and Tunisian Salafism: Understanding the Jihadi Current," *Mediterranean Politics* 18, no. 1 (2013).

85. "Experiences and Perceptions of Young People in Tunisia."

86. "Experiences and Perceptions of Young People in Tunisia," 5.

87. See Mounir Saidani, "Post-revolutionary Tunisian Youth Art: The Effect of Contestation on the Democratization of Art Production and Consumption," in *What Politics? Youth and Political Engagement in Africa*, ed. Elina Oinas, Henri Onodera, and Leena Suurpää (Leiden: Brill, 2018). Also see Nouri Gana, "Rap and Revolt in the Arab World," *Social Text* 30 (2013): 25–53.

88. Cited in Sofia Laine, Leena Suurpää, and Afifa Ltifi, "Respectful Resistance: Young Musicians and the Unfinished Revolution in Tunisia," in *What Politics? Youth and Political Engagement in Africa*, ed. Elina Oinas, Henri Onodera, and Leena Suurpää (Leiden: Brill, 2018), 63,

89. Saidani, "Post-revolutionary Tunisian Youth Art," 115.

90. "Haraka Shabab Tunis: Gamaiyaa Min Thomar al-Thawra," *Al-Masdar al-Tunisiyya*, March 16, 2011.

91. Sarah Yerkes, *Where Have All the Revolutionaries Gone?* (New York: Center for Middle East Policy, Brookings Institution, 2017); Matt Gordner, "Youth Politics in Tunisia: Comparing Land / Labor, Leftist Movements and NGO-ized Elites," *Youth Politics in the Middle East and North Africa* 36 (November 2019).

92. Silveira, "Youth as Political Actors after the "Arab Spring," 23.

93. Adeline Masquelier, interview in "Bar Book Forum: Adeline Masquelier's Fada: Boredom and Belonging in Niger," https://www.blackagendareport.com/bar-book-forum-adeline-masqueliers-fada-boredom-and-belonging-niger.

94. Conversation with Ayet and Ridaa, January 2012, Tunis.

95. Cited in Giovanni Cordova, "Challenging Hegemony, Imaging Alternatives: Everyday Youth Discourses and Practices of Resistance in Contemporary Tunisia," *Journal of North African Studies* 26, no. 2 (2021): 6.

96. Wa'il Lutfi, *Du'ah al-supermarket: al-Judhur al-Amrikiyya lil-Du'ah al-Judud* (Cairo: Dar al- 'Ayn lil-Nashr, 2019).

97. Sari Hanafi, "The Arab Revolutions: The Emergence of a New Political Subjectivity," *Contemporary Arab Affairs* 5, no. 2 (2012): 53.

98. Conversation with Ayet, January 2013, Tunis.

99. See how the young supported Bernie Sanders in the United States, or they supported the old unorthodox president Kais Saied in Tunisia who lashed out at party politics in favor of bottom-up democracy through representation through local, regional, and national councils; Tarek Amara and Angus McDowall, "New Tunisian Leader Rode Wave of Youth Excitement to Presidency," Reuters, October 14, 2019, https://www.reuters.com/article/us-tunisia-election-youth/new-tunisian-leader-rode-wave-of-youth-excitement-to-presidency-idUSKBN1WT20F.

## 7. THE SOCIAL WORLD

1. Alain Badiou, *The Rebirth of History: Times of Riots and Uprisings* (London: Verso, 2012), 109.

2. Ala'a Abdel-Fattah, "The Dream Comes First," *Al-Shorouk*, June 24, 2011. Operating in a different zone of consciousness had already been echoed by the mystic poet Rumi centuries before—"In love with insanity, I'm fed up with wisdom and rationality."

3. Mikko Jakonen, " Thomas Hobbes on Fear, *Mimesis, Aisthesis*, and Politics," *Distinktion* 12, no. 2 (2011), https://www.tandfonline.com/doi/abs/10.1080/1600910X.2011.579491?src=recsys&journalCode=rdis20.

4. Associated Press, "Egyptians Have Personal Revolutions after Tumult," https://www.youtube.com/watch?v=F4bJjmJkWR0.

5. For a more extensive analysis of the Tahrir moments on which the next two paragraphs heavily draw, see Asef Bayat, "Global Tahrir," in *Global Middle East: Towards the 21st Century*, ed. Asef Bayat and Linda Herrera (Berkeley: University of California Press, 2021).

6. See Jeffery Alexander, *Performative Revolution in Egypt: An Essay in Cultural Power* (London: Bloomsbury Academic, 2011); Alain Badiou, "Tunisia, Egypt: When an East Wind Sweeps Away the Arrogance of the West," trans. Anindya Bhattacharyya, *Le Monde*, February 18, 2011, https://thefunambulist.net/philosophy/politics-tunisia-egypt-when-an-eastern-wind-sweeps-up-western-arrogance-by-alain-badiou; Slavoj Žižek, "For Egypt, This Is the Miracle of Tahrir Square,"

*Guardian,* February 10, 2011); Helga Tawil-Souri, "Power of Place," *Middle East Journal of Culture and Communication* 5 (2012): 86–95.

7. Gunning and Baron, *Why Occupy a Square? People, Protests and Movements in the Egyptian Revolution* (Oxford: Oxford University Press, 2014), 259.

8. Cilja Harder and Dina Wahba, "New Neighborhood Power: Informal Popular Committees and Changing Local Governance in Egypt," New Century Foundation, February 14, 2017, https://tcf.org/content/report/new-neighborhood-power/.

9. This passage on Popular Committees draws on Aysa El-Meehy, *Islamist and Non-Islamist Local Activism: Comparative Reflections from Egypt's Popular Committees* (Washington, DC: Project on Middle East Political Science, 2017); Ayse El-Meehy, "Egypt's Popular Committees," *Middle East Reports,* no. 265 (Winter 2012), https://merip.org/2013/01/egypts-popular-committees; Hatem M. Hassan, "Extraordinary Politics of Ordinary People: Explaining the Microdynamics of Popular Committees in Revolutionary Cairo," unpublished paper, University of Pittsburgh, 2017. A more recent fine study is found in Cilja Harder and Dina Wahba, "New Neighborhood Power: Informal Popular Committees and Changing Local Governance in Egypt," New Century Foundation, February 14, 2017, https://tcf.org/content/report/new-neighborhood-power/.

10. The passages are drawn from "Mahaliya al-Dokki wa al-Aghouza," *Tadamun,* http://www.tadamun.info/?post_type=initiative&p=6232#.WCjGhrU-7AL.

11. Excellent analyses may be found in Mona Abaza, "Walls, Segregating Downtown Cairo and the Mohammed Mahmud Street Graffiti," *Theory Culture Society,* October 9, 2012; Mona Abaza, "The Field of Graffiti and Street Art in Post-January 2011 Egypt," in *Routledge Handbook of Graffiti and Street Art,* ed. Jeffery Ross (New York: Routledge, 2016); Samuli Schielke and Jessica Winegar, "The Writing on the Walls of Egypt," *Middle East Report,* no. 265 (Winter 2012); Ted Swedenburg, "Egypt's Music of Protest," *Middle East Report,* no. 265 (Winter 2012); Lucia G. Westin, "Tunisian Music: The Soundtrack of the Revolution, the Voice of the People," *The Phenomenon of Singing* 9 (2013); Dounia Georgeon, "Revolutionary Graffiti," *Wasafiri* 27, no. 4 (2012): 70–75.

12. Lilia Labid, "Political, Aesthetic, and Ethical Positions of Tunisian Women Artists, 2011–13," *Journal of North African Studies* 19, no. 2 (2014): 157–171.

13. Sonali Pahwa, "Making Revolution Everyday: Quotidian Performance and Utopian Imagination in Egypt's Streets and Squares," *Text and Performance Quarterly* 39, no. 1 (2019).

14. Dina Ibrahim, "The Birth and Death of 25TV: Innovation in Post-revolution Egyptian TV News Formats," *Arab Media & Society*, no. 23 (Winter / Spring 2017).

15. Euromed, *Youth Work in Tunisia after the Revolution* (Brussels: European Union, 2013).

16. *Al-Badil*, March 16, 2013.

17. "Violent Tide of Salafism Threatens the Arab Spring," *Guardian*, February 9, 2013.

18. Some of the passages in this section are drawn from the chapter 9 of my book *Revolution without Revolutionaries: Making Sense of the Arab Spring* (Palo Alto, CA: Stanford University Press, 2017).

19. Reported in the website Kefteji: Tunisian Politics, Media, and Culture, June 11, 2012.

20. *News Wires*, France24.com, posted on October 13, 2013.

21. "Saudi Police Arrest Two over 'Free Hugs,'" *Al-Jazeera*, November 21, 2013, www.aljazeera.com.

22. Fawziya Torbai, "Spread of Urfi Marriage in Universities after the Revolution," *Mahres*, February 22, 2012, https://www.masress.com/shamsalhoria/7322.

23. Conversation with Hala, May 2015, Cairo.

24. Sheera Frankel and Maged Atef, "More and More Egyptian Women Are Casting Aside Their Veil," www.buzzfeed.com, posted on November 7, 2013. My own conversations with Egyptian activists supports the claim.

25. Conversation with Hala, May 2015, Cairo.

26. Saba Mahmood, *Politics of Piety: The Islamic Revival and the Feminist Subject* (Princeton, NJ: Princeton University Press, 2005), 16.

27. Nareman Ehab Amin, "Revolutionary Religion: Youth and Islam in Post-2011 Egypt," (PhD diss., Princeton University, 2021), 278.

28. Frankel and Atef, "More and More Egyptian Women Are Casting Aside Their Veil."

29. Conversation with Hala, May 2015, Cairo.

30. Conversation with Hala, May 2015, Cairo.

31. Cited in Ghadeer Ahmed Eldamaty, "Mustaqillat: Navigating Women's Mobilities in Post-2011 Egypt" (MA thesis, American University in Cairo, 2019), 40.

32. For a perceptive analysis, see Laleh Khalili, "Women in and after the Arab Spring," Sadighi Annual Lecture (Amsterdam, 2013), 62–63. Also see Maya Mikdashi, "Waiting for Alia," *Jadaliyya*, November 20, 2011.

33. Bel Trew, "Egypt's Growing Gay-Right Movement," *Daily Beast,* May 21, 2013.

34. "Spotlight on Egypt: A Gay Blogger's POV," Gaytravel.com, February 8, 2011, https://www.gaytravel.com/gay-blog/spotlight-on-egypt-a-gay-bloggers -pov/.

35. Sarah Carr, "Of Moral Panic and State Security," *Mada Masr,* November 25, 2013; *Aswat Masriyya,* October 13, 2013.

36. "Egypt Prosecutor Orders 7 Held for Homosexuality," Associated Press, September 6, 2014.

37. "Being lesbian in Egypt is not something I can freely be. I believe this [concert] was the perfect chance for the LGBT community to say 'we are here, we have rights,' without jeopardizing our own safety," one participant said; *Egypt Independent,* https://egyptindependent.com/controversy-flies-lgbt-rights -rise-rainbow-flag-concert/.

38. https://www.alaraby.co.uk/english/indepth/2018/3/20/tunisias-lgbt -community-demand-change.

39. https://www.facebook.com/SHAMS-RAD-759151530946388/.

40. In a country where only 7 percent of the people supported homosexuality, Baatour received nearly 20,000 signatures in support of his candidacy—double the required number. Claire Parker, "An Openly Gay Candidate Is Running for President in Tunisia, a Milestone for the Arab World," *Washington Post,* August 9, 2019, https://www.washingtonpost.com/world/2019/08/09/an-openly -gay-candidate-is-running-president-tunisia-milestone-arab-world/.

41. Samar Kadi, "For LGBT in Arab Countries, 'Change Is Painstakingly Slow,'" *Arab Weekly,* May 8, 2018, https://thearabweekly.com/lgbt-arab-countries -change-painstakingly-slow

42. Nadia Idle and Alex Nunns, *Tweets from Tahrir* (New York: OR Books, 2011), 221.

43. Some estimates speak of four million adherents. The two million figure is based on Gallup Poll and the University of Michigan polls; see Magdy Samann, "Atheist Rise in Egypt," ZAM Chronicle, October 17, 2013.

44. See Samann, "Atheist Rise in Egypt."

45. Carlyle Murphy, "Atheism Explodes in Saudi Arabia despite State-Enforced Ban," *Global Post,* June 12, 2014.

46. Murphy, "Atheism Explodes in Saudi Arabia despite State-Enforced Ban."

47. In Qantarah, https://en.qantara.de/print/28282.

48. Murphy, "Atheism Explodes in Saudi Arabia."

49. Diaa Hadid, "Arab Atheists, though Few, Inch Out of the Shadows," *Huffington Post*, March 8, 2013.

50. Mounir Adib, "While Atheism in Egypt Rises, Backlash Ensues," *Egypt Independent*, September 30, 2013.

51. *Al-Watan*, October 28, 2013.

52. See Shahra Razavi and Anne Jenichen, "Unhappy Marriage of Religion and Politics," *Third World Quarterly* 31, no. 6 (2010).

53. Cited in Hadid "Arab Atheists."

54. Samann, "Atheist Rise in Egypt."

55. *Al-Ahram* daily, June 18, 2014.

56. "Egypt Lawmaker Moves to Criminalise Atheism amid Moral Panic," *New Arab*, December 24, 2017, https://www.alaraby.co.uk/english/news/2017/12/24/egypt-lawmaker-moves-to-criminalise-atheism-amid-moral-panic.

57. "Anarchists in Egypt, Will the Real Black Bloc Please Stand Up?" tahriricn.wordpress.com/2013/11/03/Egypt-anarchists. An interview with an anonymous member of this secret group.

58. Interview with activists of Feminism Attack, reported in tahrircn, "Feminism Attack!"

59. Montassir Hamadah, "Ahdas al-Fawda al-Khallaqa wa Tahavvolat al-Khitab al-Islami," *Al-Daar*, May 10, 2020, https://aldar.ma/166813.html.

60. Local observers invariably confirm the impact of the revolution on the religiosity of Egyptian population, in particular the youth; see for instance Mohammed Fotouh, *Man Yamla' al-Faragh? Al-Kiyanat al-Diniya wa al-Thaqafiya fi Masr Ba'd al-Thawra* [Who fills the void? Religious and cultural entities in Egypt after the revolution] (Cairo: Markaz Nohoudh Lil-Darasat wa al-Bohouth, 2021); Hisham Ja'afar, "Al-Shabab al-Masri wa Bada'el al-Islamyiin," *Mada Masr*, April 19, 2021.

61. Wa'il Lutfi, *Du'ah al-Supermarket: al-Judhur al-Amrikiyya lil-Du'ah al-Judud* (Cairo: Dar al- Ayn lil-Nashr, 2019).

62. See Nareman Ehab Amin's empirical research in 2018 and 2019 in Egypt in *Revolutionary Religion: Youth and Islam in Post-2011 Egypt*, PhD Dissertation, Department of Religion, Princeton University, April 2021.

63. Vickie Langohr, "This Is Our Square: Fighting Sexual Assault at Cairo Protests," *Middle East Report*, www.merip.org/mer/mer268/our-square.

64. Fatma Emam Sakory, "Being Nubian in Egypt, and in the Constitution," *Mada Masr*, December 23, 2013; Aurora Ellis, "Egypt's Nubians: We Want to Reclaim Our Homeland," *Middle East Eye*, November 10, 2016.

65. Lila Abu-Lughod, "In Every Village Another Tahrir: Rural Youth in a Moral Revolution," in *Public Space and Revolt: Tahrir Square 2011*, ed. Elena Tzelepis and Sherene Seikaly (Cairo: American University in Cairo Press, 2017).

66. For details, see "Refusing to Forgive: Tunisia's Maneesh M'sameh," interview with two activists, Wassim Aghayr and Hamza Abidi, in *Middle East Report*, no. 281 (Winter 2016).

67. Hannah Arendt, "The Social Question," in *On Revolution* (London: Penguin Books, 1963); Hannah Arendt, *The Human Condition* (Chicago: University of Chicago Press, 1958).

68. Asef Bayat, "Revolution in Bad Times," *New Left Review*, no. 80 (March–April 2013).

69. See Hannah Arendt, "A Lecture: Thoughts on Poverty, Misery and the Great Revolutions of History," *New England Review*, June 2017.

70. Famously, Arendt makes distinction between three types of activities. First, *labor* or what humans do to survive, earn living, eat; it is biological, animalistic, and so forth. Second, *work*, through which humans build the world, create, as homo-faber. "Work" is tied to the condition of worldliness; it is humanistic. Finally, there is *action*. The subject of "action" is plurality; in action, humans engage in speech, human communication, discussion, and consensus building. This is the realm of politics and its aim is "freedom"; see Arendt, *The Human Condition*.

71. Marina Sitrin, *Everyday Revolutions: Horizontalism and Autonomy in Argentina* (London: Zed, 2012). *Horizontalidad* is building popular power in society rather than seizing state power. In Argentina, it was a practical response of the working people to the economic crisis of 2001–2002. Since people had lost trust in the state, they resorted to themselves to find solutions by taking over factories to run, initiating autogestion, building autonomous associations, and neighborhood self-rule in an outlook that disdained state-centerism in favor of grassroots politics of affect, love.

72. Joshua Stephens, "Talking Anarchism and the Arab Uprisings with Mohammed Bamyeh," Toward Freedom, February 26, 2013, https://towardfreedom .org/story/archives/middle-east/talking-anarchism-and-the-arab-uprisings -with-mohammed-bamyeh/.

## 8. WHATEVER HAPPENED TO THE REVOLUTION?

1. Fuad Ghorbali, "El-Ahya al-Sha'biyya fi Tounes: Ann Siyasat al-Azal al-Moda'af" [Popular neighborhoods in Tunisia: On the policies of double isolation], *Al-Safir*, May 15, 2020, http://assafirarabi.com/ar/31179/2020/05/15/%d8%a7%d9%84%d8%a3%d8%ad%d9%8a%d8%a7%d8%a1-%d8%a7%d9%84%d8%b4%d8%b9%d8%a8%d9%8a%d8%a9-%d9%81%d9%8a-%d8%aa%d9%88%d9%86%d8%b3-%d8%b9%d9%86-%d8%b3%d9%8a%d8%a7%d8%b3%d8%a7%d8%aa-%d8%a7%d9%84%d8%b9%d8%b2/.

2. Harry Pettit, "The Cruelty of Hope: Emotional Cultures of Precarity in Neoliberal Cairo," *Environment and Planning D: Society and Space* 37, no. 4 (2019).

3. https://pressfrom.info/au/news/world/-318683-how-the-west-hollowed-out-the-tunisian-revolution.html.

4. Amr Adly, "Challenging Spatial and Economic Order: The Rise of Street Vendors Movement," in Arab Reform Initiative, *Effervescent Egypt: Venues of Mobilization and the Interrupted Legacy of 2011* (Beirut: Arab Reform Initiative, 2018), 31.

5. See "Itlaq Khamsa Marakiz Jadidah Li-Tanmiyya al-Mashari'a al-Nisaiyya," *Al-Masdar al-Tounisi*, January 22, 2015.

6. Yahia Shawkat, *Egypt's Housing Crisis: The Shaping of Urban Space* (Cairo: American University in Cairo Press, 2020), chapter 2. See also https://web.archive.org/web/20200519050431/http://www.estrdad.gov.eg/NewsDetails.aspx?NewsId=146.

7. Yahia Shawkat, "Egypt's Construction Violations Reconciliation Law," https://marsadomran.info/en/policy_analysis/2020/01/1880/.

8. Amr Abdel Abotawila, "Understanding Egyptian Social Housing Squatting Phenomenon Post January 2011" (MA thesis, Ain Shams University, 2017).

9. Based on research by the anthropologist Yasmine Ahmed; personal correspondence, September 2020.

10. For details, see Habib Ayeb, "Mohamed Bouazizi and Tunisia: 10 Years On," *Review of African Political Economy*, December 17, 2020, https://roape.net/2020/12/17/mohamed-bouazizi-and-tunisa-10-yearson/?fbclid=IwAR3NOtIfmWrGrPTWBMxB858CsI8zNCFypdGqAMADdrZlnW6H8k2_u5wMjoM.

11. Ayeb, "Mohamed Bouazizi and Tunisia."

12. Mounir Saidani, "Tunisia: Social Movements Initiate a New Revolution," *Orient XXI*, January 5, 2021, https://orientxxi.info/magazine/tunisie-les-mouvements-sociaux-amorcent-une-nouvelle-revolution,4400.

13. See Benoit Challand, "The Revolutionary Praxis of Civility in Tunisia and Its Legacies," panel presentation, MESA annual meeting, 2016.

14. See Nareman Ehab Amin's empirical research in 2018 and 2019 in Egypt; see her "Revolutionary Religion: Youth and Islam in Post-2011 Egypt" (PhD diss., Princeton University, 2021).

15. See, for instance, Karin van Nieuwkerk, "'Uncovering the Self': Religious Doubts, Spirituality and Unveiling in Egypt," *Religions* 12, no, 20 (2021), https://doi.org/10.3390/rel12010020 https://doi.org/10.3390/rel12010020.

16. Central Agency for Public Mobilization and Statistics of Egypt (CAPMAS), *Statistical Yearbook* (Cairo: CAPMAS, 2020), 9. See also CAPMAS statistics cited in Dina Helmi, "Qanoun al-Khul': al-Mottaham waal Dahhiyya fi Tafkik al-Usra al-Masriyya," *Eda'at*, November 17, 2019, https://www.ida2at.com/khul-law-accused-victim-taking-egyptian-family-apart/.

17. Peter McPhee writes how the French Revolution left an irreversible change in people's perceptions and identity even after the Napoleon's coup in 1799 and the restoration of the monarchy in 1814. People kept uttering the language of rights, freedom, and sovereignty. What served this continuity was the memory of 1789 that was transmitted from "fathers to sons"; Peter McPhee, "Daily Life in the French Revolution," in George Rude Society Conference Archives, 2006 Seminar, vol. 2 Papers (2009), p. 30.

18. According to the 2018/2019 Arab Barometer and 2019/2020 Arab Public opinion poll; https://pressfrom.info/au/news/world/-318683-how-the-west-hollowed-out-the-tunisian-revolution.html.

19. Muhammad Ibrahim, his Facebook page, January 25, 2020, on the tenth anniversary of the Egyptian revolution.

20. Ahmed Alowfi, "The Logic of Globalized Modernization: The Political Economy of Cultural Reform in Saudi Arabia," Amber Buckley-Shaklee Annual Conference, Department of Sociology, University of Illinois, Urbana-Champaign, April 10, 2021; see also Mohamed al-Akhssassi, "Reforms in Morocco: Monitoring the Orbit and Reading the Trajectory," *Contemporary Arab Affairs* 10, no. 4 (October 2017). See also "Africa Can Learn from Egypt's Educational Reform: World Bank Director," *Egyptian Street*, November 11, 2020; Mohamed Soliman, "All You Need to Know about Egypt's First High-Speed Electric Railway," *al-Ahram online*, January 17, 2021.

21. See, for instance, Thomas Friedman, "Saudi Arabia's Arab Spring, at Last," *New York Times*, November 23, 2017.

22. Samuel J. Brannen, Christian S. Haig, and Katherine Schmidt, *The Age of Mass Protests: Understanding an Escalating Global Trend* (Washington, DC: Center for Strategic and International Studies, 2020).

23. This argument comes from the entomologist Peter Turchin; see his profile in Edward Helmore, "We Are on the Verge of Breakdown: A Data Scientist's Take on Trump and Biden," *Guardian*, January 17, 2021; Graeme Wood, "The Next Decade Could Be Even Worse," *The Atlantic*, December 2020, https://www .theatlantic.com/magazine/archive/2020/12/can-history-predict-future/616993/.

24. See the interesting essay, "Onward Barbarians," *Endnotes*, https://endnotes .org.uk/other_texts/en/endnotes-onward-barbarians, followed by a Twitter discussion, https://twunroll.com/article/1338786788370997248. The essay has deployed my concept of nonmovement with somewhat different interpretation to emphasize the fluidity and fragmentation of the current global movements. But I should stress that nonmovements possess the flexibility to move back and forth from noncollective to collective and from opacity to open activism. In addition, the analysis put forward by the *Endnotes* essay disregards the role of new technologies, social media, in facilitating widespread mobilization of the fragmented subjects; see the very fine analysis on the role of new information technologies in Zeynep Tufekci, *Twitter and Tear Gas: The Power and Fragility of Networked Protest* (New Haven: Yale University Press, 2017).

25. David Kirkpatrick, "Leaked Emirati Emails Could Threaten Peace Talks in Libya," *New York Times*, November 12, 2015.

26. According to the Egyptian journalist Fahmi Huwaidi in youtube.com /jazeera1; see also Guido Steinberg, *Leading the Counter-Revolution: Saudi Arabia and the Arab Spring* (Berlin: German Institute for International and Security Affairs, June 2014); Madawi Al-Rasheed, "Sectarianism as Counter-Revolution: Saudi Responses to the Arab Spring," in *Sectarianization: Mapping the New Politic of the Middle East*, ed. Nader Hashemi and Danny Postel (London: Hurst, 2017).

27. Robert Pelzer, "Policing of Terrorism Using Data from Social Media," *European Journal for Security Research* 3, no. 2 (2018): 163–179.

28. He said he barely manage life; that he had not seen meat when it cost LE 90 per kilo; chicken is supposed to be available for the lower classes, but it cost LE 50 per kilo. "I am not afraid, I speak out. . . . A second revolution will come; it will come soon."

29. In her acclaimed study of "great revolutions," Skocpol comes to the conclusion that revolutions are not made; rather, they "happen"; see Theda Skocpol,

*States and Social Revolutions* (New York: Cambridge University Press, 1979). But as Michael Burawoy argues, Skocpol's conclusion derives from her method of inquiry that "collapses necessary and sufficient conditions" for the occurrence of revolutions; see Michael Burawoy, "Two Methods in Search of Science: Skocpol versus Trotsky," *Theory and Society* 18 (1989): 771.

30. Edward Thompson, *Whigs and Hunters: The Origin of the Black Act* (New York: Pantheon, 1975), 258.

# Acknowledgments

In preparing this volume, I have benefited from the practical assistance and intellectual insights of many colleagues, friends, and academic institutions. I am especially indebted to so many people in Egypt and Tunisia who helped me with my study during my field research. They graciously shared their experience of living through the revolutions and triggered many important ideas. They are too numerous to name here, but I wish to record my deepest gratitude to them all. I am grateful to my former colleagues at the American University in Cairo as well those friends at Cairo University who have always been welcoming and generous with their time and intellectual observations. I remain thankful for Yahya Shawkat for sharing his insights on urban Egypt with me. I had lived in Egypt and knew my way around, but Tunisia as a research site was new to me. I owe a great deal to Habib Ayeb, who opened my eyes to Tunisia by way of his personal knowledge and network of activists and intellectuals. Mabrouk Jebahi has always been gracious with his hospitality and insights. My gratitude also goes to Massaoud Romdhani, Elyssa Jalloul, Nadia Marzouki, Hamza Meddeb, Larry Michalack, and Larissa Commack for their help and hospitality.

The research and writing for this book was supported by a number of academic leaves and fellowships. Most of all, I thank my colleagues at the Department of Sociology, University of Illinois, Urbana-Champaign (UIUC) for their generous encouragement. I appreciate the Teaching Release Time awarded in fall 2020 by the Research Board of UIUC, which allowed me to focus on the final preparation of the manuscript. A Guggenheim fellowship made possible a leave of absence in 2014–2015 for research and writing, and a fellowship at

Wissenschaftskolleg in Berlin, 2016–2017, offered an intellectually stimulating environment to think, discuss, and write. At the Wissenschaftskolleg, I very much enjoyed hanging out and discussing a host of issues with Elias Khouri, Sinan Antoon, Sa'diyya Shaikh, Menaka Guruswamy, David Dyzenhaus, Michael Lambek, as well as other wonderful scholars.

Sari Hanafi and Lisa Hajjar were kind to host me at their stimulating conference on the Arab Spring at the American University of Beirut, Lebanon, in 2013. So were Lila Abu-Lughod and Amal Ghandour, who brought me to Amman, Jordan, in 2014 to participate in the workshop to debate the "woman question" in light of the Arab revolutions. I benefited greatly from the event and discussions with the participants, notably Hoda El-Sadda, Zakia Salime, Frances Hasso, and Nicola Pratt. The conference "A Century of Revolutions: Gramscian Paths in the World," Sardinia, Italy, was most instructive in connecting the Arab revolutions to Gramsci's legacy and to the broader global context. My thanks are due to Alexandria Marchi and Gennaro Gervasio for their warmth and generosity. Visiting Gramsci's childhood house in Ghilarza was an unforgettable delight.

I wrote a good part of this book in Berlin during my summer breaks, while enjoying the city's remarkable cosmopolitan culture and intellectual community. The Berlin milieu included a number of friends and associates whose company and intellectual support I continue to value. They include Georges Khalil, Cilja Harder, Sonja Hegasy, Mohammed Bamyeh, Randall Halle, Atef Boutros, Jochen Bekker, Sandra Schafer, Leila Dakhli, Jens Hanssen, as well as Viola, Hoda, Firoozeh, Nader, Tooska, Melony, Shiva, Wouter, and many more. I wish to acknowledge that portions of Chapter 5 were first published as "Plebeians of the Arab Spring," *Current Anthropology* 56, Supplement 11 (October 2015): S33–S43, © 2015 by The Wenner-Gren Foundation for Anthropological Research. I have used fictitious single names for most of the people cited in conversations.

Reflecting on Bombay, Suketu Mehta once wrote that home is where your corner store sells to you on credit. In the city where I live and work, Champaign, Illinois, probably no corner stores would sell to anyone on credit these days. What makes this place home, instead, is the convivial community of friends and comrades who have made life more than tolerable even in the midst of global despair. I have been lucky to be part of this community energized by such forerunners as the wonderful Zohreh Sullivan and Rajmohan Gandhi. The city's library, probably one of the best in the country, remains a most inspiring environment to write books.

At the university, I am fortunate to be surrounded by a number of smart graduate students, including my advisees, whose presence has added much to the intellectual vigor of the department. I wish to especially thank Heba Khalil for her valuable assistance on the Egypt part of the research and Hany Zayed for drawing the figures for this book. Kaveh Ehsani and Linda Herrera kindly read parts of the manuscript, and Zackary Lockman graciously and carefully reviewed the entire first draft. I am indebted to them as well as to the anonymous reviewers of the manuscript for their invaluable comments. Needless to say, I alone am responsible for any error of fact or analysis this book may contain. Sharmila Sen, editorial director, and Heather Hughes, associate editor, of Harvard University Press showed much enthusiasm for this book project from the very start. I appreciate their patience, professionalism, and support. I am especially grateful for my editor, Joseph Pomp, for his particular care and critical insights at every stage of the editorial review. In the end, nothing would have been possible without the support of my family, Linda, Shiva, and Tara. They remain a source of energy, sanity, and sustenance.

# Index

New Woman Research Centre
(Egypt), 66, 262n101
NGOs (nongovernmental organizations), 13, 45, 167, 170–171, 175;
civil society and, 217; social minorities and, 72; women's movement
and, 65, 69; youth activism and,
188, 206
Nicaraguan revolution (1979), 3, 11, 12
Nidaa Tounes, 9–10
9 / 11 terrorist attacks, 47, 74
nonmovements, 2, 19, 35, 46, 303n24;
digital, 31; flexible dynamics of,
34; network of, 36; networks
and, 37–38; passive networks of,
104; process of turning into
movements, 165–172; return to,
174–177; subaltern, 27, 31
Nouh, Mokhtar, 227
al-Nour Party (Egypt), 157

Occupy movements, 11, 40, 212, 243, 244
Oman, 8
Omar, Asmaa, 225
Onodera, Henry, 264n136
opacity / opaque sphere, 30, 31, 73, 74,
207, 246
Operation Anti Sexual Harassment
(OpAntiSH), 168
oral histories, 2, 4
Orientalism, 22

Palestinians, 60, 74
"parallel state," 11
patriarchy, 16, 20, 28, 63, 101, 150, 159;
backlash against feminism, 178;
Mahfouz's appeal to men, 105–106;

neopatriarchy, 23; reassertion of,
185; religion and, 69; women's
groups negotiating with, 67
"people, the," 103, 143; fight with the
police, 95; revolutionary spirit
and, 40; sectoral interests merged
into, 112–113; will of, 146; women
as part of, 150
*Persepolis* (film), charge of blasphemy
against, 218
Persian Gulf states, 44, 230
personal status, women and, 27, 28;
Egyptian activists, 67; state
feminism and, 65; in Tunisia, 68
Personal Status Code [PSC]
(Tunisia), 167, 172
police, 32, 37, 84, 144, 255n65; bribes
paid to, 50, 58; collapse of police
control, 39; everyday encounters
with, 50; killings by, 38–39; mocked
in rap music, 205; police brutality
in Egypt, 46, 51, 89, 93, 95; police
stations attacked, 86, 90, 95, 97, 115;
sexual harassment by, 64; social
minorities and, 72; Tunisian uprising and, 85; violent clashes with
riot police, 95
political class, 126, 148, 205; deradicalization of, 13; social question
and, 228
political parties, 2, 117, 187, 200, 226,
227; ancien regime, 198; as "collective actors," 32; farmers unions
and, 136; gender equality and, 156,
172; left and liberal, 139; women
and, 69; youth and, 188, 189, 191,
201, 205

suicide in, 7; class divide in, 82; farmers in, 52, 53; as rural-urban hybrid, 264n3; Tunisian uprising and, 85

Sisi, General Abdel Fattah el-, 4, 10, 127, 195; attempt to appeal to youth, 196; gentrification of Cairo and, 230; modernization campaigns of, 242; as "real man" of Egypt, 223; rise to power, 166; street vendor's castigation of, 145–146; "women's freedom" and, 174

sit-ins, 78, 106, 129, 191

Sitrin, Marina, 233

Sitta el-Heita [Women on the Walls] (Egypt), 171

Skocpol, Theda, 16, 303n29

Slasel Nefsi, 169

socialism, 147, 250n8

social justice, 5, 11, 116, 117, 234, 236; democracy and, 147; Egyptian uprising and, 127; subaltern claims for, 238

social media, 32, 55, 82, 92, 168, 246; digital divide and, 34; protests linked through, 112; Tunisian uprising and, 116; women and, 102; youth activism and, 62, 190, 191. *See also* digital technologies

social minorities, 5, 19, 20, 71–74, 105, 210, 236; Egyptian uprising and, 102–103; information technologies and, 37; revolutionary spirit and, 39

social networks, 33, 37, 147, 206

social question, the, 3, 14, 198, 211, 228–233, 244; American Revolution and, 232; "opportunism" of

the poor and, 39; political agenda and, 42, 116, 148

Soeif, Leila, 166

solidarity, 22, 40, 74, 95, 115, 239; ethics of, 33; friendship and, 24; imagined, 109, 113; poverty and, 232; revolutionary ethics of, 234; undersocieties and, 79; women and, 98

Soueif, Ahdaf, 93, 98

South Africa, 141, 166

South Asia, 18

Soviet Union, collapse of, 29, 81

Springborg, Robert, 25

squatters, 50, 54, 55, 93; in Cairo, 77, 128, 129, 131, 140; Egyptian uprising and, 95

state-centric view, 1, 3, 43, 235

state feminism, 65–66, 151, 164, 167; grassroots feminist challenge to, 168, 179; women at center of nation building, 156, 283n27

Stephan, Maria, 16

street vendors, 38, 145–146; Egyptian uprising and, 137–140; networks and, 34, 37; origin of Arab Spring and, 7, 50; permits lacking or denied to, 49, 53; police harassment of, 80; as "suspected" individuals, 50; syndicates and unions among, 41, 120, 229; with and without permits, 119. *See also* Bouazizi, Mohammed

strikes, 16, 32, 78, 99, 114, 127, 263n121; in post-revolution Tunisia, 126, 273n33; Tahrir moment, 127; during Tunisian uprising, 124–125

subalterns, 1, 37–38, 79, 126, 147; "counterpublics" and, 26; everyday